IN THE AIR

IN | THE | AIR

Essays on the Poetry of Peter Gizzi

EDITED BY ANTHONY CALESHU

WESLEYAN UNIVERSITY PRESS | MIDDLETOWN, CONNECTICUT

Wesleyan University Press
Middletown CT 06459
www.wesleyan.edu/wespress

Manufactured in the United States of America
Designed by April Leidig
Typeset in Garamond by Copperline Book Services

Library of Congress Cataloging-in-Publication Data
Names: Caleshu, Anthony, editor.
Title: In the air: essays on the poetry of Peter Gizzi / edited by Anthony Caleshu.
Description: Middletown, Connecticut: Wesleyan University Press, [2017] | Includes bibliographical references and index. | Identifiers: LCCN 2017018704 (print) | LCCN 2017019569 (ebook) | ISBN 9780819577481 (ebook) | ISBN 9780819577467 (cloth: alk. paper) | ISBN 9780819577474 (pbk.: alk. paper)
Subjects: LCSH: Gizzi, Peter—Criticism and interpretation.
Classification: LCC PS3557.I94 (ebook) | LCC PS3557.I94 Z67 2017 (print) | DDC 811/.54—dc23

LC record available at https://lccn.loc.gov/2017018704

5 4 3 2 1

CONTENTS

ACKNOWLEDGMENTS

The idea for this collection of essays came about during the "Poets and Critics" symposium dedicated to the study of Peter Gizzi's work that took place on the weekend of May 28–30, 2012, at Universités Paris Est Marne-la-Vallée, Paris 7 & 8, and Institut Universitaire de France. I'm grateful to the organizers, Olivier Brossard and Vincent Broqua, and to the symposium contributors, particularly David Herd and Daniel Katz, who have been generous in conversation and scholarship over these past five years. Additional enablers of my thoughts and writing about Gizzi include Edward Clarke and Philip Coleman; I remain especially grateful to Philip for supporting my residency at Trinity Long Room Hub (Trinity College, Dublin), where my own chapter herein was redrafted. Once the idea for a volume of essays was in the air, the poets and critics approached were enthusiastic, and I'm grateful to the contributors who made time to write so meaningfully about Gizzi's work. It must be an awkward position to be the subject of a book, and great thanks are due to Peter Gizzi, himself, for his clarification of certain points as well as his willingness to be interviewed several times over these past few years. Thank you to the publishing team at Wesleyan University Press, particularly Suzanna Tamminen, for her invaluable support of contemporary poets and poetry. Thank you to my own institution, University of Plymouth, for research time and funding, enabling various trips in the UK, USA, Ireland, and France, as well as for supporting the hosting of conferences dedicated to contemporary poetry at our home campus: Poetry and Public Language (May 18–20, 2012), and Contemporary Poetry: Thinking and Feeling (May 20–22, 2016). And finally, an acknowledgment to my family, Ciara, Parker, and Caleb, for always giving me reason to "love this ball I'm riding on . . . around my loves and my loving" (to use the words of Peter Gizzi).

SOURCE ABBREVIATIONS

AH	Gizzi, Peter. *Artificial Heart*. Providence, RI: Burning Deck, 1998.
ARCH	Gizzi, Peter. *Archeophonics*. Middletown, CT: Wesleyan University Press, 2016.
OUT	Gizzi, Peter. *The Outernationale*. Middletown, CT: Wesleyan University Press, 2007.
PER	Gizzi, Peter. *Periplum*. Penngrove, CA: Avec Books, 1992.
PEROP	Gizzi, Peter. *Periplum and Other Poems, 1987–1992*. Cambridge, UK: Salt, 2004.
SP	Gizzi, Peter. *In Defense of Nothing: Selected Poems, 1987–2011*. Middletown, CT: Wesleyan University Press, 2014.
SVLW	Gizzi, Peter. *Some Values of Landscape and Weather*. Middletown, CT: Wesleyan University Press, 2003.
TS	Gizzi, Peter. *Threshold Songs*. Middletown, CT: Wesleyan University Press, 2011.

INTRODUCTION | ANTHONY CALESHU

In the Air

The Poetry of Peter Gizzi

1

In the air Peter Gizzi finds and makes poetry. He closes the first poem in his first collection with an exclamation, "Into blouse of // Air go there!" (PEROP, 3), and in his second collection writes of "speech becoming air" (AH, 12). In his third and fourth books, language materializes in the air further, and then further again so that it takes on a determined physicality: "The font is still. / A fanfare of stone air" (SVLW, 38); "the words scroll onto air" (OUT, 25). I want to bypass his fifth for a moment and cite from his sixth single collection, *Archeophonics*, which demonstrates just how grammatically malleable a poetic space the air can provide and be. As the subject of verbs, the air is *eaten* and *climbed* (ARCH, 6, 71), *consulted* and *composed* ("I always consult the air before composing air," ARCH, 67). It is modifier and modified ("air conditioner," "Crisp air," 12), and subject of homophonic puns ("ancestral airs," from "A Garden in the Air," 49). The air can transform the hackneyed—"these trees are not real they grow out of air" (34)—and the air, itself, speaks: "Fuck, the air said" (16). As a trope, the air serves as that poetic domain where Gizzi has continually investigated the matter and manner by which the poetic tradition is extended: "I wanted out of the past so I ate the air, / it took me further into air" (59). In and through time, *air* becomes that idiomatic place of our future: "Our future is / in the air" (43). All the while, the air isn't just external to us, but "the air [is] inside me / inside you" ("A Ghosting Floral," 47). This makes the poem a place of tension between exterior and interior experience.

Which brings me back to the collection I haven't cited from yet, Gizzi's fifth, *Threshold Songs*, where to be thrust into the air is to be thrown into the songs we hear and the songs we likewise sing. "There is a spike / in the air / a distant thrum / you call singing" (*TS*, 1). Songs exist at that threshold of outer and inner reception and rendering. Like "air," "song" is not a passive term or space for Gizzi. Beyond lyric meditation or utterance, it articulates a euphonically conceived way to actively mediate and modulate the plural voices by which we constitute ourselves and our world. Or as Gizzi puts it in "The Outernationale," "So many strangers / alive in a larynx" (*OUT*, 93). Songs in the air demarcate a "threshold" between life and death, self and other, physical reality and imagined construction.

There is a long poetic tradition about sourcing poems or "songs" through the "air"— from the Greeks, to Blake, to that father of modern American poetry, Emerson: "For poetry was all written before time was, and whenever we are so finely organized that we can penetrate into that region where the air is music, we hear those primal warblings, and attempt to write them down."[1]

Emerson's air became Whitman's — and like Whitman's "every atom," the air for Gizzi is both private and public, both a literal and a metaphorical expression of the interior consciousness by which we think and feel, and the exterior world in which we live and breathe. Gizzi's is the air of Dickinson, Pound, Stevens, Niedecker, O'Hara, Ashbery — in part, it's the same air that Gizzi shares with contemporaries such as Elizabeth Willis, Julianna Spahr, Lisa Robertson, Mark McMorris. It's the air of abstracted subjects and personality — an anecdotal and yet impersonal (and plural) "I" that makes for a montage of selves and experiences, for poems that are aurally enhanced and tangibly descriptive, poems that transcend context by multiplying meaning within a tradition that appropriates and subverts its (re)written language.

Mystical expressions of sourcing poetry from the air include the mid-twentieth-century California poet whom Gizzi has edited, Jack Spicer. Less supernaturally inclined than Spicer, who self-declared his practice of "dictation" as stemming from "ghosts" or "spooks" or "Martians" (as Gizzi explores in his afterword to Spicer's *Collected Lectures*[2]), Gizzi is similarly interested in a "program of intertextuality."[3] But where Spicer argues for the poet's "passive" act as transmitter, Gizzi's implication of the "self" as "listener" to other voices seems decidedly active.[4] Gizzi's own particular take on this comes in his complex sense of the "self" as both maker and conduit, one whose *active* intervention is part of the process of modulating the voices of others through his own. In interview with Ben Lerner, he declares an "[interest] in . . . 'vamping,' or 'throwing' of the voice and placing it beside the speaker" before citing Whitman and Dickinson, the two poets to whom critics most often refer when discussing Gizzi's work.[5] To these names, Lerner adds Hawthorne (to which I'll add Emerson), before making the point that "these 19th century New Englanders often seem to me to be your most immediate contemporaries: that you've caught the voices they've thrown, that you're in some important sense coeval."[6] The "ghosts" of past voices that appear in Gizzi's work are thus the ghosts of those writers whom Gizzi has long read and loved — the ghosts of his literary predecessors[7]: as he begins one poem, "I like to read the dead" ("A Telescope Protects Its View," *OUT*, 24). The ghosts of Spicer, the fairies and angels of poets like Yeats and Blake, the "primal warblings" of Emerson (who David Herd writes of as promoting a "citational, or allusive, or aleatory [poetry] . . . in [the] spirit of circulation"[8]), enable foundational ideas about the nebulous state (and place) of poetry's beginnings which is relevant to Gizzi, who, in the tradition of Pound, begins the process of assimilating the plural voices that exist in the "air" within the "I" of a poem.

In the pun-titled "Eye of the Poem," Gizzi metaphorically renders his compositional process, concluding with lines: "I am silly with clarity. / Born of air I am . . . I remake my life. . . . / A bright patch over the roof / on the jobsite singing itself" (*TS*, 12). Clarity, and likewise a knowing sense of just how *unclear* the world can be, is not solipsistically sought; instead, the tension is fruitfully acknowledged between the desire to render the interior while being externally invested in the very air that bears poetry, an air that is both contemporary and past. In interview, Gizzi tells us,

> I am interested in what I would like to call the borderless nature of selfhood and tradition . . . the ultimate mission of the poet in the western tradition is to bring back the beloved . . . My bibliography, all the books I've read, are a huge part of my autobiography. So when I say the borderless nature of selfhood and tradition, what I'm saying is that it's not only the people I've lost who are called back through the book, but so are all these other poets that I've read through my life. They're here in the language, in the layering of voice.[9]

When Emerson writes of man's ill-fated attempt to "penetrate into that region where the air is music," he's not damning man as inadequate ("though imperfect [they] become the songs of the nations"[10]), but neither is he imagining, I think, the deliberateness with which Gizzi is literally "miswriting" or "substituting" the language he's sourcing from literary predecessors . . . not just Whitman and Dickinson, but Pound, Rimbaud, Villon, Blake, Rilke, and Solomon, all of whom Gizzi tells us, in interview, he "speaks through."[11] As quickly as Gizzi acknowledges his debt to "The old language," however, he also acknowledges that "It don't mean shit" (*ARCH*, 16). This oppositional sense of reverence and belligerence strains the poem until a new "syntax breaks down / its mangled draft" (17). In this way, Gizzi's poetics evolves into a signature use of repetition, infinitives, speculation ("If"), and the impersonal-personal "I"-verb construction: "I quantify, I loaf, I wonder, I find, I rev" ("Apocrypha," *TS*, 53–54). These are the verbs of forefathers like Whitman, Stevens, and Williams, but also the verbs that now might describe Gizzi's own poetics. Gizzi's poems *quantify* in their allegiance to science and philosophy, and yet *wonder* with a penchant for imaginative contemplation. His poems *loaf* with dedicated pacing, conveying, at times, a doleful melancholy. And yet his poems *rev* down the page with speed, manifest as intimacy and a rendering of interiority. This enables what has often been called Gizzi's "reinvent[ion] of the lyric," as John Kinsella has written.[12] The effect is a poetry of prescient affect.

Both Marjorie Perloff and Lee Upton in their respective essays in this collection use the word "prescient" to describe Peter Gizzi's poetry, in regards to Gizzi's use of language and in his poetry's depiction of the abstracted self:

> Gizzi is curiously prescient. Sampling, stealing, appropriation: these are now the norm. (Chapter 4, Perloff)

> In some ways, Peter Gizzi's poetry of recent years has been prescient about the manner in which privacy has been depleted . . . [he] resists traceable public selves, and makes of the poem a site where it is possible to recognize ungovernable and invisible aspects of human lives. (Chapter 15, Upton)

To be prescient is to be visionary. And to be visionary is to render images (and sounds) of what comes next. Gizzi's poem "Fragment (To the Reader)" is repositioned from its place in the middle of *Threshold Songs* to become the final poem in *In Defense of Nothing: Selected Poems, 1987–2011*, cited here in full:

When you wake to brick outside the window

when you accept this handmade world

when you see yourself inside and accept its picture

when you feel the planet spin, accelerate, make dust
of everything beneath your bed

when you say I want to live and the light that breaks
is an inward light

when you feel speed of days, speed of light

if one could fancy vision then let it be of you

let it be thought breaking in your view (*SP*, 221)

To "fancy" is to envision, to imagine "vision" itself, to imagine seeing oneself in a world spinning faster than one can control. The "you" addressed is both the "self" and an "other." And the "inward light" renders consciousness of "feel[ing]" both in and outside of oneself in the "speed of days, speed of light." Days and light refer to the passing of time, which is both external to us and something we make, a metaphysical construct. In a recent interview, Gizzi's speaks of "tradition" as not something that's happened in the past, but something we're moving toward: "tradition is not behind me . . . it's ahead of us."[13] Time in this sense is alinear. Or, to put it another way, time is part of our consciousness; to be visionary in terms of time is to render what we are *becoming*—a word Gizzi uses regularly, and a concept I want to arrive at through William James.

Gizzi uses James for the front epigraph of his *Selected Poems*: "The world contains consciousness as well as atoms—and the one must be written down as just as essential as the other" (*SP*, 1). In one of James's most celebrated essays, "The Stream of Consciousness," he writes, "The first and foremost concrete fact which every one will affirm to belong to inner experience is the fact that consciousness of states of some sort goes on."[14] Gizzi's interest in exposing a "state of consciousness" is clearly distinct from those poets who are "self-conscious," who are invested in rendering whole and complete selves. Just as often as he writes "I" (the pronoun often appears multiple times in a poem), he also effaces the self (the very self that might be read as a composition of disparate or myriad selves). What Gizzi takes from James most readily then is the idea that such a state of "consciousness is in constant change." "Stream of consciousness" is now a familiar trope, but James's metaphor is worth citing nonetheless: "Within each personal consciousness, thought is sensibly continuous . . . Consciousness, then, does not appear to itself chopped up in bits . . . It is nothing jointed; it flows. A 'river' or a 'stream' are the metaphors by which it is most naturally described."[15]

Just as James goes on to explain how such a "stream" enforces a "sense of belonging together, a kind of jointing and separateness among the parts," Gizzi's poetics revels in the poem as providing unified space for such fragmentation: its twisted syntax, its aborted sentences, its anaphoric clauses beginning with the speculative "when" or "if" (or that most philosophical of infinitives, "to"). Approaching the end of his essay, James introduces into his argument the idea of moral consciousness: "What he shall *become* is fixed by the conduct of this moment" (my italics).[16] "Becoming" is a realization of "consciousness." And yet becoming, as Gizzi stresses, also denotes an act of process, a span of time—a transitive verb that extends a state of transformation, as in the early poem, "Ledger Domain":

> My smile is becoming different from you.
>
> —becoming—and you crave an earlier affection
> Where was the silver becoming from?
>
> Who forgets that we dream—who forgets we dream
>
> The dark is near! That loss was dark; there that's darker!
>
> A page, we become (*AH*, 33)

The title is a homophonic pun on "legerdemain"; but the sleight-of-hand performed on the reader takes place in the "ledger," that is, on the "page." The manipulation of language—of structure and syntax (earlier we're told "Syntax bent the child / —playing on the page")—means the "becoming" can accommodate the fragment within the whole; it is not simply a linguistic experiment or experience. Instead, it has the semblance of spiritual utterance; *becoming* as a moment of enlightenment. To *become a page* is tantamount in Gizzi's world to pulling words out of the air to become a poem. And like Emerson, Gizzi conceives of the value of the poem as that very space which transcends time, that space which can accommodate our divided selves and world, our divided human condition. Marked by him here, at the conclusion of another poem:

> Like to be beside and becoming
> to be another and oneself
> to be complete inside the poem
>
> To be oneself becoming a poem
>
> ("Saturday and Its Festooned Potential," *OUT*, 60)

2

Gizzi is the author of numerous small-press chapbooks, folios, and artist books, six full-length single volumes of poetry, and a *Selected Poems*. Since his first collection, *Periplum*, was published in 1992, he's garnered significant praise from writers and critics as varied as Adrienne Rich, Robert Creeley, John Ashbery, Bernadette Mayer, Michael Palmer, Juliana Spahr, Kamau Brathwaite, Marjorie Perloff, Eileen Myles, and Nathaniel Mackey. Within a contemporary poetry scene as diverse as it is divisive about the value and purpose of poetry (in terms of aesthetics, theme, politics, and so on), the importance of Gizzi's work may well stem from his bridging of poetic "camps," an investment in avant-garde language play and yet lyric treatment of humanist themes (love, death, life), nicely summed up in a sentence by Ben Hickman in a review of Gizzi's *In Defense of Nothing: Selected Poems, 1987–2011*: "Besides being a collection of the most compelling American poems of the last thirty years, Peter Gizzi's *Selected Poems* is the story of how a poet schooled in the radical deconstructive tradition of Language poetry ended up reimagining the lyric for the twenty-first century."[17]

In interview with Ben Lerner, Gizzi talks of his voice as "a conceptual and a made thing: it's built from both my autobiography and my bibliography."[18] While it's clear that Gizzi's "bibliography" is central to his poetics, the deliberate refraction (pushing at times toward abstraction) of autobiographical material reveals that Gizzi is well outside the realm of the twenty-first century's post-confessional and anecdotal poets. He eschews the merely "personal." In interview, he may tell us he is "the grandson of Roman immigrants, and the son of an important General Electric scientist, and for stretches a strung-out denizen of the seventies and eighties Lower East Side,"[19] but his poetry favors the "impersonal personal" space[20] in order to register a tripartite level of engagement: with "the actual world," "the shattered-pane world," and "the shadow world" (to use the words of three different poems ranging his oeuvre: "Poem for John Wieners," *PEROP*, 112; "Lessons in Darkness," *SVLW*, 40; "Hypostasis & New Year," *TS*, 7). If Gizzi's is not a poetry of documentary witness, it's still one where an interior mining takes place; the reader both reads and doesn't read, per se, about what Gizzi *feels* about the death of his father in a plane crash when he was twelve years old in the early poem "Despite Your Notices" (*PEROP*, 36). Likewise, the poems of *Threshold Songs* transcend the subject of the death of the book's dedicatees: Gizzi's brother, friend, and mother. What it means to die, or to live when others die, sits alongside ontology, consciousness, time, and the will of the imagination, as themes that Gizzi both writes toward and away from, a refraction that reveals an interest in transcending subject via materially invested language throughout his work.

This collection of essays was conceived at a symposium dedicated to the study of Gizzi's work, part of the ongoing "Poets and Critics" series at Universités Paris Est Marne-la-Vallée, Paris 7 & 8 and Institut Universitaire de France.[21] In addition to myself, four other essayists herein participated in the symposium that took place May 29–30, 2012: David Herd, Daniel Katz, Cole Swensen, and Olivier Brossard (co-organizer of the symposium). The conversation that happened that weekend continues here with recognition of the international significance of Gizzi's work: extending the traditions of (especially) nineteenth-century American Romanticism and twentieth-century Modernism into a contemporary poetry that firmly reclaims the living presence of the "lyric" in its capacity to sing of the human predicament and the difficulty we have capturing it. "Life is big these days and its hard to take / its measure" (*ARCH*, 53). Although many essayists have written before on Gizzi, all but two of the chapters collected here have been written bespoke for this collection. And while these chapters are loosely structured in three sections, which serve to group those of shared concerns, the sections are necessarily fluid frames, with the hope that essays might be read as dialoguing with each other beyond their assigned spaces.

In the first section, Michael D. Snediker, Charles Altieri, Kacper Bartzak, Marjorie Perloff, Hannah Brooks-Motl, and Sara Crangle explore Gizzi's poetry for its embodiment of an American tradition and its expression of a calculated intertextuality. A national case is made for Gizzi's extension of an

American literary tradition, in particular venturing back to American Romanticism and Modernism but declarative of a contemporary filmic sensibility that enables a new grammar and syntax. Despite, or perhaps because of, Gizzi's regular reference to earlier poets, Harold Bloom's influence theory is often cited. Notably, however, the influence of Emerson, Whitman, Dickinson, Stevens, and Eliot is argued for *without* anxiety on Gizzi's part. An international tradition closes this section as Jeremy Noel-Tod explores Gizzi's "affinity . . . for modernist British poetry," most substantially W. S. Graham.

The second section brings together essays that explore Gizzi's reinvigoration of the lyric (both personal and collective) within an avant-garde aesthetics, as Olivier Brossard exposes. David Herd and Lytton Smith read Gizzi's work as of public concern and existing within the tradition of Olson. The aftermath of Modernism is the subject of Peter Middleton's essay and also Ruth Jennison's; both of them bring Oppen into the mix. Jennison and Nerys Williams, respectively, explore Gizzi's poetry in the wake of the Cold War and in the midst of our current war on terror, complicating our historical predicament. Philip Coleman's close reading of Gizzi's long poem "Pierced" returns us to one of Gizzi's touchstone subjects, poetry itself.

For all his investment in language and Modernist/contemporary avant-garde aesthetics, Gizzi's poetry is equally invested in affect. Emotion is mined and experience re-rendered with particular attention to aurality, allusion, and myriad ideas about the construction of the self, as the essays in the third section emphasize. Visceral corporality and its relationship to consciousness means that the heart and the mind are not just metaphorical places for poetry. Lee Upton's sense of the self in Gizzi as a neurological construct and Daniel Katz's understanding of Gizzi's "somatic psyche" express the tension between the body and consciousness as well as emotions felt and enabled. Beckett and Spicer, among others, are cited as providing Gizzi with a lineage of opposition to subjectivity and a tradition of failure. Dan Beachy-Quick and Anthony Caleshu explore Gizzi's work for its allusive sense of becoming; in readings that reference Gizzi's beginnings (and endings), they respectively invoke Greek philosophy (via Robert Duncan) and refer to Gizzi's use of Judeo-Christian intertexts to explore tensions between a poetics of epistemological and ontological expression. Single poems by Gizzi are given close readings by Aaron Kunin, Graham Foust, and Ben Lerner, who expose Gizzi's work as informed by its relationship to cinema, aurality, song, art history, philosophy, and linguistics.

As an afterword, Cole Swensen's hybrid essay offers a poetic/critical engagement with Gizzi's sense of sound. It closes the volume but opens up a very real aspect of the dialogue that's been ongoing between all the essayists and Gizzi. Throughout, dialogues with Gizzi come not just in citations of his poetry, but in citations of his various interviews. Gizzi's own discursive articulation of his aims and concerns serves as both resource and springboard for essayists to explore and interrogate the work. As a whole, the volume confirms and asserts the project Gizzi himself speaks so well about when he encapsulates his chosen form's place in a contemporary world that is historically vested:

> People often say that the lyric is dead, or that it's . . . an impoverished form to record the contemporary world. I would disagree. I think the lyric is an incredibly flexible form, a very durable form . . . it's always been able to dilate and to accommodate the world, which I'd like to call an unstable multiplying narrative. The lyric has always been there as this tool to investigate and to open up and to display the world in all its myriad confusion.[22]

NOTES

1. Ralph Waldo Emerson, "The Poet," in *The Essential Ralph Waldo Emerson* (New York: Random House, 2000), 287–306: 301. Gizzi's work could well be read in relation to another Emersonian tradition, as written about by David Herd in his book *Enthusiast! Essays on Modern American Literature* (Manchester: Manchester University Press, 2007). Herd argues that Emerson "inaugurated Modern American Literature . . . by mobilizing what one can call, a tradition of enthusiasm" (22); "[t]o be in the mental state known as enthusiasm is to be ready to receive words, intimations and ideas, but it is also to be in a state to pass them on" (5). It could be argued that Herd's authors, Thoreau, Melville, Moore, O'Hara, and Schuyler, provide a particular lineage for Gizzi.

2. Peter Gizzi, afterword to *The House That Jack Built: The Collected Lectures of Jack Spicer*, ed. Peter Gizzi (Middletown, CT: Wesleyan University Press, 1998), 189, 197.

3. Gizzi, afterword, 179.

4. Anthony Caleshu, "In Conversation with Peter Gizzi," *PN Review* 209, 39.3 (Jan.–Feb. 2013): 50. Also, see Gizzi's edited volume of Spicer lectures, *The House That Jack Built*. Spicer's idea that "poetry [comes] from the outside rather than the inside" (5) manifests as "textual mirroring" and, as Gizzi argues, "reiterate[s] [Spicer's] view of poetry as a tradition based in copying" (219). For Spicer, "the poet is essentially a passive receiver of messages from beyond, which he copies or translates" (174).

5. Ben Lerner, "Poetry at the Threshold," *Poetry Foundation*, www.poetryfoundation.org/article/243686, accessed Jan. 18, 2015.

6. Ibid.

7. "When I say the ghost has begun/ you understand what is being said," Gizzi begins his poem "True Discourse on Power" (*TS*, 61).

8. David Herd, *Enthusiast! Essays on Modern American Literature* (Manchester Manchester University Press, 2007): 22.

9. Caleshu, "In Conversation with Peter Gizzi," 50. Note: Whitman, of course, and many of Gizzi's sources are more loved than "unread, unsung."

10. Emerson, "The Poet," 301.

11. Caleshu, "In Conversation with Peter Gizzi," 50. Note: Gizzi is speaking about the poem "Apocrypha." Also, I'm only stressing literary intertexts here; it's important to qualify that nonliterary, contemporary, and cultural "voices" abound, from pop music to the sound bites we hear on TV.

12. John Kinsella, *Australian Book Review*, Best Books of 2007.

13. Anthony Caleshu, "An Interview with Peter Gizzi," Periplum Video, www.plymouth.ac.uk/periplum, accessed May 11, 2016.

14. William James, "The Stream of Consciousness," in *The Principles of Psychology*, ed. George A. Miller (Cambridge, MA: Harvard University Press, 1983), 140.

15. Ibid., James (bold in the original).

16. Ibid., James is considering a question about how man resolves to act when confronted with an ethical dilemma: "When he debates, Shall I commit this crime? choose that profession? accept that office, or marry this fortune? — his choice really lies between one of several equally possible future Characters."

17. Ben Hickman, "A Believable Foothold," *PN Review* 220, 41.2 (Nov.–Dec. 2014), www.pnreview.co.uk/cgi-bin/scribe?item_id=9214, accessed Jan. 15, 2015.

18. Lerner, "Poetry at the Threshold."

19. Ken Babstock, "Off the Shelf: Echoes of Empire: Rachel Kushner, Peter Dyer, and Peter Gizzi," *Nuvo Magazine*, nuvomagazine.com/magazine/autumn-2014/off-the-shelf-echoes-of-empire, accessed Jan. 9, 2014.

20. Caleshu, "In Conversation with Peter Gizzi," 50.

21. "Poets and Critics," Peter Gizzi symposium, Universités Paris Est Marne-la-Vallée, Paris 7 & 8 and Institut Universitaire de France, May 29–30, 2012. See www.poetscritics.org/poets-and-critics-program, accessed Jan. 9, 2017.

22. Caleshu, "An Interview with Peter Gizzi," Periplum Video.

PART I | TRADITION AND INTERTEXTUALITY

1 | MICHAEL D. SNEDIKER

Gizzi's Romantic Exportance

To say that Peter Gizzi writes in an Emersonian vein only begins to suggest the arresting literalism with which his poems encounter and assimilate objects and sensibilities exported from American Romanticism. That the ends of this curating are not always clear is unsurprising, because the uncertainty (in Dickinson's sometimes less worried word, the possibility) of one's ontological implication with objects is as generative for Emerson as it is for Dickinson and Hawthorne. I am thinking about sensibility, here, as itself an object to be approached, tried on and out. My sense of this hypostasizing export-effect is pretty loose. For present purposes, we might just call it *washing up*—curating as the installation of cultivated, entropic movement—an effort to move away from the poet-centered business of influence for the sake of thinking about the lyric traffic of objects themselves. Some version of this revised account of objects and author informs "The Custom House," Hawthorne's preface to *The Scarlet Letter.* That "The Custom House" mortifies the scene of a writer writing in favor of fabricating the aleatory felicity of a custom-house agent finding an artifact suggests the quite literal importance for American Romanticism of its objects, to which Gizzi's *exportance* corresponds. Beyond vestigial, Bloomian flinch, I prefer "export" over "influence" because the scale of the former's mobility seems more adequate than the latter's artisanal inflexibility to the sieve-like porousness with which Gizzi's poems are shot through not just with echoes of Dickinson or echoes of Emerson, but with American Romanticism writ large. If something among a given set of mid-nineteenth-century American writers was, as we say, in the air, one proof of it is the allusive cross-pollinating with which Gizzi's writing seems alternately echoed, saturated, riddled.

In invoking "one's uncertainty,"[1] I'm referring to neither author nor generalized subject so much as the poem itself in its elliptical movement between registering as a text and an utterance. An utterance, in this case, is neither equivalent to a voice, per se, nor metonymic for an author. Less than the nominally autobiographical speaker of "The Custom House" but more than many of Dickinson's decreating experiments in lyric speech, the utterance of Gizzi's poetry approximates a lyric self or perhaps more accurately approaches one:

I standing
feet on the ground
not under it
I frozen and
I can feel it
to meet incumbent
death we carry
within us a body
frozen ground (*TS*, 3)

That these lines *nearly* conjure a voice or speaker — or alternately, that the poem's voice nearly seems assignable to something like a speaker — is a Dickinsonian effect learned from the likes of "After great pain, a formal feeling comes":

This is the Hour of Lead –
Remembered, if outlived,
As Freezing persons, recollect the Snow –
First – Chill – then Stupor – then the letting go –

"After great pain" is an utterance without a first-person singular, a poem that both theorizes and enacts the vicissitudes of lyric speech as it is at once sponsored and infringed upon by the self's felt absence. Almost implicit in the poem's allusion to the pain preceding it is a person particular enough (or perhaps, risking tautology, enough recognizable as such) to experience the pain at all. In the wake of the pain, personality gets displaced — or maybe dilapidated; less clear than *what* has happened is that it *has* happened, the consequence of which being the poem's task to trace — leaving less a voice than this formal feeling, an auratic vacuousness that attempts to take itself as its own principal object. That the utterance falls ontologically short of being a speaker makes the freezing persons, invoked analogically in the poem's last stanza, all the more spectrally captivating. In a sense, the auto-personifying echo of these lines in Gizzi's "I frozen and / I can feel it" speaks less from the living or the dead than from Dickinson's analogical interior: "we carry / within us a body / frozen ground."

The relation between these concentric selves and the "theory" of objects by which they are sensible if not understandable to each other informs Dickinson's project and by extension Gizzi's, not least because the latter seems to understand itself as an articulation of the same concentric legacy. Without quite knowing the implications or stakes thereof, let's try to piece together what such a theory might venture were its elements able to articulate themselves to each other, not in sole relation to one poetic enterprise or the other, but as that which illuminates the movement between them. In this way, to meditate on the vividly harrowing meditation that concludes "After great pain" is to learn something about Gizzi's own circling of what in *Artificial Heart* he calls "the truth of winter" (*AH*, 56). Here is an early vision of Gizzi's interpretation of implication in the Dickinsonian universe, from "Despite Your Notices" (whose titular homage to Spicer's *Billy the Kid* reminds us that Spicer was, along with everything else, an incisive Dickinsonian):

> For it was me they stuck out there in that winter hole. Earth so frozen it came up in slags that still get caught in my throat every time you tell me you love me. So don't. I mate with these voices on the other side. Their memos become the mottos of my solo walk into emblem. As the torn metal of all industrial accidents flowers in my brain. (*PEROP*, 37)

The particularity of "for it was me" suggests the clarifying of some earlier unresolved misperception, as though for some time we—or you, or they—had thought perhaps the one in the winter hole might otherwise have been *you*. When the earth breaks up as frozen slags "in my throat," the spatial rhyme of the hole and the throat turns the burial not only into a living burial, but a living burial nearly inside one's self. Gizzi's semantic preference for "stuck" over something like "buried" helps us hear the dialectical complexity lodged in the strandedness. Burials or funerals occur from the vantage of a mourner. They take the buried body as an object, even as the rites of them are followed for the sake of extending what seems in the object still human.[2] By contrast, "being stuck" casts an analogous scene from the vantage of one being buried, even as it idiomatically suggests one is being treated like an object: as an experience of depleted options, being stuck might well describe the experience of subjectivity so much at an impasse that feeling like a subject or object is moot. The difficult syntax of the poem's "me they stuck" further compresses this problematic in a way that recalls the poem's having already twice declared "this is my poem," as though that propriety were itself in question if not under duress. The distinction between a subject and an object is further undone (turned inside out) by the poem's landscape, experienced simultaneously as "out (there)" and "in (my throat)."

The prosaicness of "stuck" is important to these lines precisely for its difference from the lyric landscape that the speaker inherits (in which he's been buried). "A History of the Lyric," a poem from *Some Values of Landscape and Weather*, rehearses this synecdochally pastoral lexicon in a way that clarifies my sense of the way lyric objects are often in Gizzi's poetry without being of it: "what were we hoping to say: / ailanthus, rosebud, gable / saturnalia, moonglow, remember" (*SVLW*, 6). Unlike this later catalogue, the offhand Old English of "stuck" comes from a demotic seemingly meant to stave off the Romantic universe signified by moonglow. We might take it as a kind of vernacular "motto" salvaged from "memos," the things jotted down as opposed to *written*. Along these lines, however, we along with the poem might nervously note that "stuck" as colloquialism is undermined by the archaism implicit in the line's syntax (*for it was me they stuck out there*). The echo chamber of "every time you tell me you love me" convulses the poem both deeper in and further from both its need and its capacity for communication. The shattering force of these words is inseparable from one's own, insofar as the cruelty of "I love you" provokes the amazing peristalsis — or is it nausea, or sobbing, or speech? — of imagining the same formulation coming from the slags of one's own throat. We aren't told if these words are unbearable because they are true or because they aren't. What we are given is that someone else's words tear up a frozen landscape that the poem's voice both is and is embedded in.[3]

Even as "they stuck me here," like Keats's "belle dame sans merci," has the effect (characterizing and psychically tenacious) of a motto, it has a memo's ring. It's offhand, like Hart Crane's "memoranda, baseball scores / The stenographic smiles and stock quotations,"[4] the latter of which can't help but conjure the very kinds of lyric convention it tries to circumscribe. (Crane would be amused and perhaps unsurprised that we contemporaries of Gizzi might well hear "stenographic smiles and stock quotations" as its own stock quotation.) The ruthlessness of Gizzi's vernacular "stuck," then, is all the more awful in its attempt to strip the predicament it describes of the lyricism by which it's constituted. That memos could become mottos only to end up again as memoranda is the temporal vertigo — a cyclical air like the compulsive swirls that make up a Van Gogh sky — in which the poem's spatial vertigo (self becomes object and back again) takes place.

This peristalsis of frozen earth recovers the fearful urgency of the task Whitman sets himself in the preface to his 1855 *Leaves of Grass*. "The proof of a poet," Whitman writes, "is that his country absorbs him as affectionately as he has absorbed it."[5] Often, when discussing this line with my students, I think my attention too often moves to the nearly science-fictionally scalar scene of mutual absorption at the expense of that deceptively slippery (or is it jagged?) adverb. To take "affectionately" as epithetical (when isn't Whitman affectionate?) or tautological (is not mutual absorption a way of describing if not what affection is, then how it feels?) misses the affective precariousness that prompts Whitman so repeatedly (in both preface and subsequent poems) to assert it. And so Gizzi's poetry, time and again, finds itself encountering objects (including feelings and words) it doesn't quite know how to handle, treat, or claim, the figure for which is a hand neither closed nor open so much as learning as it obsolesces a new relation to the things it might have held. For Dickinson and Gizzi, it is a hand frozen (if only by the elements of the poem itself) into the incompletable act of letting go. "Sad nothing can be held," says an earlier line from "Despite Your Notices,"

> so thoroughly we might assimilate it. Only in the letting go will the full concentration of tone bleed into the periphery of our lives and settle into a patina that can never be altered. I surrender my vision thus. Because I don't understand. That joke isn't funny anymore. It cuts me precisely where laughter is a departure from this parlor. I live on flight 405 departing into an icy altitude — cold and detached. I'm here despite notices and obituary. That plane didn't crash. It still hovers around my head. The constant hum of its

engine reminds me I still haven't landed. I know this by the way a hand like a landing strip will reach over to wave here, here, here. (*PEROP*, 36–37)

The strangeness of a hand waving like, as opposed to directing one to, a landing strip is difficult to parse beyond the oneiric disjointedness that isolates it from either a body to which it might belong or the world with which it might make contact. At the same time, the doomed flight 405 codes the contact above which it postponingly hovers as disastrous. Even as the plane of the poem "didn't" and therefore (at least in the time of the poem) doesn't crash, it's both doomed with the knowledge that landing equals wreck and unable, mid-flight, to return to any earlier destination. The plane of the poem is suspended like a hand indefinitely holding the grenade it's pulled. Along these lines, the thrice-repeated deixis is unassuaging because the "here" of the poem isn't locatable so much as interstitial between equally (but differently) unreachable locations. Such a suspension informs the simultaneously stalled and discombobulated temporality of Dickinson's "After great pain": "'Yesterday, or Centuries before?'" The voice that asks this question both is and isn't the voice of the poem, in the way that Gizzi's hand both is and isn't directing that poem's "I" to a place it already occupies. *This* place both internal, external, and beside itself, is the "here" of one of Dickinson's most compulsive locative — which is to say *echolocative* — gestures, as in "Wrecked, solitary, here — ."

Or as Emerson analogously asks at the opening of "Experience," "where do we find ourselves?"[6] The hand that leads us *here, here, here* is as impossible as an M. C. Escher drawing. As Gizzi writes in a poem from *Threshold Songs*, "I, artifact. In this age the hand is a voice" (53).

Threshold Songs titularly recalls Hawthorne's account of the threshold in "The Custom House," where — recalling "this parlor" in which is envisioned the "full concentration of tone bleed[ing] into the periphery of our lives"— Hawthorne (or rather, a speaker who is and isn't Hawthorne) sits in a "deserted parlour, lighted only by the glimmering coal-fire and the moon, striving to picture forth imaginary scenes, which, the next day, might flow out on the brightening page in many-hued description."[7] In this scene of Romance where "the Actual and Imaginary may meet," Hawthorne dreams of a "warmer light" that "communicates, as it were, a heart and sensibilities of human tenderness to the forms which fancy summons up. It converts them from snow-images into men and women." Gizzi's poetry, like Dickinson's, is both an archive of and tribute to the snow-image, Hawthorne's "citizen of somewhere else," Orpheus as the outernationale.

These pages have sought to describe the improvisatory protocol by which Gizzi's poetry negotiates the possibility of its own voice not as a given but as the transaction of objects of which the self isn't the opposite so much as the most acutely available — because, metaphysically speaking, so saliently unavailable — example. That subjectivity and interiority (especially in the context of Romanticism) are synonymous underwrites the poetry's understanding of this serial operation in terms of a chronically recrudescent interiority. When it comes to lyric poetry, we take for granted that a poem has or more simply is an interior. In Gizzi's poetry, by contrast, the occasion of a poem often seems to occur when something like interiority most feels itself, which is to say encounters interiority as though it were different from either itself or the self that only nominally contains it. Gizzi twice revisits the peristalsis of "Despite your Notices" in *The Outernationale*: "It's true, the horizon empties into / a throat" (*OUT*, 12) is the opening of that collection's second poem, "The Quest." More succinctly, one of the book's two title poems laconically notes "So many strangers / alive in a larynx" (93). Something in such moments — call it voice, or feeling — is attentive to an interior that may or may not be ontologically coextensive with it, and which equivocally gets experienced as neither quite lyric source nor impinging antigen.

The difficulty even in a given instance of parsing the qualities of this inner object (or world, or psyche, or self, or not-self, and so on) might well be constitutive of it. Compared, for instance, to the identifiable pathos of "Earth so frozen it came up in slags," these later lines from *The Outernationale* seem distilled or emotionally evacuated, as though the earlier profession of feeling were replaced by relationality. We are given less a tangible sense of the qualities of a self or its objects than the frequency if not fact of relation. The opening lines of the book's second "The Outernationale" pose an analogous model of relations in terms whose self-deflating investment clarifies the ambivalent lyric gesture of take-it-or-leave-it:

So the bird's in the hand
and now what?
The penny shiny
in the dark belly of mr. piggy. (92)

As miniature *ars poetica*, these lines (I think pretty brutally) translate something like lyric salving into savings. That the penny (or even a piggy bank full of them) is doomed, as far as savings go, to (an infantilizing pathos of) insufficiency informs the poem's later turn on the "oikos" at the heart of "economy": "Such cruelty comes / from lack of everything / or so I imagined, / having failed / to save anyone / from anything / in this empty house. / From this empty empty house" (*OUT*, 93). The Romantic downgrading of "shiny" makes it simultaneously cheap and precious, a preciousness on the cheap we might well describe, following the suit of this poetry's predilection for the related cheapness of tautology, as *precious*. This is the conundrum of Gizzi's post-Romantic poetry, tersely recounted in a later poem, "Pinocchio's Gnosis," whose own punning title conjures not just the fraudulence but the un-concealable, theatrical fraudulence with which this poetry associates, almost in spite of itself, the interiority of its own insight:

> It was a simple mallet. It spoke simply, whammo, blam, I understood perfectly. Its oscillations filled the dark in waves of blue, some green and felt like no other mallet in my life. Its use was not significant only its shape, after all it was a tool.
>
> Sunday, the silver of asphodel will not save me. If only I were rich. I could write "happiness." (*TS*, 32)

This is the conundrum of post-Romantic poetry, but it is also the conundrum of Romantic poetry. After all, Gizzi's piggy bank — the bird in hand — can't *not* conjure the following equally brutal poem by Dickinson:

> Split the Lark – and you'll find the Music –
> Bulb after Bulb, in Silver rolled –
> Scantily dealt to the Summer Morning
> Saved for your Ear when Lutes be old.
>
> Loose the Flood – you shall find it patent –
> Gush after Gush, reserved for you –
> Scarlet Experiment! Sceptic Thomas!
> Now, do you doubt that your Bird was true?

Although Linda Freedman is not alone in arguing that this poem "uses the story of doubting Thomas to satirize a failure of faith in experience,"[8] I think

Virginia Jackson hits closer to the mark in noting the poem's bizarre and not entirely stable subjection of itself to satire.[9] It's not only that lyric poems are as unlikely to contain silver bulbs as a lark is, but that the fantasy of lyric interiority as silver bulbs is as precious as Gizzi's silver asphodel (rated by the poem's own economy if not as cheap as a shiny penny, then perhaps a dime a dozen). The send-up of doubting Thomas who vivisects a poem in hope of finding its mechanics or source is a foil, as it were, for a poem whose inability to distinguish avowal from disavowal (heads or tails) operates with the swiftness of a first principle. I might have written "resistance" instead of "inability," because the agential oscillation between inability and resistance is the Emersonian axis along which these dialectical stanzas crystallize: "This is a hard hat area. / The image of the spectator trapped / in a mirror, the relationship of spectator, object / and the space within love's bent axis" (*SP*, 43).

Dickinson's "Scarlet Experiment" is a precursor to Gizzi's iconoclastic mallet, which doesn't smash the piggy bank to bits ("its use was not significant") so much as coerce preciousness[10] into uncomfortable proximity to the mallet's vernacular: *whammo, blam* ("shiny," "stuck"). On the page, the efficacy of the mallet would seemingly require that the "silver of asphodel"— a lyric cousin of the aforementioned "ailanthus, rosebud, gable"— precede it. That the asphodel follows the mallet implies that the silver interior object is a kind of zombie; or to stick with the horticulture to which Gizzi and Dickinson resort, an unkillable weed.

That the weed might "look like" a "real" flower or even be one describes the intractable if not irresistible force of what Daniel Tiffany calls poetic kitsch, the guiding emblem of which, for Tiffany, is Keats's "silver planet." As Tiffany notes of Pound (whose *Periplum*, of course, Gizzi takes as the title for his first collection), "Even as it symbolizes the fetishized materials of Pound's borrowed diction, the color silver subtly infuses the ornamental nature of Pound's monotonous 'planet'; the floating world of kitsch is laced with references to 'silver shafts,' 'silver harness,' and 'silver hounds'; to the 'silver of the leaf,' to 'a silver reed,' and 'the silver rustling of the wheat.'"[11] We might add to Tiffany's catalogue the myriad references to silver across Gizzi's oeuvre, including "Collocated with clouds and silver" (*SP*, 27); "A morning's silver announces sky" (49); "The page is silvery — almost as silver / — announced a child — " (50); "over the mountain face // empurpled, its silhouette / ragged, silver // unquantifiable in pixie dusk" (79); "now a silver wisp winking on the roof / silver imp waving from a long shaft ago" (135); "what silver world mirrors tarnished lenses /what fortune what fate / and the forms not themselves but only itself the sky / by water and wind shaken / I am born in silvered dark" (176).

Like Hitchcock planting himself in one of his own films, Tiffany takes evident pleasure in noting as evidence of Robert Herrick's involvement in a seventeenth-century proto-kitsch poetics that he "appears to be intrigued by various translucent media (such as the luxurious and diaphanous 'tiffany'—a gauzy, linen veil) through which the world, especially nature and erotic objects, appears to be essentially ornamental and illusory" (38). Along similar lines, "Gizzi" becomes an inadvertent echo of "gauzy." "In poem after poem," John Palattella writes in a blurb for *The Outernationale*, "nerve flares into shimmering gauze." Palattella's account echoes lines from *The Outernationale*'s opening poem, "if in the auroras' reflecting the sea, / gauze touching the breast" (3). Its rococo extravagance conveys the alacrity with which these poems convert phenomenological experience into aesthetic encounter (and, inevitably, vice versa). The nerve flares initially register as something to be felt, something external (a pain, an emotion, a pressure) brought inside. The shimmering gauze reverses this direction of information (what Emerson more plangently might call ductility if not *education*) such that what was felt is being viewed: the shimmering gauze operates in terms of a visual exclusivity resonant with Tiffany's account of tiffany as a medium of eroticizing translucence. As both the setting and effect of a poetic of precious fraudulence, gauziness injects the scene it covers ("makes one's nerves sharpen to the point / of a syringe" [*SP*, 44]) with a delicacy or intimacy immediately countermanded as ersatz. Something similar is at work in Gizzi's equivocal turn to lace,[12] which conjures the possibility of (that is, capacity for) beauty always on the verge of threatening, it seems, to dismantle itself:

> But after a fashion
> which when you're dead
> is an eternity I begin
> to settle into painterliness
> and the grace vivant
> of moonlit brushstrokes
> and the true depth
> of that moonlight.

Silver and old lace
and its relation to music
listing at nature's mirror.
But the empty center
of whitish marks
its indelible air
arctic and sharp
whizzes through me. (*TS*, 45)

The terms of these lines — the arctic blast, the whizzing — ought hopefully by now to be familiar. A few pages later, Gizzi reiterates: "So the lace and downy light / undoes me. Because looking / at your face here as it changes / the gemmed scene / I am also changing love" (*TS*, 75). To ask whose voice this is (to wonder if it counts as one) returns us to the haunting accuracy of "I artifact. In this age the hand is a voice." Tiffany writes that "[a]lthough the work of classification and definition is essential to establishing the exact contours of poetic kitsch, formal analysis must be supplemented . . . by efforts to understand the term 'kitsch' as designating not simply a particular kind of artifact, but a distinctive *relation* to artifacts . . . a relation that is consistently negative, derogatory, paranoid."[13] Gizzi's poetry is a constellation of artifacts and decoys, encountered by a self whose searing flair for fraudulence underwrites equivocal relation (even at its most undermining) as the formal feeling it can't do without. "What could we do now our gaze / had been altered, and constantly. / The shiny spot's decoy, sometimes / emotive, sometimes in bright digression." (*SVLW*, 24) What we could do, Gizzi's line implies, isn't hampered by our not knowing if the bright digression is what we are or follow, if the aura on the landscape is the one we gave it.

NOTES

1. My recent thinking about uncertainty's aesthetic ecology is informed by Leo Bersani's essay "Ardent Masturbation (Descartes, Freud, Proust, et al.)." "Rather," Bersani writes, "the mind has become a secret object to itself; the inventory of the most banal steps in the conduct of an excavation of this hidden mind underlines the difficulty and the strangeness of entering a territory at once native to and distant from the exploring subject. The Proustian narrator explicitly recognizes the uncanniness of this psychic doubling: 'What an abyss of uncertainty, whenever the mind feels overtaken by itself; when

it, the seeker, is at the same time the dark region through which it must go seeking and where all its equipment will avail it nothing.'" (Leo Bersani, *Thoughts and Things* [Chicago: University of Chicago Press, 2015], 44). Along the lines of my interest in lyric export and curation, Bersani's "inventory" suggests that the "banal steps" by which we excavate the secret object of the mind are encountered as objects in their own right (even as the ontological relation between these objects and the object of the mind remains unclear).

2. That a funeral is experienced from the outside in compounds the uncanny self-estrangement that is the event of Dickinson's "After great pain a formal feeling comes."

3. Looking ahead to Gizzi's *The Outernationale* and its provocatively inverting nod to the Left's late nineteenth-century anthem, it's useful to hear this poem's lament — at once excoriatingly personal and (not only impersonal but) anti-personal — beside a poem like Volker Braun's "Property," two of whose lines Charity Scribner translates as "What I never had is being torn from me. / What I did not live, I will miss forever." (Charity Scribner, "Object, Relic, Fetish, Thing: Joseph Beuys and the Museum," *Critical Inquiry* 29.4 [Summer 2003]: 634).

4. Hart Crane, "For the Marriage of Faustus and Helen," in *Complete Poems of Hart Crane* (New York: Liveright, 1986), 26.

5. Walt Whitman, *Leaves of Grass; The First (1855) Edition* (New York: Penguin, 1986), 24.

6. Ralph Waldo Emerson, *Essays and Lectures* (New York: Library of America, 1983), 471.

7. Nathaniel Hawthorne, *The Scarlet Letter* (New York: W. W. Norton, 2005), 29.

8. Linda Freedman, "Touching the Wounds: Emily Dickinson and Christology," in *Emily Dickinson Philosophy*, ed. Jed Deppman, Marianne Noble, and Gary Lee Stonum (New York: Cambridge University Press, 2013), 76.

9. Virginia Jackson, *Dickinson's Misery: A Theory of Lyric Reading* (Princeton: Princeton University Press, 2005), 187.

10. One example is the ingenuousness with which Freedman understands Dickinson's "silver bulbs" in terms of "pure[ness]" and "protected delicacy."

11. Daniel Tiffany, *My Silver Planet: A Secret History of Poetry and Kitsch* (Baltimore: Johns Hopkins University Press, 2014), 145. Subsequent references are cited parenthetically in the text.

12. Tiffany would appreciate the kitsch sensibility of laciness, which I've been ruminating on since visiting an exhibit in one of the upper rooms of Basilica Cattedrale Patriarcale di San Marco. Vitrines of fifteenth-century lace in which disintegration so often seamlessly bled into the meticulousness of the original labor gave way to a visit, a few days later, to Burano, a Venetian island whose penchant for lace making found expression in the local market's profusion of handmade lace cozies for every imaginable object, including rolls of toilet paper.

13. Tiffany, *My Silver Planet*, 3–4.

2 | CHARLES ALTIERI

Gesture and Philosophical Reflection in the Poetry of Peter Gizzi

As I was working on a book about Wallace Stevens, I came to think that two of his central preoccupations might be increasingly important in contemporary poetry — as distinctions among poets and as distinctions that dramatize competing forces within a single poet's work. Let me call these forces explorations in the power of expressive gesture and elaborations of what philosophical reflection can do — and not do — in lyrical modes of establishing significance for our affective states. Each of those forces must be defined against a powerful antagonist: the task of gesture is to ward off submission to a sense of pathos about the self and the world; the task of philosophical reflection in poetry seems to be to explore possibilities of belief that transcend the specificity of historical explanation. Philosophical reflection brings meaningfulness to pathos itself.

Stevens's *Harmonium* exemplifies what gesture in lyric is and what it can accomplish. He casts gesture as the overcoming of the pathos that occurs when the writer cannot find an adequate verbal response to fear and suffering, and so surrenders to what Stevens would later call "the pressure of reality."[1] The pressure of reality is everything that makes imagination feel powerless, so that the agent submits to all that mortality and society demand. Think of how often in *Harmonium* Stevens confronts the fear of death and the "inarticulate moan" of a life without a sense of how value can be established. Then think of lines such as "the only emperor is the emperor of ice cream" or "out of the tomb we bring Badroulbadour" (a name whose sonic delights are asked to resist the despondency of the poem's content).[2] One might even include in the logic of gesture how the single sentence in "The Snow Man" makes "nothing that is not there and the nothing that is" at least the accomplishment of the mind's powers to sustain intricately folded acts characterizing one's own suffering.[3]

Lyric gesture is the relying on inventive and theatricalized language to direct compassion, find release from suffering, or gain power over a troubling situation. It is not the enterprise of sustained thinking or reasoned judgment in the process of testing possibilities for belief. If one adapts J. H. Prynne's argument about Pound's version of the image,[4] one can see the centrality of gesture emerging as one aspect of Modernism's deep suspicion of any mode of argument or sustained reflection. Instead, lyricism in the Imagist vein cultivates a sense of instant discovery or resolution that frees a sensibility for other experiences. There is little comparison and almost no effort to assess the gesture or place the liberating moment within larger temporal frameworks. By this logic, the fullest heirs of early Stevens and early Pound are O'Hara and Creeley, each in his own way a master strategist of just the tone and sense of detail that will allow immediate resolution for intricate states of mind.

The opposite of gesture is what I am calling the reflective philosophical mode that tries to generalize the situation of the poem as an instance or type of more capacious relations between mind and world, so that the poet's treatment of a situation can be seen as testing and eliciting belief in some truth about the world. The reflective mode has two primary concerns. First, it must get the substance of the world down correctly. It must find names for what persists, so that naming itself is a demanding and powerful act of imagination. Second, it must accept an obligation not just to use names, but to speculate on how and why it matters that we have this power of naming. This is poetry bound to correlating the consciousness that looks outward with the activity of self-consciousness that looks at how its own capacities might be grounded.

One might say that where gestural poetry attends primarily to the effective phrase or sentence, the poetry of philosophical reflection is oriented toward grammar, to how individual phrases gain their power from underlying structures in the language—think of Stevens's concern with "as" and Eliot's with "now." More generally, each mode accepts different kinds of responsibilities for interpreting situations. O'Hara's gestural "The Day Lady Died" develops an intricate set of relations among diverse details, all synthesized but not explained by the final line. And Creeley's "Something" offers a wandering narrative of a sexual encounter until its last line, "What love can learn from such a sight," offers a perfect tonal shift allowing the speaker to find witty praise for the lady and abolish all rhetorics of shame.[5]

How different the pacing is in philosophical poets such as A. R. Ammons, Geoffrey Hill, and Jorie Graham, all working in the shadow of Stevensian speculation of lines like the conclusion of "Esthétique du Mal":

> As if the air, the mid-day air, was swarming
> With the metaphysical changes that occur,
> Merely in living as and where we live.[6]

None of these poets seek explanations for phenomena, but they also do not trust single resolving leaps of imagination. Their work thrives on studied repetition and variation that tries different names for phenomena and resolves itself by establishing what might be called satisfying balances between the claims of the world and the claims of self-consciousness. This ambition places such poets in a fraught relationship with Romanticism: they completely distrust the rhetoric of genius and symbolic readings of how the mind comes to a sense of power by honoring the many sides of its objects, and yet they continually find themselves repeating Romantic rhetorics of how the mind builds exemplary modes of sensibility. For the poem is ultimately a war with sheer narrativity, and only the achievement of exemplary states will sustain claims that history lacks the authority to interpret the powers that the poem exhibits. The poem wants to define why it can assume responsibility for the names it composes.[7]

I worry that my distinctions create more problems than possibilities for discussing contemporary poetry. But I risk suggesting this framework because it seems to me to fit a good deal of the work of Peter Gizzi, one of our most interesting practicing poets. In a superb review of Gizzi's second book, *Artificial Heart* (1998), Marjorie Perloff emphasizes what I want to appropriate as two fundamental features of gestural poetics — the capacity to develop strikingly concrete resolutions for complicated affective situations and the ability to hear and to deploy the history of poetry in English as influencing and making possible those gestures.[8] I am concerned primarily with gestural endings. In Gizzi's volume, these endings seem to play two basic roles — to allow the poems to cover an immense range of attitudes and details without collapsing into that multiplicity, and to test the powers of synthetic imaginative intelligence to develop comprehensive attitudes without having to claim to have discovered some sustaining belief.

"Will Call" is short enough to quote:

> There is an order to the skyline. Beyond this
> a ragged blank. The present evaporates
>
> into day. Settles about shoulders and cries.
> The phone rings. A car honks. Others
>
> pass in the outline of slate. It was an average day.
> An arrangement of place. A state of report
>
> or a state of grace. For centuries weeds have hidden it.
> Now autumn. Silence is what we make
>
> of eyes, trees and growing vine. It pierces.
> And these are the stories they will bring in boxes. (*AH*, 53)

Notice how the poem emphasizes its fragmentary present by persistent enjambment, as if the condition of things here either (or both) rushed into the next line or lacked the energy to complete the line it belongs to—"a state of grace" or "a state of report." In this regard, "Others" is marvelously both vitriolic and melancholic in its lonely beginning of a sentence. But the "it" variously possessed by all these attributes will not go fully into the silence. So the poem has to address it, preferably in a mode that will complement the tension between "report" and "grace." The poem's last line offers an elegant solution because it honors refusing to be silent while providing a completely ambiguous attitude toward that refusal. That the stories are in boxes suggests a funereal quality to what we resurrect of our average days. But it also honors the care that it takes to memorialize anything without transforming it into the stuff of extraordinary days, and thus lying to ourselves about our ordinariness.

I think "The Question of Scale" is an even better, more tonally complex example of the work gesture can perform because the poem so manifestly deploys the variety of aspects of scalar relations as a challenge to develop an attitude that comprehends and addresses those relations. But the best example of the role gesture plays in this volume occurs in its first poem, largely because Gizzi also asks the final poem to engage much of the same materials in a radically different, philosophically reflective tone. And in doing this, he introduces much of the project that will occupy his next book, *Some Values of Landscape and Weather*. The first poem in *Artificial Heart*, "New Picnic Time," offers a quasi-catalogue of an earth unwriting itself into a variety of images. Then it challenges its own figures with the question of how self-recognition might be possible for these pieces of a world without an appropriate rhetoric. Finally, the poem turns to the issue of the speaker's own self-recognition:

> When will they say they hear me. It was a dream. It was a tin can.
> It was a funny thing to feel. And the children. Or beyond this
> for posture, a simple garden, evergreen, a green car out front,
> the picket fence is white, what color are the flowers
> unwritten in a day. There is no space. Only sky and water.
>
> Uncanny earth. A funny thing to feel. (*AH*, 13)

After "uncanny earth," the repetition of "a funny thing to feel" produces a very different emotion from its initial statement. In fact, it produces an emotion bearing a very different attitude about emotion. The first statement is reportorial, an aspect of the catalogue of events. The second is the extension of "uncanny earth" and so syntactically an absolute construction rather than a narrative report. Now all the tension in the poem between a kind of absurdity and a kind of caring is summarized in the "uncanny" unstable balance between "funny" and "feel." The primary feeling now is for the inarticulacy of these details that nonetheless want to present themselves, even if their modes of presence are less than compelling. Their being "funny" seems capable of being included within a much more capacious level of care, so long as it does not try to take itself very seriously.

I do not even have to comment on how different the earth becomes in the last poem of the volume, "The De-Evolution of the Father," with its reach toward a Romantic comprehensive act of blessing and its loss of the intimate ambiguities of adjusting to sheer fact:

> here it comes now   give   give it to me
> the page is upon you   beautiful page
> disclose solace   offerings of
> an evolving library   an avowed earth (*AH*, 93)

This evolution is away from the father's will toward a different kind of custodial relationship toward the earth — based on will and testimony.

Now look at the introductory poems to Gizzi's next volume, *Some Values of Landscape and Weather*, a title clearly marking a concern now for what endures and what invites philosophical reflection rather than gesture. Gizzi seems to be trying out the possibility of an avant-garde rendering of philosophical lyrics strongly indebted to Romanticism. The first section of the volume is titled "Forensics," consisting of one poem, "A History of the Lyric," with several sections that in effect analyze the corpse that lyric may have become. Here revitalizing the lyric entails absorbing the history of styles rather than reporting on them. That process of absorption consists largely in the interplay of two dispositions.[9] One is pervasively ironic and gestural, defending itself against the pompousness of the title and the even more pompous claim to speak for the lyric. The other takes its key from the opening reflection on objects. Apparently one of the ways to restore values of depth and intensity to lyric experience is to concentrate directly on the interface where objects take on reality because of what the mind can bring to them and for them. At first, however, the poem seems to resist any return to a Romantic meditation on these processes. The first section, for example, quickly subsumes objects into lyrical attitudes, stressing how these objects appear to "your mess." We get gorgeously crafted phrasal balances, but that beauty has to compensate for a lack of any actual attention to how experience might be grounded, as if the avant-garde had to retrace the cost of its ambitions to deny Romanticism any existential traction. The conclusion of this first section can at best muster a responsiveness to twilight (a central figure in this book) that entails gesturally acknowledging the historical challenge this book faces:

closer than power lines
casting shadows on brush.

breath, heart ticking
the prepared delay

as twilight settles
in waves and crests

a water fowl, hooded owl

•

an avant-garde
a backward glance (*SVLW*, 5)

The ending here must be content with a range of floating appositions because twilight has come to dominate both the physical and the metacritical stages. Perhaps the avant-garde would be willing to extend its own sense of possibilities by taking this backward glance at what lyric might offer in a space beyond the affordances of historical analysis? (The backward glance seems to parallel the forward playful sounding of "a water fowl, hooded owl.")

Initially, "A History of Lyric" seems to offer no alternative to this kind of gestural conclusion, at once gathering the situation and avoiding further thought about it. But there soon emerge exploratory movements toward some other ideal of poetic labor. The speaker crosses the river and begins to occupy an "other side" (*SVLW*, 6) where one can say, "Every thing is poetry here" (7). Yet "here" is not defined and perhaps cannot be defined without resolving whether avant-garde still prevails or the lateness of the desire for lyric in this book can foster a different sensibility. "Here" may refer to the world across the river, or be merely a tautological reference the poem itself, or be a hope that this tautology itself can come to bear significant meaning as writing explores the sites it labors to develop.

Once the river has been crossed, there can be a dialogue between avant-garde and romantic dispositions. The first opening is to replace "here" as the space of artifice with a particular challenge to artifice — an actual garden that seems capable of inspiring a fresh way of addressing the sense of desperation with the present that pervades the volume:

Lateness is a dark and luminous thing
so true of early twilight.

I have known the morning to be darkest
upon waking. The pictures go away

and one is back to the thing of living.
Things to handle and attend:
. . . .

If the dark speaks what does it say
in a dark time. As words choose me

are they mine, and the counterpointing wind. (*SVLW*, 8)

Philosophy for Gizzi begins in the fluid (and sensually gorgeous) movement between "lateness" as an abstract condition and the strange and beautiful conjunction made with this "early twilight," a surprisingly apt concrete realization of such lateness. In the first of a series of doublings, "lateness" refers to both a general historical sense and the problem of being avant-garde now. Then the opening phrase divides. "Darkness" quickly becomes a condition of waking, because to wake is to feel responsibility for all that resolutely refuses intimacy with the self. (The echo of Eliot's "April is the cruelest month" is palpably but gently in the background.) Then the dark gets to speak. Its questioning affords a path back to the concrete world, where it now seems possible to sustain relationships that might repair remembered damage:

What way? The goodly silence
returns to its music as lateness falling

falls back into nerve.

So things come together, one
and one. And if one, and if

an overwhelming sense of rescue:
fallen leaf. Broken acorn. Schoolyard tears. (*SVLW*, 9)

Now the luminous can also enter as the darkness affords the possibility of speech, and of mediating what the questions it raises generate as attention to the unfolding scene. Lateness modulates into darkness, and darkness introduces conditions of recurrence that make the status of objects an abiding concern.[10] Lyric too becomes something other than simply a historical question.

But this volume offers a series of poems that cannot find much in the world to sustain that lyricism. Social conditions that might have allowed lyric to provide a sense of truth, as Adorno puts it, now separate beauty from truth so that poetry can only be an indictment lamenting its own limitations. Gizzi seems forced once again into the gestural.[11] Many of these gestural poems offer moving poetry brilliantly articulated. But this reader, at least, wants more variety in the poems' senses of the work they can perform. Or perhaps I want this because I think Gizzi wants me to appreciate fully how the last section of the volume turns toward possibilities for song, and so finally extends the volume's sense of the possible satisfactions a historical consciousness about lyric might produce. In this final section, the lyrics emphasize what attention to objects can establish as modes of sensibility not satisfied by gestural moments. There are three poems in the sequence, each specifying different kinds of naming that will become crucial to Gizzi's next volume.[12] Naming becomes a condition of song because it can picture what is an aspect of the world's constancy while at the same time making manifest the roles of human desire and human hunger for values invested in that constancy.

The first poem, "It Was Raining in Delft," begins as a statement of longing for his wife because he is in Europe on her birthday. Gizzi is quite moving in his effort to combine self-disgust at the conventionality of his lyric plight with the effort to make that conventionality speak anew of love and need. The poem eventually speaks anew by revitalizing sheer attention to objects as emblems of his desire for the beloved. The resulting sense of focus makes clear how the power of love recalled can illuminate any landscape. This is still a conventional thematic echo of Romantic sensibilities. But the poem also takes on a projective dimension because of how the naming involved manifests so different a relation to the world from Gizzi's typical gestural mode. Such shifts demand self-consciousness, and Gizzi proves a powerful inquisitor of just what it takes to accommodate the self to this labor of naming. His conclusion turns outward, not as an effort at emotional mastery but as an admiration for how things both contain their history and afford new attitudes toward that history, attitudes that challenge an avant-garde emphasis on change:

There is so much stone here. And grass. So beautiful each
        translucent electric blade.
And the noise. Cheers folding into traffic. These things.
        Things that have been already said many times:
leaf, zipper, sparrow, lintel, scarf, window shade. (*SVLW*, 81)

The second poem, "Fin Amor," offers an intricate sequence that I must oversimplify in order to emphasize what Gizzi does with the motif of naming. (I cannot even capture the intricacy of the title, which involves the end of love as something passing and the end of love as an ideal part of loving, with echoes also of "finally love" as a partial private resolution for a volume tormented by what seem insoluble public issues. In addition, there are numerous sound equivalences like cries for "more.") The crucial change is embedded in the work Gizzi asks anaphora to accomplish as an intricate form of naming. Unlike gesture, anaphoric structures treat names as elements within more capacious frameworks, setting the stage for our recognition of the roles objects might play in our lives. Anaphora makes material and instrument utterly codependent, and thereby virtually forces the poems to become philosophical if they are to take responsibility for what they make possible. In effect, Gizzi adds a grammatical dimension to Romanticism as his way of fusing avant-garde sensibility with respect for past ambitions for what lyric can accomplish.

Three of the six sections work with anaphoric structures (and a fourth achieves intense plenitude by repetition of "blue" in several registers). The anaphoric poems establish for forms of expression what the repetition of "blue" does for a sense of objectivity. Together the blend of forms and names offers a new definition of the old power of song — that it makes articulate the forms of desire underlying repetitive syntax, as if attention to such structures intensifies the sense of need that desired objects can satisfy. Anaphora in Gizzi is necessarily abstract: the poem tests what desires a syntax can sustain. But the abstraction is not in tension with objects. Rather it raises them up to the kind of satisfactions that can occur when the objects become the instruments eliciting the song in the first place.

Notice, for example, how repeating "if" produces a sense of substance for the hypothetical space the grammar establishes:

> If love if then if now if the flowers of if the conditional
> if of arrows the condition of if
> if to say light to inhabit light if to speak if to live, so
> if to say it is you if love is if your form is if your waist
> that pictures the fluted stem if lavender
> if in this field
> if I were to say hummingbird it might behave as an adjective
> here (*SVLW*, 82)

We see the spirit of "here" returning with all its combination of particular and abstract force. Now its role is to designate this complex site of habitation where form modulates from characterizing the very space of "if" to designating the locus of desire in the waist that pictures the fluted stem.

The second of the anaphoric poems in this section, "Plain Song," emphasizes simpler linguistic structures, so in one sense the poem is more concrete than "Château If." But that very simplicity opens another vein of abstraction. This is the conclusion after three pages of various acts of summoning and of summing up:

> Some say "the good way," some "stuff"
> some say yes we need a form
> some say form is a simple thing some say yes the sky is a
> form of what is simple
>
> •
>
> some say molecular some open others porous some blue
> some say love some light some say the dark some heaven
> (*SVLW*, 91)

The poem identifies with the naming rather than objects eliciting the names, and so finds a simple yet powerful way to celebrate multiplicity as well as the degrees of involvement that constitute basic differences in our modes of valuing. More important, by varying punctuation and the presence and absence of quotation marks, the various sayings seem somewhat independent of formal linguistic concerns, as if the repeated sayings were capable of constituting substance.

Finally, "Reverse Song" has to be quoted almost in full for us to recapture the force of Gizzi's complex understanding of how names participate in grounding our desires and satisfactions. Here the history of lyric invents a Romantic sensibility that seems capable of subsisting by meeting all the demands the avant-garde might muster:

> Not because there is a road
> and a woman walking
> nor the trees lining this road,
> the light at half-mast
>
> not the birds in *v* crayon
>
> not the uneven houses lit up from within

not even the clapboard's chipped paint

nor the fact she is not alone
in the cricket sound

not the sun setting nor a first star . . .

not the catcalls making one stranger
nor the river gaining volume
making all sentient things still
crossing a bridge

not the lamp's sudden flame

but the type of daisy
robins live among,
circle of light found on the table,
her gait, her motion, her speed. (*SVLW*, 92–93)

I think this poem asks us to enter a space where the negative is much more forceful than the positive at the positive work of naming. In effect, the series of negations develop a virtual plot. It seems as if no details can satisfy—probably because the possibility of song depends on something other than detail. It depends on focusing and expanding this energy of negation, as if only what one can desire but not name provides an adequate frame for what can satisfy. Against that backdrop, against that dissatisfaction with event, the poem postulates the importance of the type of the daisy. (Gizzi is not one to miss the link between type as category and type as a medium.) Then "her gait, her motion, her speed" are not just observations about her but revelations of what is essential to her—her type and what it would take to type who she is against a background of all that she is not.[13]

Looking forward to the final and probably the best poem in the volume, "Beginning with a Phrase from Simone Weil," one could say that as Gizzi turns to the idea of Song, his poems offer explicit encounters with how song can become a mode of valuing. Song establishes a distinctive form of the present tense because it does not carry an epistemic relation to the world. We do not sing because something proves true, but because it comes to overwhelm us with a mode of presence that calls for celebration. Song directly evokes what can appeal intensely to imaginative needs. To make this condition visible, Gizzi has to negate and bypass our myths of immediate presence (and the gestures of imagist writing that make that presence available in lyric time):

> when we lose sight of a present,
> when there is no more everything. No more presence in
> everything loved.
> . . . .
> Is there no better presence than loss?
> A grace opening to air.
> No better time than the present. (*SVLW*, 95–96)

Ultimately, the history of lyric might be in large part constituted by an intricate series of negations in order to make present what is more than can be observed by acts of attention to the practical world. Once we see that one basic quest of self-conscious lyric is for something we can imagine as the type of intense particularity, we can understand how poets of every generation have to negate the present in honor of an ideal of presence that must combine that ideality with that specificity. This is the core of poetic naming, something well worth risking the effort to combine lyric and philosophical intelligence.

I have two remaining tasks. I want to represent Gizzi's fullest understanding of how poetry and philosophy might share common ends, and I want to propose one reason Gizzi ultimately cannot be satisfied by philosophy's ways of naming, even though he fully recognizes the full interdependence between two constitutive factors in experience — the interchanges between frame and observation and those between absence and the kinds of presence absence can afford. His latest book, *Threshold Songs* (2011), casts philosophical typing as simply too cavalier with history. This typing has to minimize the pains and vulnerabilities that call upon the presence of a needy individual as the focus for testing the resources poetry has to help us work through these conditions.[14] The important acts of naming in this volume are not frames for objects but concern the capacity to treat the subject as object without losing compassion and hope for the individual life. Naming the threshold does not matter much; feeling its danger and power is what the individual needs.

It is *The Outernationale* (2007), the book preceding *Threshold Songs*, that develops this transition away from philosophical reflection in romantic modes.

Its opening poems perfect what I am calling the naming powers of grammatical romanticism, only then to explore what those powers cannot bring about. Consider "Stung" first because it so clearly echoes in grammatical terms the structure of "Tintern Abbey." Its first of three sections presents the child free to absorb the world within himself: "If I became this light / it wasn't luck. It was easy" (*OUT*, 13). This sense of ease makes it possible for the subject to take in everything; nothing remains outside of his sense of power and possession:

> I held one true thing.
> This scene moved through me,
> a seesaw. A picture
> inside a question inside
> the coming night. (13–14)

The second section adjusts to seeing things as they are "outside in the grass / in March," "outside memory." This mode of seeing makes love possible in a variety of conditions (*OUT*, 14–15). But love for this poem is not the fullest state of consciousness, precisely because it so depends on what can be seen and felt, without self-consciousness. The third section offers Gizzi's version of Wordsworth's "paradise within greater far." Notice the way inside and outside generate one another's possibilities for plenitude of being (carried in part by the anaphoric use of "to," a great operator of possibility):

> To be and not to understand.
> To understand nothing
> and be content
> to watch light against
> leaf-shadowed ground.
> To accept the ground.
> To go to it as a question.
> To open up the day inside the day,
> a bubble holding air
> bending the vista to it.
> To be inside this thing,
> outside in the grass place,
> out in the day
> inside another thing. (*OUT*, 15–16)

Intelligent as "Stung" is, the poem seems somewhat stiff in its three-part structure and somewhat flat in its intricate and beautiful sound structures. So I prefer as Gizzi's probably richest statement of his possibilities for an overtly philosophical poetry the intricate concreteness of the last section of the volume's opening poem, "A Panic That Can Still Come Upon Me." Again, the basic concern is for anaphora to establish how names and the world can fuse with one another while at the same time honoring those differences between domains that have been the cause of so much suffering. And again, the key operator is "if." But now "if" structures what seems a synthesis between the virtual and the existential, each completing the other's mode of naming:

> If we struggle for a name
> if colors change
>
> if mood is connected to naming, to color
>
> If say a ship's in deep water
> and a piece of sky empties the mind
>
> or when I was frigate-tossed
>
> If I wanted to go all over a word
> and live inside its name, so be it
>
> There is my body and the idea of my body
> the surf breaking and the picture of a wave (*OUT*, 11)

One has to ask how Gizzi can invoke such traditionally warring elements as body and idea while seeming to refuse all tension between them. The answer has to involve the power of the hypothetical, aligned with the poet's desire to so flesh out virtual space that he can live inside a name. Living inside a name means internalizing all the power that the name can muster — to refer but also to determine what become the appropriate contexts by which reference might be elaborated. At this level of identification with the name, one has to correlate the body and the idea of the body: each would seem empty without the other.

The same case is harder to make for the division between the surf breaking and its picture of a wave because the wave is only at best a metonymy for the surf. Overcoming that difficulty gives the poem its distinctive power. The difference between surf and wave introduces a time lag between the event and its picture. Differences multiply, but the multiplication provides routes for a synthesis. The picture of the wave is not potentially identical with the surf, as is the idea of a body with the body. The picture does, however, come to symbolize or represent the surf, giving it another kind of ideal existence, and providing another sense of how the mind's constructs serve complex naming functions. Here the reader rather than the poem has to do the work of the negative. And that work, I think, provides an even richer sense of complex presence, reinforced by the poet's choice to end the poem so abruptly that we have to attribute powers of closure to this final phrase. Poets typically condemn mere pictures as only representations that lack the force of will and desire. Here by concluding with the picture, Gizzi gives it an abstract concreteness and sonic extension that seems to be a celebration of how surf might evoke a full range of concrete satisfactions. The poem insists not only that the picture of the wave is as real as the surf breaking, but also that it evokes a particular power to embrace the sense of picture as a fundamental force making repeated experience possible and pleasurable.

As *The Outernationale* develops, it elaborates the negative dimension of the within-without relation basic to its strange title. It becomes increasingly difficult for the volume to consider selves as representative or names as capturing types that will carry exemplary value. "Beacon," for example, demands of reflection that it capture not the choices that seem free but "the ones you are made of" (*OUT*, 32). And this poem beautifully articulates the kind of personal name that evokes primarily a private history:

> I heard my name
> one day from the road.
> It startled me, that alias
> bringing me inside. (37)

Romantic naming also fails in a more surprising way in "Vincent, Homesick for the Land of Pictures." Here what can satisfy the painter because of its qualities as picture constantly frustrates the poet who is addressing Vincent and demanding meanings rather than the constant barrage of images:

> But felt things exist in shadow, let us reflect.
> The darkness bears a shine as yet unpunished by clarity
> but perhaps a depth that outshines clarity and is true. (*OUT*, 48)

The considerable power of the poem lies in Gizzi's efforts to make language have the same supplemental extension of seeing as brushstroke can give a painted image:

> To step into it as into a large surf in late August
> to go out underneath it all above and sparkling.
> To wonder and to dream and to look up at it (*OUT*, 49)

But the poet gets distracted by this reliance on the "I." Poetry has to grapple with darkness and stress questions rather than celebrate images.

Not surprisingly, all of these refusals of Romantic values, even those suitable to an avant-garde consciousness, come to the fore at the conclusion of the volume, where Gizzi characteristically defines the grappling that will occupy his next book. The second "Outernationale" dwells on the pains of having to be this isolated "I," however many its facets. The poet's home has to be in the dark, if only because the drama of coming into the light makes sense of the poet's art. The poet does not find names and frames but brings artifice to bleak truth:

> The wanting that keeps us
> looking hard into the dark.
> The dark we hope to unpack
> and move into
> that one day
> we might find ourselves lit up. (*OUT*, 102)

Craft might not quite light up the self, but it brings stunning pleasure to the possibility of such lighting. Notice first the preponderance of monosyllables, as if the speaking would go to any length to sustain an impression that it has gotten to bedrock conditions. Then this version of truth starts to light up. "Wanting" gets concretized by "looking," which in turn establishes the long "o" of the next two verbs. "Dark" gets concretized by its echoing "hard" and so becomes inseparable from the looking and so the wanting. The passage then moves from internal rhyme to assonance, all dominant effects because of the economy of the presentation. But all this is only preface to the brilliant final line. "Lit up" is a large claim bordering on visionary heroism. Yet here, the preparatory series of "I" sounds occurs in the most modest possible syntax: being lit up does not depend on will but on chance that makes us "appendages to evolution" (*OUT*, 107). Yet we know from the sound effects how to recognize such grace when it might occur. And grace is one thing the Romantic philosophical imagination must ignore in its confidence that mind and world structurally reflect one another. We may need the darkness if it can lead us to challenge the hubris of such a faith.

NOTES

1. David Fite in *Harold Bloom: The Rhetoric of Romantic Vision* (Amherst: University of Massachusetts Press, 2009, 110–15) does a good job of showing how Bloom leads us back to the roles these terms played in classical rhetoric. I think it is fair to say that ethos in a rhetorical performance tries to get the audience to identify with the speaker, while pathos exhibits the speaker's capacity to identify with the suffering of his or her audience.

2. Wallace Stevens, *The Complete Poems of Wallace Stevens* (New York: Knopf, 1971), 64; 49.

3. Ibid., 9.

4. See J. H. Prynne, "Image and Figure in Twentieth-Century English Translation of Chinese Poetry," May 1991, babylon.acad.cai.cam.ac.uk/students/study/english/chinese/imaglect.pdf, accessed Sept. 8, 2008.

5. Robert Creeley, *The Collected Poems of Robert Creeley 1945–1975* (Berkeley: University of California Press, 2006), 281.

6. Stevens, *Complete Poems*, 326.

7. One might say that John Ashbery becomes a philosophical poet because of the abstract self-consciousness he brings to his ways of gesturing. And perhaps it takes Ashbery's indirection now not to feel the limitations of a poetics so bound to the accuracy and generality of the naming process. This poetry has to ignore, or has to claim the power to ignore, the troubling density of historical particulars, which also haunt the gestural as that which might challenge the effort to resist pathos.

8. Marjorie Perloff, "To Wonder without Becoming Dry," *Boston Book Review* 5–6 (Aug. 1998): 34–35. I am heartened by this observation from Robert N. Casper in an interview with Gizzi in *Jubilat* 14: "I find your poems have a signature gestural quality — certainly rhetorically, but also in terms of theme, and in the way they address the present and the past. Stylistically, they gesture toward a range of influences as well, and yet they are tonally uniform. Your last two books, *Some Values of Landscape and Weather* and *The Outernationale*, seem to extend this gestural quality" (n.p.). One might also note that just the title of Gizzi's volume offers a marvelously intricate gesture. At one pole it refers entirely to the pressure of reality: even the heart is mechanical and controlled from elsewhere. Yet the poems the volume contains involve another kind of artifice that comes close to producing a living heart, just because here artifice may be necessary to produce a range and depth of feeling not readily available within our culture.

9. I prefer the concept of dispositions in conflict rather than voices because a disposition seems to me to encompass more of a complete perspective, but unlike perspective, a disposition is a modality toward action rather than toward efforts at knowledge.

10. I omit from my reading how the mildly anaphoric use of "if" here continues the activity of complicating what allows objects to appear. We will have other occasions to take up what the anaphoric involves for Gizzi.

11. Let me cite three consecutive endings to make concrete the role of gesture as the negotiation of historical dilemma in Gizzi's poetics. From "Imitation of Life: A Memoir": "We live pedaling into the sunset, looking for the sound / coming from an abandoned parking lot" (*SVLW*, 35). From "Take the 5:10 to Dreamland": "The Green of Night is upon the door. / today a girl asked if doves / blow into old bottles to call to us / Small things are what prey upon sleep" (*SVLW*, 37). And from "Edgar Poe": "Winter's the thing / I miss. The font is still. / A fanfare of stone air" (*SVLW*, 38).

12. In his interview with Robert Casper, Gizzi says he likes to conclude a volume with poems that look forward to the new possibilities to be taken up by his next book.

13. I am "buoyed" (*OUT*, 76) by the fact that Gizzi returns to the type motif as a mode of praising the singularity of the beloved in "Lines Depicting Simple Happiness" (*OUT*, 45): "With you nothing is simple yet nothing is simpler / About you many good things come into relation."

14. Gizzi's interview with Ben Lerner provides a very useful context for the pressures Gizzi is responding to in *Threshold Songs*. See "Poetry at the Threshold: Peter Gizzi on Lyric Selfhood and the Perils of Singing," *Poetry Foundation*, www.poetryfoundation.org/article/243686, accessed Apr. 27, 2016.

3 | KACPER BARTCZAK

The Artifice of Personhood and the Poetics of Plenitude in Peter Gizzi's Archeophonics

The Whitmanian strand of American poetry, to which Peter Gizzi belongs, evokes the themes of excess and plenitude. There are various plenitudes, of course. Harold Bloom reaches for a kind of plenitude when he proposes a reading of Freud and formulates his theory of influence. Here, plenitude is the Plotinian *pleroma*, a fullness from before the fall into belatedness.[1] But to the extent to which Bloom's "influence" evokes Emerson's thought, Bloom is part of an American tradition that predates psychoanalysis; call it Emersonian-pragmatist. Richard Poirier speaks of it when he remarks on Emerson's "superfluousness" as "an effort to refloat the world."[2] In a similar vein, Stanley Cavell returns to the Emersonian excess when he mentions a "form of breathing . . . that opposes the breath in my body to the ideas that fill the common air."[3] This comment by Cavell relates to a passage in "Fate," where Emerson claims, somewhat cryptically, that "the air is full of men." The task of reading Peter Gizzi, a contemporary heir to this tradition, is to begin to sense the literal meaning behind this apparently metaphorical splicing of the realm of ideas with the realm of physical stimuli.

In Gizzi, the physical presence of the world cannot be distinguished from a consciousness of it. His way of characterizing this poetics has been to speak of poetry as dictation taking, and his fascination with Jack Spicer suggests that his openness to dictation taking may be a part of what Robin Blaser has called "the practice of outside."[4] It remains to be discussed, however, how Gizzi's poems differ from Spicer's in negotiating the evanescence of the poetic self as it comes to participate in the plenitude of the outside. For Blaser, the poet becomes a medium letting the otherness of language speak through, a gesture the tradition of which goes back to Blake via Yeats. I see Gizzi's poems as a further exploration into what happens to the medium itself, an exploration that brings back the Emersonian reverberation of the Not-Me. With Emersonian exteriority the stakes differ: dispersal is accompanied by a painful return of a self, as the poem's artifice offers a model of personhood. To see what Gizzi's latest volume, *Archeophonics*, contributes to this poetics is to ask about the poem's conflict-ridden participation in the external excess and notice its modulation into a specific kind of self that emerges in the process.

The participation begins on the material level. Cole Swensen sees Gizzi's poems as concerned with the question of "how things [are] put together" and "how they hold,"[5] and she tries to show how he abandons the epistemological model. While I think this is correct, it also seems to me that we have yet to catch up with the radicalness with which Gizzi leaves behind the dualisms of traditional epistemology. As Swensen notes, Gizzi invites us to think beyond the "conceptual frames"[6] that keep the world and language separate. However, such removal of the inside-outside barrier also requires us to step beyond the scheme-versus-content model of representation, which means giving up on the question of seeking kinds of "order" beyond language.[7]

To probe Gizzi's radical answer to the question of how things hang together, we should return to William James's assertion, in his *Pluralistic Universe*, that they do so in many ways, and that the connective possibilities depend on the human inquirer. What James means is not lack of order but the indelibility of the human participation in any order whatsoever. To ask how things keep together is the same as to ask how we compose them.[8] Joan Richardson traces this line of thinking from Edwards to James, and names it "the natural history of pragmatism." Richardson shows convincingly how the American transformation of Puritan religiousness toward the stance of openness to the potential of the world, a stance that James called "the will to believe," means that the world of human beliefs and desires interpenetrates with the world of matter.[9] Here, inquiry becomes a composition of the world, conducted by organisms endowed with a spectrum of purposive reactions, beyond the barrier between the organic, the mineral, the spiritual, and the cognitive.

In Gizzi's poems, this stance is realized in the formula of the "song." The poem as song is the experience of the birth of knowledge, an event generating intelligent sentience, a nexus of the psychological, the physiological, the somatic, and the cognitive. Writing poetry beyond the scheme-versus-content distinction means being permanently in touch with the world,[10] but the poem as song is not a neutral realization of this post-Cartesian proposition. It becomes a state of intensity that not only signifies sentience but causes its rise to the level of pain that belongs to a person. *Archeophonics* continues this non-Cartesian poetics, but it also tests its processes by searching out moments when the world-disclosing descriptions stall. When they do, Gizzi becomes a Stevensian scholar of "the nothing," but with this difference, however: that his reductions to "nothingness" reject Stevens's abstraction and reveal the poem as painfully personal.

Archeophonics continues the themes of the poems' emerging from the excess of stimuli. In this mode, the inside-outside barriers vanish to enable a larger voice that belongs to poetic enhancement of the inquiry. The emerging voice, as before, transcends personality and individual contour. "I am just visiting this voice," reads the first line of the new volume, establishing a connection with previous such moments in Gizzi. In "Human Memory Is Organic," for instance, we find a similar trope of a powerful external visitation: "I am just a visitor to this world" (*OUT*, 27). Now, however, the "visitor" is even more external, signaling that it is different not only from the dead, geological matter of the world (which it haunts and pushes toward life), but even from the "voice" of the poem. The increase in the distance increases the invading force. In an important poem of the new volume, "A Garden in the Air," Gizzi's cryptic syntax identifies the locale of the poem as "here on the terra forming" (*ARCH*, 48), as if the poem itself were a planet going through its geological and organic convulsions. In all these poems, the *poesis* of world-disclosure/world-making injects poetic movement into matter, mineral or organic, as the action of the poem is found at the geological levels of "glass" and "salt" (*OUT*, 27), or it is identified with the work of atoms, genes, organic chemistry. In a poem from *Archeophonics* called "the winter sun says fight," an apparently personal voice suddenly loses contour, as the speaker is distributed over an expanse that confounds any division between inside and outside:

Where
do I actually live so far
outside my head deep
inside the chemical
wash of my genes. (*ARCH*, 32)

Such distributions testify to a merger of two traditions: the Romantic perception of nature as presence and the twentieth-century dispersal of presence by increased textuality. Gizzi submits the poem to large external forces of a natural kind, locating the sources of poetic speech — in Whitman-like fashion — in the midst of elemental natural phenomena: electricity, air masses, geology, light, or gravity. Such forces are called upon to organize the flow of poems, which is perhaps especially clear in some minimalistic lyrics. In a short poem "Fragment" from *Threshold Songs*, the spaced-out lines cohere only, if they do at all, if we see them as intervals within, or traces of, gravitational spinning (*TS*, 18). Yet these natural elements, when so evoked, are never far from the forces of lexis, syntax, and textuality. Those poems in *Archeophonics* that resemble "Fragment" in their form — by their overall minimalism, the anaphoric repetitiveness that bespeaks control and economy — point clearly to this enmeshing. In "How to Read," for instance, the sparse formulations give the poem over to systems of exchange that project fusions of large masses, thermodynamics, and gravity. The poem registers "a syntax of heat and dynamism," "a giganto space of silence, time," physical entities that the progression of lines recognizes as part of the same order that also contains human psychology raving between its extremities: "A human world mewling in the dark" and "A mind on fire in the heat of the quest." Such combination is then revealed to be a result, or the very essence, of a poetics, as the poem becomes aware of its own prosody and rhetoricity ("rhythm, percussion, assonance") and modulates toward the idea of "a textual nimbus, air born" (*ARCH*, 52). Textuality replacing physical presence does not signify idealism: material nature does not disappear. Far from it. Gizzi's poetics of exposure to external excesses is faithful to the Emersonian-pragmatist line in which nature is inseparable from a purposive, focused inquiry of it. In poetry this means an enhancement of natural forces as they are now smoothly connected — through rhetorical action — to psychology, both communal and individual.

Accessing psychology through rhetoric signifies the presence of a specific rendering of poetic influence. Gizzi's poems proliferate within the medium of "air"— the word signifying the literal physical mass, but also a transmission and a communication channel. The air as medium is a depository of the message, a recording and storage device. Poetic speech as breathing is entering an "archive," as we are reminded in the opening lyric, but there is a constant sense in this volume that it is not just the human mouth that utters the sounds, but the "air" itself. Natural presence is inseparable from the way it has been described by previous poetic speech acts. "All the stars are here," we read within a series called "A Winding Sheet for Summer," "that belonged to whatever was speaking" (*ARCH*, 62). This means that the brushes with matter in the volume are brushes with poetic predecessors. *Archeophonics* is an archeology of the layers of sound deposited in so-called nature; some of this sound has already been a poem, a poem by Dickinson, by Whitman, or by Stevens.

Such an approach modifies Bloom's idea of influence away from an internal drama of one poet-person's psychology, whereby this psychology takes shape in opposition to a rhetorical-psychological formation belonging to a predecessor poet. In Gizzi, this Freudian text is subsumed under the Emersonian-pragmatist one in which the influence is received from the physical presence of the world, a materiality not to be distinguished from the earlier poetic achievement. Gizzi accepts the existence of an already formulated rhetorical-psychical space. He welcomes it as poetic environment proper, to be entered and participated in, just as a physical surrounding is entered and specifically "participated in" by an inquirer. Such modification to the notion of influence also changes the mode of poetic being: from the struggle with the predecessor to a kind of accelerated involvement in the network that connects the material and the psychical. Yet, the element of struggle does not vanish: now the struggle is not against the internalized image of a predecessor, but against the increased capacity of the poem as a situation to receive or intercept the stimuli of various kinds, what we might call the heightened receptivity of the act itself.

And just as in the Bloomian poetics of influence, it is the struggle that leads to individuation. A poem by Gizzi is a specific disturbance of externality through which an artifice of personhood emerges and is endowed with sentience, cognition, memory, historical consciousness. We may return at this point to the already quoted "the winter sun says fight," in which the personal moments are contaminated and distorted by their openness to the external forces whose mere physical presence points to the text of the previous poet. Thus, the admonition to "fight," contained in the title, alludes to Stevens, with his northern lights, here evoked early on in "the arctic blasts [that] say fight" (*ARCH*, 31). But the figure points not so much to an "anxiety" resulting from another poet's priority, as to an anxiety of expecting that a mere presence of physical phenomena will hit soon with a wave of rhetorical radiation that puts the self in touch with itself, calling it into existence, at the price of being simultaneously spread and scattered amid various ontological orders.

Private selves emerge in the rays of lexical, syntactic spectrums, emanating from matter, and their human emergence testifies to the unity of natural evolution and human historicity. In a beautiful short poem called "A Social History of Mercury," the scattered lines link up a moment of private self-recognition to the dimensions of historicity and mineral nature. The speaker obtains a narcissistic self-reflection in a domestically carved moment, governed by a constellation of light. Domestic materials become a mirror, but so involved in human self-recognitions that they are also revealed in their historical moldings, subject to the mutations of human history—describable, contingent, prone to language. Language is the medium of change, a source of history, a kind of natural deposit itself: "Simply primeval / Words live here / Take root / Their vocative flourish" (*ARCH*, 30).

This is the poetics of the human-nonhuman reciprocity in which poetry is an insight and enhancement of a total evolution of whatever exists. *Archeophonics* gathers its motifs from the previous volumes. But the new collection proposes a gesture that, although also present before, now becomes more pronounced. A poetics of excessive reciprocity needs defenses with which the poem can find its shape and contour against all kinds of externality. In *Archeophonics*, the poems often work against the increased capacity of the poetic process, trying to put it on halt, searching moments of the fault in the process, rethinking their own emptiness or "nothingness."

One of the dominant tropes of "Field Recordings," the opening longer series of the volume, is the metaphor of "the old language." It is interesting to hear from a post-Language poet of the medium itself becoming "old." In some moments the trope signals a break in the transmission of the otherwise widely opened and increased poetic receptivity, what Gizzi calls "calibration," and the failure of the medium. "The old language," we learn at one point, "don't mean shit." The medium is revealed in its low orders and states, close to the gutter, dirt. Or even close to a lie; the indices of language, we hear at one point, its categories, have been "a lyre" (*ARCH*, 6). Our categories and concepts — the grounds and mechanics of knowledge — were formed within the medium of a melody produced by language as the poetic instrument — a lyre, which is the source of sound, and also the primary vehicle of poetry. Yet such poetry-as-knowledge is also a "liar," its very action and movement departing from any form of the stone-dead literal. But a poet of language as evolutionary force has to be careful accusing language of being a lie. The poetic element as the driving force is a necessary "lie"— a power of diversion from whatever refuses the metamorphic rhetoricity in the name of however understood literalness. Gizzi's poems, after all, feed on misnaming and error — on the lie in the vitalistic, Nietzschean, and Emersonian sense.

Thus, here, language's lie must mean something different, for instance its saturation with some discourses that, perhaps, want to sever their genetic relations to mutability and experiment, instead professing infallibility. Politics is a candidate, as a discourse of a specific kind of failure to which all poems of contemporary externality must be exposed. Here, "the old language" means threadbare ideological prattle, a language that mocks the normal commitment, so important to the Emersonian-pragmatist. It is "The old language / [that] renews the pundits' / chatter," and the poem must work against it (*ARCH*, 14).

But poems in *Archeophonics* go further in challenging their normal element of increased rhetorical flows between various ontological realms. They at times question the flows themselves. A number of poems in the volume contain the gesture of saying "no" to things, to matter. The gesture itself appeared earlier, in a poem in *Threshold Songs* called "A Note on the Text," where we read, "the good poets defy things / with their heart" (59). However, in that poem such heartfelt defiance went against things as reified meanings, in fact fueling the metamorphic operations of poetic rhetoric. In *Archeophonics*, in contrast, the denial turns against these operations themselves. We notice how poems seek breaks in transmission and its de-acceleration. One such moment occurs early on, in a section of "Field Recordings," when a parking lot, one of Gizzi's favorite localities, undergoes an unexpected freeze of connections:

> A sun-slashed parking lot,
> thinking a poem
> stalled

in the broken
surround. (*ARCH*, 9)

The stalling is part of the general slowing down dominating the section, and it is uncharacteristic. More usually, an exposure to light, especially the sun, helps the fluency of the poem in Gizzi, making it a more expansive construct. Here, interestingly, the sun's rays "slash" vision, thwarting the movement of composition.

The poem returns us to some earlier parking-lot compositions in Gizzi, and likewise tests the results of their Stevens-like reductions. Gizzi's parking-lot poems are modern-day "Snow Man" exercises, in which a sharp intake of light blinds the speaker, revealing in return the power of the mind to take its own constructions apart. As we well know by now, in Stevens such reductions result in the increase of the poetic power itself.[11] Stevens moves later in his career, notably in "Notes Toward a Supreme Fiction," from a simple decreation of a winter landscape to reimagining the Sun in a Romantic flexing of imagination. Gizzi writes in the same vein when, in his earlier parking-lot scene, "In Defense of Nothing," his ability to accept the scene's poverty indicates a sort of faith in the poem — to say that the intercepted aesthetic scarcity of the scene "will have to do" (*SVLW*, 53) is to imply imagination's self-sufficiency. It is this mood that is reevaluated in *Archeophonics*, where poems of the sun contain reductions to "nothing" of a different sort, more ambiguous, less assertive, more private, concretely human.

A whole group of poems in *Archeophonics* recalibrates the abstract Stevensian nothingness as trope of poetic power to a nothingness that belongs to moments of existential distortion. Where Stevens achieves imaginative strength that allows him to redescribe physical forces, he does that at the modernist price of replacing a person with a "mind." But the kinds of sentience we have seen emerging within Gizzi's poems swerve away from such abstraction and reveal a self. It is a self within closed, private surroundings, consulting the poverty of its enclosure, finding its reflections in creaking floorboards or house interiors. Stevens's triumphant "nothing that is"— a poetic substance that brags its priority over any ontology — gives way to jumbled local bits and pieces, "erratic nothings," nothingness as error, misnaming, in which the self sees its "warping" and strangeness, as it finds itself "do all the talking" (*ARCH*, 49).

The powerful poetic processes that invade the poem do not erase the self, as they do in Spicer or Stevens; a self is in fact emerging here — but it is tainted with all the intensity, artifice, and contingency of the poetic process. It is "dearrange[d] and uncompose[d]" (*ARCH*, 8). This warped and deranged self speaks from many of the poems in *Archeophonics*. Although emerging in opposition to the poem's fluid passage amid ontological orders, this self is aware of its affinity to the process and the external forces ushered in. In its loneliness and strangeness, it still sees itself as belonging to them. Floors of all kinds, wooden or geological, revolve in Gizzi's plenitudes, and so do the artificial, touched, emerging selves of these poems: "The fact I spin and it spins and everything is spinning close up" (*ARCH*, 26).

The poetics of external excess changes into a poetics of plenitude. Here, by plenitude I mean something different from sheer excess: a transformation of all sorts of excesses — textual, linguistic, cultural, mineral, and organic alike — into a fresh multidimensionality of a self, redeemed, as it comprehends its artifice and strangeness. In Gizzi, Stevens's "listener," who is "nothing himself," is given a voice and power to personalize his nothingness as significant distortion that he is now able to acknowledge. Although painful, the acceptance is an achievement — it gives us a truer, more authentic, Western self for today. When so revealed, there may be a community of such selves — others who will identify with the ironic self-limitation and courage of this poetry's voice, as it begins to reconcile with its human connections:

> I came from a different world.
> I will die in it.
> Someone saw it, I love them for seeing it.
> I love seeing it with them. (*ARCH*, 66)

NOTES

1. For an earlier discussion that connects Gizzi's poetry to my concept of the poetics of plenitude, see Kacper Bartczak, "The Poetics of Plenitude and Its Crisis in Wallace Stevens, Rae Armantrout, and Peter Gizzi: A Pragmatist Perspective," in *Exorcising Modernism*, ed. Mikołaj Wiśniewski (Warsaw: SWPS Press, 2014), 254–97.

2. Richard Poirier, *Poetry and Pragmatism* (Cambridge, MA: Harvard University Press, 1992), 40.

3. Stanley Cavell, *Philosophical Passages: Wittgenstein, Emerson, Austin, Derrida* (Oxford: Blackwell, 1995), 171.

4. Robin Blaser, "The Practice of Outside," in *The Collected Books of Jack Spicer*, ed. Robin Blaser (Santa Rosa, CA: Black Sparrow Press, 1999), 271–326.

5. Cole Swensen, "Peter Gizzi's City: The Political Quotidian," in *American Poets in the 21st Century: The New Poetics*, ed. Claudia Rankine and Lisa Sewell (Middletown, CT: Wesleyan University Press, 2007), 111–12.

6. Ibid., 113–14.

7. On abandoning the scheme-content distinction, see Donald Davidson, "On the Very Idea of a Conceptual Scheme," in *Inquiries into Truth and Interpretation* (Oxford: Clarendon Press, 1984), 183–98.

8. I am referring to the conclusions to *A Pluralistic Universe*, in which James develops the idea of a "strung-along type" of the connectivity of things, by which he means a multitude of the possible connections, each however involving a "concretely felt experience," which presupposes the presence of an inquirer; see William James, conclusions to *Pluralistic Universe*, in *Writings 1902–1910* (New York: Library of America, 1987), 778.

9. See chapter on William James in Joan Richardson, *A Natural History of Pragmatism: The Fact of Feeling from Jonathan Edwards to Gertrude Stein* (Cambridge: Cambridge University Press, 2007), 98–136.

10. Davidson writes, "In giving up the dualism of scheme and world we reestablish unmediated touch with familiar objects." Davidson, "On the Very Idea of a Conceptual Scheme," 198.

11. For the discussion of Stevens's reductive poetics resulting in the increase of the imaginative, world-disclosing power, see Harold Bloom, *Wallace Stevens: The Poems of Our Climate* (Ithaca: Cornell University Press, 1977), 173–74; and Joseph N. Riddel, *The Clairvoyant Eye: The Poetry and Poetics of Wallace Stevens* (Baton Rouge: Louisiana State University Press, 1991), 184. These critics show how Stevens's abstraction and his reductions to the "first idea" beam back on the creative powers of the poem.

4 | MARJORIE PERLOFF

Peter Gizzi's Poetics of Contingency

If exit is merely a sign. . . .

Suppose the "if" clause in this epigraph is valid; suppose the "EXIT" sign in the building you're trying to leave, or in the maze-like parking garage in which you're circling, points to nothing outside itself, that it is merely a rectangular piece of aluminum or plastic bearing the four letters E-X-I-T. *No Exit*: Sartre's drama by that title in English — the French *Huis Clos* means "behind closed doors"— is the tale of three "guilty" people whose punishment is to be confined in a room together, mentally torturing one another throughout eternity. Peter Gizzi's "A Panic That Can Still Come Upon Me," the poem that poses the question "If exit is merely a sign," avoids the pessimistic dissection of bad faith found in "No Exit." Rather, his "if" clauses — and they are, as various critics have noted,[1] a central device in his poetry — are left suspended even as the poet's "I" never quite gives up hope for something better — or at least something different — to come. Indeed, despite his association, during his Buffalo years and his editorship of *o-blēk*, with Language poetry and related French experimental paradigms, Gizzi's is a poetics of contingency squarely in the American tradition — the tradition, most immediately, of William Carlos Williams and Hart Crane, as well as of the intersection of these two great modernists in the lyrics of Frank O'Hara.

"*If* I when my wife is sleeping," we read in Williams's "Danse Russe," the unstated "then" clauses, describing the secret pleasures of being alone, only to conclude, with wry bravado, "Who shall say I am not / the happy genius of my household?"[2] And O'Hara's "Music," which begins with the lines "*If* I rest for a moment near The Equestrian / pausing for a liver sausage sandwich in the Mayflower Shoppe," finds the poet trying to brace himself against the passage of time and death by insisting that "my door is open to the evenings of midwinter's / lightly falling snow over the newspapers."[3]

But Gizzi's particular brand of *openness* differs from his precursors', in that, on the cusp of the twenty-first century, the desire for transparency finds itself always already mediated by the discourses that incessantly impinge on our consciousness. What is there, after all, that hasn't already been said or documented? Then, too, after 9/11, issues of the dissemination of information have taken on a new urgency. Two of Gizzi's long poems of the 2000s—"Revival" (2002) and "A Panic That Can Still Come Upon Me" (2006)—are a case in point. The first appears in *Some Values of Landscape and Weather* (2003), and the second is the lead poem in *The Outernationale* (2007), but both were originally published as chapbooks—a format especially appropriate for Gizzi's lyric, inflected as it is by the spatial design of the visual arts.

Panic Days

"A Panic That Can Still Come Upon Me" gives a new spin to the question of transparency. Since the bombing of the World Trade Center, keeping one's door *open* no longer seems such a ready option: secrecy, protection, security, identity theft are now issues of daily life, triggering their share of panic attacks. The chapbook's cover design by Anna Moschovakis and Genya Turovskaya (figure 1) is masterly: what looks like a large sun, its rays of light covering the page in reddish-brown, is also an empty circle, the blank face of a human being, arms outstretched into the nothingness beyond.

The five-part sequence, now reprinted in his Wesleyan University Press *Selected Poems*, begins:

> If today and today I am calling aloud
>
> If I break into pieces of glitter on asphalt
> bits of sun, the din

if tires whine on wet pavement
everything humming

If we find we are still in motion
and have arrived in Zeno's thought, like

if sunshine hits marble and the sea lights up
we might know we were loved, are loved
if flames and harvest, the enchanted plain (*SP*, 121)

The independent clause does not come until line 9 and solves nothing, for the seeming resolution, "we might know we were loved, are loved," immediately dissolves into the next "if" clause. And indeed, a note of curious irresolution is there from the start in the doubling of "today and today," the repetition implying that the need to "call aloud" is ongoing: it is felt today and then again today, even though it is not clear that anyone is hearing the poet's call. The self dissolves "into pieces of glitter" hitting the asphalt, "bits" of that sun we see on the cover, an unspecified "din." In lines 5 to 6, the muted monosyllables give way to allusion: "wet pavement" refers to the Ashbery poem by that title, and "everything humming" echoes two O'Hara poems — the already mentioned "Music" ("and I am naked as a table cloth, my nerves humming") and "A Step Away from Them," where "Everything / suddenly honks." But whereas O'Hara's "I do this, I do that" poems still feature a determinate speaker moving through a particular landscape in a coherent temporal sequence, Gizzi's lyric shifts ground without warning, soon taking up Zeno's Paradox and then the possibility of some kind of momentary escape to a realm where "sunshine hits marble and the sea lights up"— a realm of love.

But the moment of breakthrough is quickly dissipated:

> If our wishes are met with dirt
> and thyme, thistle, oil,
> heirloom, and basil
>
> or the end result is worry, chaos
> and if "I should know better"
>
> If our loves are anointed with missiles
> Apache fire, Tomahawks
> did we follow the tablets the pilgrims suggested (*SP*, 121–22)

Here the references to "missiles / Apache fire, Tomahawks" function as a reminder of the relationship of contemporary violence (the Iraq war raging at the time) to its "Pilgrim" heritage. But the catalogue that precedes it complicates this rather predictable linkage: the medicinal herbs mentioned are the very opposite of "dirt"; both "thyme" (with pun on "time") and basil have strong literary associations with healing: in Keats's "Isabella, or the Pot of Basil," the head of the heroine's lover is hidden in a pot and covered with the protective herb. And wounds were regularly bathed in oil to assuage the pain. "Our wishes" may be rebuffed by dirt and thistle, but the pain is also palliated by thyme, basil, oil. As for "heirloom," the noun is equivocal in the context: the heirloom may be a comfort, or again it may be an irritating reminder of an obsolete ways of doing things. Either way, the confusion is such that the "end result is worry, chaos, and . . . 'I should know better.'"

Gizzi's is thus a kind of ode on what Samuel Johnson called "The Vanity of Human Wishes." But how to convey the complexity and confusion of contemporary life without making the poem itself confusing? How to ensure that "every song touch its origin / just once" (*SP*, 122)? The poet's urgent tercets culminate in a mock-Romantic gesture:

if in the auroras' reflecting the sea,
gauze touching the breast

Too bad for you, beautiful singer
unadorned by laurel
child of thunder and scapegoat alike (123)

Wallace Stevens's "Auroras of Autumn," with their intimations of immortality, fade into the recognition that the "beautiful singer" (an allusion to Stevens's "Idea of Order at Key West") is here "unadorned by laurel," a scapegoat of society as well as Zeus's child. No transcendence here, where "trains / run next to the freeway"— a particularly unpleasant but accurate image of transportation glut and crowding as we know it today, where there is no escaping an incessant movement that seems to lead nowhere. And now, without the necessary "then" clause, we come to that separate line, "If exit is merely a sign."

No sadness, just disaster, as John Cage put it in talking about Jasper Johns's "In Memory of my Feelings." The poem avoids descending into bathos by making its options and eventualities so compelling that we are swept along by the lyric momentum of Gizzi's abrupt couplets and tercets. The auxiliary verb "is," for example, finds its mirror image in the first two letters of "sign," suggesting that there is no way out of this closed circle: it merely *is*. "A Panic That Can Still Come Upon Me" proceeds from these premises, coming to a climax in the death wish of Part 4, where branch, pine scent, stones, creek, hair, water, and "one crow skating by" remain startlingly separate, and the poet, in lines alluding to Whitman's "As I Ebb'd with the Ocean of Life," contemplates "saying goodbye to myself."

But that's not the end of it. In the remarkable turn of Part 5, the poet suddenly remarks "I am not stupid," and from here on out, more hopeful possibilities suggest themselves. "Why," the question is posed, playing on a well-worn cliché, "shouldn't I come in from the cold"? He can now lampoon the romantic notion of being "frigate-tossed"— a reference to Thomas Chambers's great melodramatic mid-nineteenth-century painting *Storm-Tossed Frigate*, but also to the great shipwreck poems of the nineteenth century from Coleridge's "Ancient Mariner" to Rimbaud's "Bateau ivre." And "A Panic" concludes:

if I wanted to go all over a word
and live inside its name, so be it

There is my body and the idea of my body
the surf breaking and the picture of a wave (*SP*, 129)

The first line here is, as Rob Stanton notes, a renewed avowal of the poet's vocation.[4] To "go all over a word / and live inside its name" is to declare oneself firmly in the corner of poetry: "so be it." In the poet's consciousness there is, finally, no difference between "my body and the idea of my body," between the "surf breaking" on a "real shore" and "the picture of a wave." The art/life division, Gizzi declares, is false, and in that sense, "EXIT" is never only a sign.

The Revival of Panic

A similar thematic complex is at the heart of a second Gizzi ode, this one more properly an elegy, bearing the understated name "Revival." Written for Gregory Corso, the famed Beat poet who died of cancer in 2001, "Revival" was first published by the Phylum Press, whose cover image (figure 2) was designed by one of Gizzi's youthful heroes, the artist-musician David Byrne. What look like bits and pieces of armor — a helmet, a vizor, an armpiece, that have sunk into marshy ground — could also be the debris of a plane crash. What is it, the color photo asks, that survives the blast? What is that open book doing near the metal arm? And where did the bronze derby hat at rear center come from?

Broken metal plate, airplane debris: these are, in any case, suitable emblems for Gizzi's oddly impersonal elegy. In the Phylum Press version, "Revival" has an epigraph from Corso's own elegy ("Elegiac Feelings American") for Jack Kerouac: "What happened to you, O friend, happened to America." For *Some Values of Landscape and Weather*, Gizzi removed the line, perhaps because Corso's statement is a bit too histrionic, too predictable. But the American allusion turns out to be important: "Revival" is Gizzi's own elegy for what Allen Ginsberg called, with reference to Whitman, "a lost America of love." That lost America, in Gizzian terms, is defined by those great American movies another one of his heroes, Frank O'Hara, commemorated in "To the Film Industry in Crisis" and related poems. But Gizzi's "America" is darker and more global than O'Hara's; indeed, it is no longer confined to the actual United States. His America is one where Hollywood film images pop up only to lose their author-

ity very quickly as memories of the literary works that have shaped the author's consciousness interfere with the palpable *presence* of the celluloid world.

"It's good to be dead in America." The opening line of "Revival" is startling: we expect, of course, to read "It's good to be alive in America," as the TV ads for the Ford Cherokee or Celebrex tell us. Is the aphorism supposed to comfort the dead Corso? Hardly, and indeed Gizzi never quite writes the proposed elegy, his concern being not with Corso's death or even with his own, but with the death signs of our culture that make the writing of poetry such a problematic enterprise.[5] It's good to be dead in America, because being alive here and now is so painful. Then again — and here Gizzi's conditional mode returns — it's also good to be dead to the outside world in America, happily ensconced in the movie theater, seeing one's fantasies played out on the screen:

It's good to be in a theater waiting
for The Best Years of Our Lives to begin.
Our first night back, we're here
entertaining a hunch our plane did crash
somewhere over the Rockies, luggage
and manuscripts scattered, charred fragments
attempting to survive the fatal draft. (*SP*, 93)

In its layering of complex items, this is vintage Gizzi. It's nice to be watching a film called *The Best Years of our Lives*, but of course its title is ironic: William Wyler's classic tale of three World War II veterans trying to adjust to civilian lives in the small town to which they return is largely a dark one. Indeed, "the best years of their lives" are the ones they gave up when they went to war. And then the seemingly realistic reference to "Our first night back" modulates into another film narrative, perhaps Sylvester Stallone's "Cliffhanger," in which a plane crashes "somewhere over the Rockies, luggage / and manuscripts scattered, charred fragments." The pun on "fatal draft" in the last line links the two plots: it was the fatal draft in *Best Years* that made the young Homer Parrish lose his hands in a shipboard disaster. And, in the first decade of the twenty-first century, "fatal draft" also alludes to the permanent war the United States is seemingly fighting.

Throughout "Revival," the poet tries — but fails — to connect past and present, the literary universe in which he has lived since college, and the absurdly fantastic, melodramatic and riveting "present" of the movies.

To be dead in America at the movies
distracted by preview music in dimming lights.
I never once thought of Alfred Deller
or Kathleen Ferrier singing Kindertotenlieder.
It's good to be lost among pillars of grass.
I never once thought of My Last Duchess
or the Pines of Rome. Isn't it great here
just now dying along with azaleas, trilliums,
myrtle, viburnums, daffodils, blue phlox?
It's good to be a ghost in America. (*SP*, 93–94)

The layering here is complex. The first two lines set the scene and might have been written by O'Hara or even Corso himself. But then, in the space of eight lines, at least eight references to artists and artworks, both musical and poetic, are worked in: the art music of Alfred Deller (singing Bach or Purcell?), Kathleen Ferrier singing Mahler's *Kindertotenlieder*, Ashbery's "They Dream Only of America," where the line "to be lost among thirteen hundred pillars of grass," in its turn, evokes Whitman's *Leaves of Grass*, Robert Browning's *My Last Duchess*, Respighi's familiar *Pines of Rome*, and finally, Wallace Stevens's "The Man on the Dump," in which lassitude and despair give way to an unexpected epiphany:

> Now in the time of spring (azaleas, trilliums,
> myrtle, viburnums, daffodils, blue phlox),
> between that disgust and this, between the things
> that are on the dump (azaleas and so on)
> and those that will be (azaleas and so on),
> one feels the purifying change. One rejects
> the trash.[6]

The citation is not acknowledged: Stevens's words simply become part of the fabric of "Revival," the echo subtly transformed into something equivocal. For Gizzi, it's not so easy to "reject / the trash," and the "dump" seems to be all there is. But dump is also compost heap: the fantasies of pop movies are everywhere inflected with the high art notes, mostly of European derivation, that have been so central to this poet's life — from Renaissance song and the gorgeous music of Mahler, to the specter of Rome raised by the Respighi composition, to Browning and Stevens. Gizzi's items are carefully chosen. In "The Man on the Dump," the cited lines suggest renewal. Stevens, writing in the tradition of Emerson and William James, "rejects the trash," and, in his poem, "That's the moment when the moon creeps up." But in Gizzi's version, it is the death note that dominates: the Mahler *song* Ferrier is singing comes from *Kindertotenlieder*, leaves of grass have been transformed into pillars, and Browning's Last Duchess is the victim of a murder plot.

Perhaps, then, "It's good to be a ghost in America." Ghosts — think of Wallace Stevens's "A Rabbit as King of the Ghosts"— can do things the rest of us can't. Being dead, they have the privilege of "never coming back to the same person / who knew certain things, certain people, / shafts of life entering a kitchen / at the end of an age of never coming back now" (*SP*, 94). And they have no memory of "A hard, closed, linear world at the edge / of caricature," (*SP*, 94) no bother with the urgent questions raised in Vico's *New Science* or Darwin's *Origin of the Species*. Better to be caught up in the movies, even when they depict painful things like Montgomery Clift being "beaten / for reading Ulysses," (*SP*, 95) presumably by the antisemitic bullies in *The Young Lions*.

But the revival of old films with its revival of old memories is not satisfactory either. The burning question comes in lines 50 to 52:

> How come all the best thoughts
> are images? How come all the best images
> are uncanny? (*SP*, 95)

What, asks the poet, *is* the relation of thought — or, more properly, *word*, for there are no thoughts except in words — to *image*? It seems, at midpoint of Gizzi's meditation, that the image is enough, that, say, the homilies and maxims in Isaac Walton's *The Compleat Angler* can never be as moving as the following image:

> searching for effects at the bottom of a lake
> next to a shoe slick with algae, at the base of a cliff
> with pine needles and a rotting log (*SP*, 95)

This description could refer to any number of films — perhaps the police search-for-evidence scene in that other Montgomery Clift film, *A Place in the Sun*. But, whatever the source, it fires the poet's imagination, allowing for any number of exciting and mysterious plots.

But there's the hooker: we know this lake incident only through the poet's *words*; indeed, no image, film or otherwise, can be *known* except through words: it is this fact that makes "the best images uncanny." Someone has to translate image into language, has to note that the log is rotting. And here the poet comes in, "rending, reading, rewriting / what is seen" (*SP*, 95). Consequently we should not miss the irony of the declaration, in line 58, that "I want an art that can say how I am feeling." This is not quite Wordsworth's "Poetry is the spontaneous overflow of powerful feeling," in that Gizzi's emphasis is on the *saying* of that feeling, which is the poetic vocation. Every image is always already mediated, always already charged with meaning. And those magic names — Jeanne d'Arc (whether in the famed Carl Dreyer film or its countless variants), Cinderella, Helen of Troy — must be reimagined and recontextualized before they can matter.

The irony, Gizzi suggests, is that the contemporary poet can draw his own image pool from any source, whether the classic narratives of Homer's *Odyssey* and Dante's *Vita Nuova*, or some ordinary film image:

> No, I am thinking
> blurry faces, a boy, girl, looking
> at New York harbor for a first time,
> soil in pockets, missing buttons,
> needing glasses, needing shoes. (*SP*, 96)

It is the familiar Ellis Island scene, as we know it from countless movies including *The Godfather* — a scene that spells out promise, the American Dream. However often we see that image, whether on film or in photographs like Stieglitz's *The Steerage*, we are moved by its natural pathos. "It's good not to break in America," good to make one's own way.

Yet "Revival" is nothing if not surprising. No sooner have we had the pretty immigrant picture than we read, "It was war. A capital experience!" (*SP*, 95). However violent and unpleasant the subject matter, the appeal can be equally strong. The poet's role, then, is to display "just courage to accept the facts / that poetry can catch you in the headlights / and it's years refocusing the afterimage." The relation of word to image is nothing if not precarious. So powerful is a given image that refocusing its poetic afterimage is all but impossible. Indeed, the image is "untranslatable, part missing line" (*SP*, 97).

Hence the difficulty of writing poetry, of being a poet. "All the codes have been compromised." Writing these words in 2002, before the Internet revolution, Gizzi is curiously prescient. Sampling, stealing, appropriation: these are now the norm. "The privileged nostalgia of a toy boat," no doubt Rimbaud's in "Bateau ivre," is now known from a diagram. The "monuments and trophies" are gone. Flowers smell only like paper, but because paper doesn't smell at all, the dialogue on the bottom of page 98 is meaningless. And now "Revival" modulates into its striking coda. Having left the movie theater and book lists behind, Gizzi poses an impassioned question:

> What does it mean to wait for a song
> to sit and wait for a story?

For want of a sound to call my own
coming in over the barricades,
to collect rubble at the perimeter
hoping to build a house, part snow, part victory (*SP*, 97)

Increasingly, in our own century, inspiration is uncertain and there are no sounds to call one's own. Echoing Stevens, Gizzi therefore chooses the garbage dump, the "rubble at the perimeter"; amalgamating "The Snow Man" and "Like Decorations," he knows that "the wise man avenges by building his city in snow."[7]

The only certainty is thus of uncertainty, contingency, surprise. The "parts," made as they are of dust along with sheet music, "open, flake, break open, let go." There are no rags "to embellish the holes in my sonnet, / no tracks leading beyond and back." American life: the tag can only be improvised. And yet there is hope. However obsolete our national anthem —"o say, can you see?" has been cited a few lines earlier — the poet still "gathers" "American lives . . . into an anthem we thought to rescue us, / over and out." And the poem concludes on a note of bravado with the words, "On your way, dust" (*SP*, 98).

Over and out: the Whitmanian poet must sing American life; *even today* (the two words are found in the Phylum Press version, where the last line reads, "over and out, even today") the anthem composed may rescue us, may send the dust flying. Like the "whispers antiphonal in azure swing" that conclude Crane's *The Bridge*, like O'Hara's "Ode to Joy," whose last line, set off from the rest, is "No more dying," and like his own "A Panic That Can Still Come Upon Me," "Revival" ends on a note of hard-earned optimism. More ode than the elegy it purports to be, more *ars poetica* than personal meditation, "Revival" takes its title all the way: it's a revival of old movies and books, of lost images and feelings, but in the end it is especially a revival of *hope*.

Gizzi is one of the few contemporaries to carry on the lyric tradition of the great Romantics — although of course his is romanticism with a small "r" and a large dose of irony, a romanticism "for want of a sound to call my own," that looks ahead to the new conceptualism in its reliance on remix, mash-up, borrowing, and appropriated text. Revival, he understands, is the best way to fight panic — a revival everywhere calibrated to Make It New.

NOTES

1. See, for example, Aaron Kunin, *Rain Taxi Interview* (2003), on Peter Gizzi's homepage, www.petergizzi.org/further-reading.html; and Rob Stanton, review of "A Panic That Can Still Come Upon Me," *Jacket* 33 (July 2007), jacketmagazine.com/33/stanton-gizzi.shtml.

2. William Carlos Williams, "Danse Russe," in *The Collected Poems of William Carlos Williams*, vol. I, 1909–1939, ed. A. Walton Litz and Christopher MacGowan (New York: New Directions, 1986), 86.

3. Frank O'Hara, *Collected Poems*, ed. Donald Allen (Berkeley: University of California Press, 1995), 210.

4. Stanton, review of "A Panic That Can Still Come Upon Me."

5. In "The Mask of Elegy: On Peter Gizzi's 'Revival,'" *Modernist Review* II, 1 (2006), 75–76, Tyrus Miller writes that "Revival" "is about the impossibility of writing the elegy [Gizzi] thought he should write for Gregory Corso.... What returns in 'Revival' and what we witness only in the uncanny sense of repetition, is the absence of real duration, connection, habit, memory." Miller's is an excellent analysis, though I don't see the poem as being quite as dark as he suggests.

6. Wallace Stevens, "The Man on the Dump," in *Collected Poems* (New York: Alfred A. Knopf, 1961), 202.

7. See Stevens, "Like Decorations in a Nigger Cemetery," *Collected Poems*, 158.

5 | HANNAH BROOKS-MOTL

Gathering the Poem

On Peter Gizzi's "A Telescope Protects Its View"

Peter Gizzi's short poem "A Telescope Protects Its View" gestures toward a writing practice fundamentally concerned with reading; it also suggests reading as a kind of writing (*OUT*, 24). How it stages these suggestions or provocations will be the focus of my discussion here. "A Telescope" creates its sense of conflation between terms — generating a quality of both/and rather than either/or — in a variety of ways, including the use of white space between lines as a kind of gutter or pause, echoing or allusiveness to predecessor texts, and what might be described as notation or overheardness: the poem seems to scrawl and patch itself together, creating an effect akin to the commonplace tradition. What "commonplaceness" might mean for readers of Gizzi's work will round out this affectionate consideration of a poem that declares its own affection —"I like to read the dead"— and then redeclares it, and then declares it once again. I'm using "affection" purposefully: one doesn't fall into or out of affection, yet the gentleness of the term belies its necessity. Without affection, would art even make sense? One says, "I like to go to the movies"; "I like to read." To say, as this poem does, that "I like to read the dead" locates in reading-as-writing a literal hinge, an activity that brings "I" into common purpose and relation with "the dead."

Granting the poem agency here — alleging that *it* might be the thing doing the liking — I take from Isobel Armstrong's assertion that "what thinks" in art is "the artwork itself, not the individual subject, self or consciousness"[1] as well as Barbara Guest's notion of "the poems' concealed autobiography. A memoir of itself which is released as it becomes a presence existing in time."[2] Gizzi's poem provides a model — or a particular kind of memoir — of reading and of writing. Left to its own devices, the poem employs various devices of writing to create both a scene of reading and its defense: through floating, turning lines, the poem stages an experience of reading as self-revelation ("I'm plucky but thankful") as well as enacts a process of reading itself, tracing an encounter with poetry that will turn out to have much to do with commonplaceness.

The poem's triplicate repetition doesn't make narrative. What happens in this poem is also how this poem happens: as a series of utterances, definitions, observations, allusions, speech acts. And in its final lines, as a qualification or rebuttal:

> She said but what of their sad work
> by the river's edge
>
> sad way of working the moth paper light
>
> trellis of dented garbage cans
> and debris at dawn. (*OUT*, 25)

For now, let's note that "she" can't pose a question (no question mark) because the issue being queried — *what of* the dead's "sad work," their "sad way of working"? — is answered in part by the poem's form. The dead's sad work is the work of poetry and poetry's "way of working" is collection, gathering, quotation, echo. Poetry is thus a commonplace, a term I will attempt to reclaim for Gizzi's poem not just as formal analogue but as thematic prizing. What this poem prizes, that is, is precisely the commonplace of poetry: poetry as a site in which a sense of what's common — general, belonging equally to many — is created by the writing of poems, a writing that can occur only through the experience of reading, and of looking. In fact, the poem suggests reading is a kind of looking, a form of observation, and thus life.

I will avoid some easy derivations, however; while forms of community and communing mark much of Gizzi's work, and figure in his own luminous discussions of practice, commonplaceness seems distinct. In this poem especially, it refers to what John Bailey, in his 1919 Warton Lecture on "Poetry and Commonplace," described as the dual application of the word, how commonplace always signifies "in a good sense and in a bad."[3] The "good" sense, for Bailey, shares ground with the object bearing its name — commonplace books are those books that collect quotes, citations, and other "striking or notable passages," according to the *Oxford English Dictionary*. The "bad" sense of commonplace, scholar Ann Moss notes, began in the seventeenth century as scientific evidence replaced the authority once ceded to classical writers; commonplace books as collections of received wisdom failed to conform to the new rigors of empiricism. The term's degradation, says Moss, "accelerated in the eighteenth century, and was irreversible by the nineteenth."[4] Commonplaceness becomes cheap once it comes to mean ordinary, taken for granted, even trite. What everybody knows and accepts, but also what everyone might *say* about what they know: commonplace thus as banality, or a form of unthinking. Yet the two senses are inseparable. The very act of selection creates the conditions in which the ho-hum begins to foment.

Bailey's pamphlet *Poetry and Commonplace* — very much of its time — nonetheless suggests the tension between originality and commonplace as an abiding one for poetic practice: rather than "discovery," Bailey suggests that poets engage in "re-discovery," finding "the life that lies concealed in what are called commonplaces."[5] Yet while Bailey acknowledges the Latin roots of the term, he ignores the older meanings of commonplace as *locus communis* or "finding-places" that produce arguments. From Aristotle, commonplaces were yoked to rhetoric, and reasoning. Such "places" of argument were multiple: they were headings or subjects that certain sets of rhetorical skills were drawn from (in terms of processes of argumentation) and deployed for (the proposition making that created areas of philosophical and scientific inquiry).

Commonplace books as organs able to *produce* knowledge eventually fell to the use writers like John Locke and even Emerson put them to —"background noise to their more focused concerns," in Moss's phrase.[6] Poetry might remain a site where commonplaceness suggests the place not only of quotation but of analytics, a mode of retrieval and recording as well as construction. Poetry as a place recalls the spatial metaphors dear to Gizzi and those poets close to his heart — one thinks especially of Robert Creeley, who spoke of certain poems as "not only tokens but evidences of a place, a very distinct and definite *place*, that poetry not only creates but itself issues from."[7] "A Telescope Protects Its View" flirts with all these modes and meanings of "commonplace." The poem's lines aren't distinctly labeled, though they are loosely grouped along such invisible headings: the first lines cluster around ideas of distance, the next silence and reversal, then circulation, and so on. The poem proposes not an argument but an inquiry into liking, reading, and the dead (authors) who found its moments of writing.

Gizzi's poetics statements as well as other individual works explore the ways in which poems might negotiate predecessors. In "A Telescope Protects Its View," form itself becomes a way of navigating commonplaceness. On one hand, the poem seems to send us away. Its allusions and citational hints move outward, into an elsewhere tangentially related to the poem and to literature, "the ones I like who are dead," in W. S. Graham's formulation — a formulation the poem's first line echoes. Such textual echoes, Gizzi himself has said, are a form of "rescue." In an interview with Aaron Kunin, Gizzi describes how writing "can bring together sensibilities, perspectives, things, nouns, intertextual references to things that are important to you; you can activate a syntax and a vocabulary that will deploy them in some way and give them life."[8] Such life can seem, above all, to be literary life. The poem returns us to more literature; in a sense, it's full of invisible footnotes. The title cribs Ashbery's poem "Clepsydra," which itself alludes to Dickinsonian "circumference."[9] In Gizzi's own lines, we might hear further cribbings from Graham, Dickinson, Hawthorne ("black ribbons" suggestive of the short story "Sunday at Home"?), perhaps Stevens (in "debris at dawn" the hint of "Debris of Life and Mind"?), and Emerson (could "who hasn't found themselves" turn on "Experience": "where do we find ourselves"?). Conceivably each line could reverb with predecessors. Yet the poem resists the open closure of post-structuralism, where writing signifies merely more writing.

For rather than laborious reference, Gizzi gives us high-spirited homage. For Dickinson's "There is no Frigate like a Book," see the wit in "A book or a boat?" Gizzi's reworking here condenses as it foregrounds the visual and aural similarity of Dickinson's original simile. He quotes to adjust, to "deploy" or position his poem as record *and* response. This too is a commonplace of the commonplace book. Moss describes Seneca's ideas about the proper use of quotation. Seneca's understanding revolves around metaphors of incorporation (bees, digestion), as well as the injunction to resemble writers one loves "as a son, not as a portrait: a portrait is a dead thing, not a living likeness."[10] To make a portrait a "living likeness," to quote so that you do not merely regurgitate but revivify, then might be to forego verbal and visual language altogether: "A portrait of you from what you aren't saying." The portraiture of the poem is at once its collage of speech acts and the sense of frame accommodating them.

Gizzi's poem exists as a gathering or collection of scraps, shards, "things, nouns, intertextual references"—a place where heterogeneous materials align with and adjust one another. The Dickinson echo, for example, follows another depiction of transit, the random circulation crucial to writing and reading both: "Letters from an old bottle, / junk in space." This metaphorical turning of trash and treasure might also link backward—to the previous line's equation of death, the imagination, and "life itself." What describes what here? Phrases tumble forward but also separate out:

> I'm plucky but thankful.
>
> Death and the imagination equals life itself.
>
> Letters from an old bottle,
> junk in space. (*OUT*, 24)

It is tempting to take the utterances singly, to make meaning of each fragment rather than attempt an account of meaning *as* fragments. The commonplace book suggests meaning works within and across individual items; this poem of parts is concerned with how particular experiences of text and world get reformulated, picked up, pondered, and turned back out. Walter Ong noted in his discussion of the form that commonplace books are at once reading that is also writing (copying), and writing that is also oral—speech meant to be circulated, "sayings" that might easily have come from speech.[11] "A Telescope" likewise operates in the space where reading is writing and writing shuffles back and forth between notation and speech. The eye, for example, rhymes glyphs that phonemes can't: read/dead, letters/bottle, book/boat. The voices in the poem seem at once personal—"I like"—and professorial in their use of aphorism and definition. We're presented with language that's been telescoped, zoomed out and focused in upon, caught in orbit or rotation. The gaps between lines suggest entries as well as pauses—the poem as commonplace book or notebook. The title, after all, presents us with the image of a telescope and the poet as astronomer (echoing Keats reading Chapman's Homer) reading "dead" stars. Creating a sense in which direct and vicarious or bookish experience mix and mingle, the poem ends in an instance of saying that it isn't the "I" but an other the poem finds unexpectedly and accommodates, a "she" who might be always present and speaking in the common place of poetry too.

While I want to think about this work formally as a kind of "commonplace poem," I also think the second "bad" sense of commonplaceness is worth investigating here. Gizzi's poem recuperates or revises banality through form; by setting off individual phrases, the poem invites us to linger with each. Yet that attention can seem to be at odds with any individual statement's content ("The bridge is up"; "There's so and so going by"). The lines become a mode of inscription (they "scroll onto air") that nonetheless leaves open the possibility that banality is potentially poetic; indeed, language might be made striking precisely because it has been selected, set off and apart, looked at or investigated.

Such language is not always either obviously banal or poetic. Language here takes up a *variety* of utterances and speech acts, including those sudden definitions in the poem's second half. Such assortment captures a sense of the line as dash or jotting—as a kind of notation not beholden to the absolute logic of what's come before but that might exist in groovy associational or observational relation. The speed each line generates within itself as a matter of linked or substituted glyphs and internal, recombinatory rhymes (mawkish/awkward) confronts the white space in which the phrases all hang, together and apart. Again, we seem to be reading entries: a quasi-quotation from a particular passage, but also (perhaps) observations scrawled down as they flash before the eye or the mind's eye. And it's here where Gizzi's title, unmoored from as well as connected to Ashbery's intertext, gains traction. The commonplace book is a kind of notebook; not all notebooks are commonplaces. What connects them is less the kind of knowledge being recorded (direct versus vicarious or mediated experience) than the form that recording takes: the jot, dash, or note. Notebooks are common in a way poetry might not at first blush seem—that is, they are a form everyone might do because their doing seems to require no special expertise. It is in this mode of poem as note taking that "A Telescope" eventually extends beyond the initial form of self-contained lines as units. As the lines bend and drift over the white space, the eye itself looks up and out, to see "everyone outside / everyone."

Gizzi has utilized the poetic form most closely aligned with commonplace—the cento—in his long poem *Ode: Salute to the New York School, 1950–1970*. "A Telescope Protects Its View" is not a cento, but is organized around multiple senses of commonplace that in part find thematic expression in its notational form. That notational aspect, along with the poem's title, suggests a scientific and technological shiver. Commonplace books as systems of knowledge (in Moss's phrase, they are "machinery of verbal production"[12]) relate them on one hand to technology and on the other to the recording devices supplementing that technology — to notebooks. A notebook might account for sudden definitions ("Synecdoche: act of receiving from another") and memory ("She said but what") alike. Notebooks, as anthropologist Bruno Latour has said, "try to grasp some recalcitrant objects through some artificial device with utmost accuracy, even though this enterprise may very well come up empty."[13] Notebooks here sound like telescopes. The telescope, Isaac Asimov once remarked, helped Galileo first differentiate planets from stars, marking "the beginning of *seeing* other worlds rather than merely thinking of them."[14] Telescopes bring those most "recalcitrant objects" of all — stars, planets, satellites — into some new kind of relation to the one observing them. They require seeing and thinking the thing at once, bringing it into focus as a trick of light, an image or vision captured by the consciousness recording it. And in this, of course, notebooks and telescopes resemble poetry.

Notebooks and commonplace books might be forms that necessarily precede poems. They provide, as for Emerson and Locke, the "white noise" out of which a symphony springs. "A Telescope Protects Its View" draws on other such writing devices as a way of formulating issues at the heart of Gizzi's poetics: affection, affiliation, or in his own words to Levi Rubeck, "the animated and affective kinship you simultaneously discover and build in the construction of voice — your own voice."[15] How we read ourselves into the works of others, how we write that reading, and how we use reading and writing both to bring "recalcitrant objects" into focus anchor the floating phrases of this poem. We might recognize our own habits of observation and notation in the generous white spaces here, a move that reminds me of Gizzi's generosity in assuring the commonplaceness of his poems and poetry generally — its availability to all. As Alice Notley has written, "poetry's so common hardly anyone / can find it."[16] In Gizzi's poem, poetry's commonness is in fact elemental, part of the atmosphere that "words scroll onto." Poetry is made out of "dented garbage cans" as well as networks of allusion and echo; it's a form of writing that requires a kind of living, looking, and reading — of liking to look, live, and read. Affection doesn't mean mastery, which is another way of assuring poetry's commonness.

In linking commonplace traditions to oral culture, Ong noted that the memorable sayings circulated were also almost always authorless: "Everybody is quoting everybody else, and has been for tens of thousands of years before the written records began, on purpose and with a feeling of achievement."[17] We might find this in Gizzi's poem as well, in its definition of "Synecdoche:

act of receiving from another." Such acts of reception, a matter of choosing but also being chosen or gripped — by a line, a scene, a life — are those moments in which our own language or subjectivity might be momentarily replaced, undergo a "change of name," as we spout a commonplace, recite a line, recount a story "on purpose and with a feeling of achievement." What are the stakes of thinking about poems as commonplaces, of considering this poem as an example of commonplaceness? As a reading practice, it might propose that letting one's own attention wander through the poem's shifting registers, tones, and hints of suggested further reading is a way of enjoying, which is to say finding delight *with* rather than *in*, the poem's "gathering" of unsimilar (even uncommon) elements. The poem's ethical orientation — its view toward the world as a site of reading-as-writing — likewise encourages us to consider acts of keeping, copying, reciting, and building as those that found poetry as an activity in which we all might have both stake and share.

NOTES

1. Isobel Armstrong, *The Radical Aesthetic* (Malden, MA: Blackwell, 2000), 65.

2. Barbara Guest, *Forces of Imagination: Writing on Writing* (Berkeley: Kelsey Street, 2003), 40.

3. John Bailey, *Poetry and Commonplace* (London: Oxford University Press, Warton Lecture on Poetry, 1919), 2.

4. Ann Moss, *Printed Commonplace-Books and the Structuring of Renaissance Thought* (Oxford: Clarendon Press, 1996), 2. Moss's book is one of the few devoted entirely to thinking through the implications of commonplace books to intellectual practices that continue to dominate Western thought. In particular, she connects the form to encyclopedias and other information-retrieval systems that continue to structure our relation to knowledge.

5. Bailey, *Poetry and Commonplace*, 3.

6. Moss, *Printed Commonplace-Books and the Structuring of Renaissance Thought*, 279.

7. Robert Creeley, *A Quick Graph: Collected Notes and Essays* (San Francisco: Four Season Foundation, 1970), 63.

8. Peter Gizzi, "In the Moment of Looking," interview with Aaron Kunin, *Rain Taxi* 8, no. 4 (Winter 2003).

9. See also Annette Gilson's discussion of the influence of Dickinson on Ashbery's poem in "Disseminating 'Circumference': The Diachronic Presence of Dickinson in John Ashbery's 'Clepsydra,'" *Twentieth Century Literature* 44, no. 4 (Winter 1998), 484–505.

10. Moss, *Printed Commonplace-Books and the Structuring of Renaissance Thought*, 13.

11. Walter Ong, *Interfaces of the Word: Studies in the Evolution of Consciousness and Culture* (Ithaca: Cornell University Press, 1977), 161.

12. Moss, *Printed Commonplace-Books and the Structuring of Renaissance Thought*, vi.

13. Bruno Latour, *Reassembling the Social: An Introduction to Actor-Network Theory* (Oxford: Oxford University Press, 2007), 135.

14. Isaac Asimov, *Eyes on the Universe: A History of the Telescope* (Boston: Houghton Mifflin, 1975), 26.

15. Peter Gizzi, interview with Levi Rubeck, *Bomblog*, Nov. 23, 2011, bombmagazine.org/article/6301.

16. Alice Notley, "C. '81," in *Mysteries of Small Houses* (New York: Penguin, 1998), 66.

17. Ong, *Interfaces of the Word*, 160.

6 | SARA CRANGLE

"Tradition & the Indivisible Talent"

criticism is as inevitable as breathing
— T. S. Eliot, 1919[1]

I don't know what there is (any longer) to say about Eliot.
— Wallace Stevens, 1938[2]

Paradox asks so much from us
we often experience it as grace.
— Peter Gizzi, 2003 (*SVLW*, 94)

Peter Gizzi shares Whitman's passion for the green, green grass that grounds; his attentiveness to natural detail echoes Dickinson ("I heard a fly buzz. I heard revealed nature" [*SVLW*, 96]) and, to a lesser degree, Williams. He is openly indebted to Wallace Stevens, as in the concluding lines of *Threshold Songs*; on occasion, Stein's voice can be heard in Gizzi's work: "The apocalypse is not a cereal" (*SVLW*, 33). When considering high modernist influences on Gizzi's sincere poetics, T. S. Eliot's alternately satiric and melancholic verse — verse infused with dour cityscapes, miserable masses, impotent men, dissatisfied women — does not immediately spring to mind. Yet Eliot's writing surfaces in Gizzi's *Periplum* in details small ("you of the carbuncle gaze") and grandiose: "It's been said that the burial of the dead / is the beginning of culture."[3] These allusions continue in *Artificial Heart*, where "The heart of poetry is a hollow man," and the blind prophet of Thebes, Tiresias, appears "on an open road reading signs" (66, 19). In the much-lamented footnotes to *The Waste Land*, Eliot argues that Tiresias is the cohering consciousness of his poem, a poem now metonymic for modernism. In Gizzi's hands, Tiresias's modernist lineage is one that continues to orient: "The dead are useful [Tiresias] said / to tell us where we are" (*AH*, 19). And Eliot, who died when Gizzi was six, determines the coordinates in the poem from Gizzi's *Threshold Songs* that is the focus here, namely, "Tradition & the Indivisible Talent."

Eliot's essay "Tradition and the Individual Talent" provokes a paradoxical reading experience. The title confers privilege to the singular writer, but in what follows, Eliot famously elides the poet's distinctiveness: "Poetry is not a turning loose of emotion, but an escape from emotion; it is not the expression of personality, but an escape from personality."[4] In "Tradition & the Indivisible Talent," Gizzi reverses Eliot's terms: Gizzi's change in diction adds the possibility of inseparability, even mutuality, to Eliot's title, but the poem itself is determined by an avowed "I." Where Eliot subsumes the poet into a larger artistic history, Gizzi affirms the minutiae observed by the perceiving self. What this self discerns is the natural world: flowering trees, the wind, vegetable or mineral objects, a sun-drenched path, birdsong, dirt. These observations offer a second layer of paradox: why write a pervasively pastoral poem referencing a poet almost inseparable from the metropolis of London, one incontrovertibly influenced by the über-urban symbolists and decadents who preceded him? Eliot is rarely aligned with the pastoral.[5] That said, paradox itself—absurdity, self-contradiction, disbelief—is fundamental to the pastoral. Consider:

1. "For Rousseau, the paradox of the human condition is that our very freedom to transform and transcend the state of nature is the source of our enslavement. . . . We are born free, but we are enchained by a society which we try and fail to transform, so we seek instead to return romantically to the state of nature."[6]
2. "The first condition of Pastoral is that it is an urban product."[7]

Pastoral writing longs for a natural state that predates or negates literature; the rural becomes self-conscious subject matter only as a consequence of an emergent cityscape. These paradoxes are furthered in Gizzi's "Tradition & the Indivisible Talent," where Eliot is the urban signifier against which the rural is measured. Eliot stands for a modernism that Gizzi's anti-elegy refuses to pronounce dead, or to accept as a purely metropolitan or highly cultivated construct.

"Tradition & the Indivisible Talent" draws directly from *The Waste Land* (1922) and the first of Eliot's *Four Quartets*, "Burnt Norton" (1935). Pentalogies both, Hugh Kenner describes how Eliot put the latter long poem in direct conversation with the former, as when the hyacinth garden and desolate seas at the outset of *The Waste Land* become rose garden and drained pool in the first section of "Burnt Norton." For Kenner, following these initial replications, Eliot continues by building the entire *Quartets* on the same foundations as *The Waste Land*:

> Each *Quartet* carries on this structural parallel. The first movement, like *The Burial of the Dead*, introduces a diversity of themes; the second, like *A Game of Chess*, presents first "poetically" and then with less traditional circumscription the same area of experience; the third, like *The Fire Sermon*, gathers up the central vision of the poem while meditating dispersedly on themes of death; the fourth is a brief lyric; the fifth, a didactic and lyric culmination, concerning itself partly with language, in emulation of the Indo-European roots exploited in *What the Thunder Said*.[8]

Teetering on oversimplification, Kenner adds that the *Quartets* depict the movements of the seasons and concern themselves, in turn, with the elements: air, water, fire, and earth.[9] Gizzi's "Tradition" brashly enters Eliot's lifelong interrogation of the form and content of these now-canonical poems, replicating, most obviously, Eliot's quinary structure. Gizzi also interweaves references to *The Waste Land*: its memory and desire, its polyphonic registers, its affirmation of lyric music: "Sweet Thames, run softly, till I end my song."[10] And he returns to the incertitude that frames *The Waste Land*: its initial assertion that we can only know "A heap of broken images[11]"; its concluding chorus summoning the incomprehensible.

Fundamentally, however, it is the deliberately cultivated world of "Burnt Norton" that most preoccupies "Tradition." Gizzi's first stanza reads,

> If all the world says something
> we think then we know something
> don't we? And then the blank screen
> or memory again. You crazy.

No, you crazy. It's like this
but almost always
when time-lapsed words
and weather-swept flowering trees
move in empathetic wind.
I am rooted but alive.
I am flowering and dying.
I am you the wind says, the wind. (*TS*, 46)

Gizzi's allegiances are signaled by the introductory, conditional, "if" and cemented by that inquiring "don't we?" "Burnt Norton" starts in earnest on line 4, which begins, like Gizzi's poem, with an "if" that leads to the positing of "a world of speculation."[12] "[S]hall we follow / The deception of the thrush?" asks Eliot's questioning speaker while descending into an echo-laden rose garden of memory.[13] This garden embodies the central concerns of the poem: it is a place to be moved through and to be still, a site to consider past and future in relation to the present, a place of desolation and hope. An empty pool may stand at the center of the garden, but children can be heard laughing in the adjacent foliage, and it contains a "heart of light."[14] Eliot returns to these latter motifs in the final section of "Burnt Norton," and the light recurs throughout as an encapsulation of his speaker's ideal state, which is one free from desire and compulsion, "yet surrounded / By a grace of sense, a white light still and moving."[15]

Gizzi's speaker is similarly preoccupied by the relationships between stasis and flourishing; pasts unbearable and futures unknowable; and with mortality. But this speaker rejects Eliot's garden in favor of a windswept landscape. We are in an emphatically uncultivated world replete with an "empathetic wind." This wind is inseparable from the poetic voice: it projects its personality into the speaker, and strives to comprehend that individual. In its reach and behavior, it is a wind that directly counters the third section of "Burnt Norton," which is defined by the city, or "a place of disaffection" filled with "strained time-ridden faces" consumed with distraction and meaninglessness.[16] In Eliot's poem, the wind appears as a force that shapes humanity, but it is less empathetic than vicious:

Men and bits of paper, whirled by the cold wind
That blows before and after time,
Wind in and out of unwholesome lungs

Time before and time after.
Eructation of unhealthy souls
Into the faded air, the torpid
Driven on the wind that sweeps the gloomy hills of London[17]

These masses imbibe and are belched out in turn by a mephitic, battering wind. In response to this perceived horror, Eliot's third movement closes by envisioning a descent into a world of solitude and stillness, a deliberate abstention from the moving, bustling world. But just as Gizzi redefines Eliot's urban wind, his third stanza emulates this individual submersion without replicating Eliot's static darkness and destitution. For Gizzi, self-submersion is also levity:

When a thought's thingness
begins to move, to become
unmoored and you ride
the current with your head,
feel yourself lift off like
birdsong caught in the inner ear
even the curios seem animated
in their dusty shelves —
the song is alive. (*TS*, 47)

Gizzi rejects the fear of death by water in *The Waste Land* and the deceptive, didactic thrush of "Burnt Norton." In "Tradition & the Indivisible Talent," to be driven by a contemplative intellect is to be unavoidably embodied yet buoyant, and Gizzi's internalized birdsong is inevitable, embalancing, vibrant. Quite unlike Eliot's, Gizzi's vast and minute natural world works almost too symbiotically alongside processes of recollection and speculation. Where Eliot's speaker frets about abstractions and "perpetual possibilit[ies],"[18] Gizzi's enjoys drifting, finding himself stuck, and the "pleasant sensation" of "loving abstraction" (*TS*, 46). Even the bewilderment that marks the outset of "Tradition" appears easily resolved. Samuel Johnson defined "bewilder" as "To lose in pathless places, to confound for want of a plain road."[19] In his second stanza, Gizzi's speaker finds a road awash in Eliot's tantalizing light; a path emerges offering an "angled view / so dramatic in boisterous sun" (*TS*, 47). In a reversal of traditional pastoral, Gizzi's Golden Age is not lost, but exists here and now.

With Gizzi's "boisterous sun" in view, it might be plausible to suggest that it is Eliot's "Burnt Norton" that offers us the utopian yearning (or in Eliot's diction, "appetency") customary to the pastoral speaker. Eliot's fourth section — Kenner's "brief lyric"— is defined by questions, and seeks affirmation from the sunflower, the clematis, and the yew tree — all of which, it is hoped, will turn and bend toward us, en heliotropic route to the daylight now buried at the earth's center. The speaker wants nature to cling to and clutch us, to "cur[l] / Down" in our direction. Nature — its flora and its fowl — should gravitate round, and meet our needs: here also "the kingfisher's wing" proves capable of bringing together stillness, motion, and Eliot's much sought-after light.[20] But these are hoped-for actions; they are yet to come. Gizzi repeats Eliot's terms in his fourth stanza, raising questions, and conflating natural life and light, a combination less descentive and entombed than grounded, leveled. Unlike Eliot, he offers answers reassuring, reassured, and of the present moment:

> Birdsong and daybreak,
> are they not the same at the root?
> Twigs torn from brambles
> nest and house this cooing thing. (*TS*, 47)

This particular root does not clutch, but consoles; Eliot's impossibly silent, moving bird is now a diminutively "cooing thing." These lines might satirize Eliot's complex and angst-laden approach to his too-tidy and too-categorical natural world. If so, this critique could explain the quick movement in Gizzi's stanza from soft murmurs at sunrise to combustibility: "And now the word is fire, / fire in the heart, fire in the head" (*TS*, 48). This is a return to *The Waste Land*, and the fascination with incandescence as destroyer and purifier that concludes "The Fire Sermon," where the ancient city of Carthage burns. Gizzi draws on a full and various range of Eliot's references to the natural world, refusing its complications, and insisting upon its enduring presence within and around Eliot's pervasive metropolises.

In his fifth and final stanza, Gizzi continues his critique of Eliot's desire for a natural world that nevertheless remains resolutely ordered around and for humankind. He does so by continuing to straddle both of Eliot's long poems and their concluding explorations of language; in "Burnt Norton" in particular, Eliot considers language music, mortal, enduring, and limited. Gizzi's last stanza borrows from *The Waste Land* colloquial registers, springtime cruelty, and Eliot's attentiveness to detritus. But this stanza is a very direct response to the final section of "Burnt Norton" and offers a sustained critique of Eliot's cautious yet demanding relationship with the natural. Gizzi writes:

> How about dirt? I love you
> like dirt. I miss you dirty mouth,
> dirty smile, oh, and my dirt
> is your dirt is nice also.
> Closer to the ground, perhaps,
> on the ground, that's real enough
> and those goddamn spuggies
> are fledged and it's spring
> and the books in my shelves
> in my head have all turned. Nothing
> but earth and peat and mold
> and rich soft living manna
> you can breathe. The must
> at the root of it all, desire
> and wanting, must know. (*TS*, 48)

The abject rats, sandwich papers, cigarette ends, bones of the dead, rotten teeth, and rejected women that populate *The Waste Land* return here in Gizzi's frank love of dirt, which he refuses to domesticate by calling it dust, as Eliot so often does. In "Burnt Norton," the speaker expresses anxiety about "Disturbing the dust on a bowl of rose-leaves"[21] and notes, at the poem's end, that although dust persists, its unpleasant pervasiveness (like the mortality it represents) is mitigated by grace-giving sunlight and idyllic children laughing among plants and trees. Gizzi is not interested in an ideal beyond; the ground is "real enough." In conjunction with the fledged spuggies that follow, this assertion counters the first movement of "Burnt Norton," where Eliot's imperious thrush informs the speaker that "human kind / Cannot bear very much reality."[22] For Gizzi's speaker, a fulsome reality bolsters; Gizzi exchanges Eliot's ill-omened urban wind for sustaining inhalations of earth and mold.

Waste is both what we reject and what rejects us in expanses of uninhabited or uninhabitable geography; in Eliot, it signals purposelessness and devastation, and is the despairing refrain by which he concludes "Burnt Norton":

"Ridiculous the waste sad time / Stretching before and after."[23] In Gizzi's "Tradition," waste becomes compost: the ground in which love grows, an element inseparable from language and reading, which, like dirt, must be turned, sprouting fresh thoughts about old ideas shelved in the mind. Dirt is imperative and commanding; dirt is stale, rotted: "The must / at the root of it all." This mold is reaffirmed in Gizzi's "must know"— from our urgent, desiring present we enter the fusty past, which in turn nourishes our need to understand. Gizzi explicitly counters "Burnt Norton," where Eliot does not share Gizzi's confidence in decomposition:

> Words strain,
> Crack and sometimes break, under the burden,
> Under the tension, slip, slide, perish,
> Decay with imprecision, will not stay in place,
> Will not stay still.[24]

Slipperiness and decay distress Eliot's speaker, as they speak to the uncontrollable abjection shared by the natural and the civilized world. Revulsion emerges in response to things that lie "Between un-being and being"[25] — objects and experiences that fall outside the purview of categorization and cultivation. Again, Gizzi refuses these distinctions and this longing for order; in stanza 3, he diminishes Eliot's concern about these parameters of existence with the all-too blasé: "Being, / it's a small word" (*TS*, 47). Like his perfect, symbiotic natural world — one broken at last by the irritated curse at the sparrows as the poem nears its end — Gizzi's characteristic ease is exposed here as an artifice deployed to challenge Eliot's great formality. In so doing, Gizzi draws on the pastoral tradition of openly engaging with the low and the vulgar, while maintaining the paradox that this "lowness" is embedded within the most venerated of literary genres, poetry.

"[I]t's spring / and the books in my shelves / in my head have all turned" (*TS*, 48). Is Eliot just a corpse in Gizzi's mental garden, sprouting and blooming? And, with blooms now foregrounded, is "Tradition & the Indivisible Talent" merely Gizzi's husbandry of the anxiety of influence, a means of diminishing Eliot's signature angst, a reduction of Eliot's (admittedly slender) output to one of many volumes contained on shelves within the librarious head? In "Tradition and the Individual Talent," Eliot permits Gizzi's return to well-tilled ground, telling us:

> We dwell with satisfaction upon the poet's difference from his predecessors, especially his immediate predecessors; we endeavour to find something that can be isolated in order to be enjoyed. Whereas if we approach a poet without this prejudice we shall often find that not only the best, but the most individual parts of his work may be those in which the dead poets, his ancestors, assert their immortality most vigorously.[26]

Eliot further acknowledges the urgency of Gizzi's "desire / and wanting" and the imperative of his final "must know": "Someone once said: 'The dead writers are remote from us because we *know* so much more than they did.' Precisely, and they are that which we know" (52). Gizzi's "Tradition" longs for that assured intimacy with the past, even as it is a poem that asserts, repeatedly, the familiarity of its author with the mainstays and forays of Eliot's major works. But Gizzi's language belies this certainty, and not just in a wilderness posed and then too-expertly navigated, but in more sincere moments of longing. There are two direct references to loss in "Tradition." We've seen one, in stanza 5: "I miss you dirty mouth, / dirty smile, oh, and my dirt / is your dirt is nice also" (*TS*, 48). There is a ring of Stein here, and the "you" may well be the (lovably) crazy individual of the first stanza — the tone is certainly similar. More importantly, it is an external and absent otherness that the speaker addresses and desires. A nostalgia for the irrational, coupled with the natural —"you dirty"— emerges, one potentially associable with the pastoral tradition, its "time-lapsed words / and weather-swept flowering trees" (46). The second example occurs in stanza 2. Within its allusive discussion of abstraction, perception, and ready dismissal of the term "being," Gizzi's speaker states: "After all absence makes / the particles move faster" (47). Given that Gizzi's titular "indivisible" means both an inseparable mass and "an infinitely small particle or quantity," these lines speak to feelings of diminution and agitation in the face of Eliotic tradition. After all, it was Eliot's goal, via depersonalization, to have "art . . . approach the condition of science."[27] In this regard, he argued: "The poet's mind is in fact a receptacle for seizing and storing up numberless feelings, phrases, images, which remain there until all the particles which can unite to form a new compound are present together" (55). In Gizzi's "Tradition," Eliot's absence, which stands for the loss of the high modernist tradition writ large, facilitates the productive movement of these particles in the speaker's poetic mind.

Contemporary critics, on the hunt for twentieth-century versions of pastoral, suggest that the tradition has been productively subverted to include faux nostalgia, parody, and, inevitably, continued homage.[28] Those focusing on the modernist period in particular suggest that during this era, the rural became the absent or degraded other within the urban modernist canon. As Maria Farland writes: "modernist versions of pastoral frequently evoke a natural landscape of disintegration and declension, whose simplicity is a function not of its unspoiled purity, but its debased position in the hierarchy of civilisation."[29] Gizzi's "Tradition & the Indivisible Talent" foregrounds the rural other discernible within Eliot's defining cityscapes. The poem allows Eliot himself to act as a repository for the formalities, civilities, and angst of a cityscape that Gizzi will not countenance as the assumed or lauded center of cultural innovation. In Gizzi's paradoxical "Tradition," the lost Golden Age is urban and modernist, and the present is a highly artificial pastoral ideal. For Gizzi, it is not the light at the center of "Burnt Norton" but paradox that is our saving grace. Gizzi's "Tradition" is no pastoral elegy: instead, he proclaims the vibrancy of Eliot's tradition even as he reconsiders its parameters. This realignment may well be just another return to tradition, as in Gizzi's work more generally, the natural world is nothing short of consolatory. At the end of *The Waste Land*, Eliot shores cultural fragments against his ruins — among them, the debris of a collapsing London bridge. Though no stranger to cultural fragments, Gizzi insists that his internal and external worlds are maintained by the glorious dirt in which Whitman's green grass grows, and just about any tree. As Gizzi writes in *The Outernationale*, "These trees rang / round my head, shored / up the sky" (14).

NOTES

1. T. S. Eliot, "Tradition and the Individual Talent," in *The Sacred Wood: Essays on Poetry and Criticism* (London: Methuen, 1960), 48.

2. Wallace Stevens, "Homage to T.S. Eliot," in *Wallace Stevens: Collected Poetry and Prose* (New York: Library of America, 1997), 801.

3. For a carbuncular gaze in Eliot, see "The Waste Land" in his *Collected Poems 1909–1962* (New York: Harcourt, Brace and World, 1963); in Gizzi, see "Life Continues" (*PEROP*, 16). Eliot's subtitle from *The Waste Land*, "The Burial of the Dead," is included in "Blue Peter," a poem that also describes the world as fragmented (*PEROP*, 26).

4. Eliot, "Tradition and the Individual Talent," 58.

5. Sandra M. Gilbert likens *The Waste Land* to a pastoral elegy because it contains

loss, vengeance, cursing, repeated questioning, mythology, and bereavement rituals. But Eliot's poem is not a pastoral elegy, according to Gilbert, because it is too fragmented, too aware of the monstrosities of World War I, to properly offer the reader the images of succour and resurrection crucial to the genre; ultimately, the writer is not consoled by his literary prowess, and traditionally, this is how the pastoral elegy should end. ("'Rat's Alley': The Great War, Modernism, and the (Anti)Pastoral Elegy," *New Literary History* 30, no.1 [1999], 179–201.)

Gizzi has at least one notable predecessor: Mary Butts's neglected pastoral novel *Armed With Madness* (1928) is set in Dorset in the 1920s; at its heart is the grail quest. Butts and Eliot published in *The Dial* and *The Egoist*, and moved in similar literary circles. *Armed With Madness* exemplifies the modernist fascination with mythology, but also comments directly on *The Waste Land*: a high modernist pastoral fiction to Eliot's urbane poetic epic, the story foregrounds questing, drought and impotence, magic and sacrifice, postwar trauma and tragedy, as well as failed and unrequited love. As in Gizzi's poetry, Butts's novel does not exclude the satiric: at the novel's end, the so-called grail turns out to be an Egyptian ashtray.

6. Jonathan Bate, *The Song of the Earth* (London: Picador, 2001), 45.

7. Frank Kermode, ed., introduction to *English Pastoral Poetry from the Beginnings to Marvell* (New York: Norton, 1972), 11–44, 14.

8. Hugh Kenner, *The Invisible Poet: T. S. Eliot* (London: W. H. Allen, 1960), 262.

9. Kenner, *The Invisible Poet*, 262.

10. Eliot, *Collected Poems 1909–1962*, 70.

11. Ibid., 63.

12. Ibid., 189.

13. Ibid., 190.

14. Ibid.

15. Ibid., 191.

16. Ibid., 192.

17. Ibid., 193.

18. Ibid., 189.

19. All quoted definitions are drawn from the online *Oxford English Dictionary*.

20. Eliot, *Collected Poems 1909–1962*, 194.

21. Ibid., 189.

22. Ibid., 190.

23. Ibid., 195.

24. Ibid., 194.

25. Ibid., 195.

26. Eliot, "Tradition and the Individual Talent," 48.

27. Ibid., 53.

28. See, for instance, David James and Philip Tew, eds., "Introduction: Re-Envisioning

Pastoral," in *New Versions of Pastoral: Post-Romantic, Modern, and Contemporary Responses to the Tradition* (Madison, WI: Fairleigh Dickinson University Press, 2009), 13–30.

29. Maria Farland, "Modernist Versions of Pastoral: Poetic Inspiration, Scientific Expertise, and the 'Degenerate' Farmer," *American Literary History* 19, no. 4 (2007): 905–35, 911.

7 | JEREMY NOEL-TOD

"To Speak in This Place"

Peter Gizzi, W. S. Graham, and English Poetry

In his study of John Ashbery and English poetry, Ben Hickman observes that "if anything defined [the New York] group of poets, it was their reading habits"— specifically, "their commitment to European literary and non-literary avant-gardes, and a unique appetite for the undiscovered and marginal."[1] Peter Gizzi, author of *Ode: Salute to the New York School* (2012), is an American internationalist in the same tradition.[2] He has taken a particular interest in what happened to modernist poetry in Britain after World War II, and found an especially sympathetic voice in the Anglo-Scottish poet W. S. Graham (1918–1986). In 1946, Graham wrote of his belief that poems have "the power to release a man into his own completely responsible world larger [. . .] than outward solid geography."[3] Gizzi has long been concerned with a similar notion: that lyric poetry reimagines the idea of "home" in a way that exceeds the given limits of any tradition. "I am interested in nostalgia," he has written, "but I would renovate its use: it's not just a return to home (or origins, the texts that inform me) but a survival of home (the process of individuation)." The aim is to arrive at a point where it is possible "to build a comprehensive music" again.[4] Through his echolalic response to Graham and other postwar English poets, Gizzi — author of a collection called *The Outernationale* (2007) — has found a way to expand the ambit of his language beyond the music of the modern American tradition.

Ideas about poetry, nation, and home are essayed explicitly by the poem "Ding Repair" in *Artificial Heart* (1998). In American English, "ding repair" refers to fixing small dents in a car, and this may be a clue to the poem's allusive method, which involves the rewriting of other American poems about home.[5] Its first lines—"There are too many skateboards here, too many / waves to negotiate, the graded hills fall / too suddenly into the sea" (*AH*, 78)—dreamily misremember the beginning of Elizabeth Bishop's "Questions of Travel": "There are too many waterfalls here; the crowded streams / hurry too rapidly to the sea." Bishop's poem, which reflects her relocation to Brazil in the 1950s, goes on to wonder, "Should we have stayed at home and thought of here?" and ends with the traveler asking herself, "*Should we have stayed at home, / wherever that may be?*"[6] Gizzi's substitution of "skateboards" for "waterfalls" suggests that we are still in 1990s North America in "Ding Repair," as he puts Bishop's questions to the political imagination of its "sunny bureaucracy, / shiny country":

> Imagining another home far from here
> not from where we have come but where we imagine,
> where vulnerability won't reproduce cruelty.
> A home in the act of finding a home in the act of
> what will suffice? No place was set
> at the table but you are invented to listen
> even if silence is a condition of mind
> you will never be forgotten here, where to learn
> the speech of the place is to earn to speak in this place. (*AH*, 78)

Replacing the word "poem" with "home," Gizzi alludes to Wallace Stevens's "Of Modern Poetry," which begins,

> The poem of the mind in the act of finding
> What will suffice. It has not always had
> To find: the scene was set; it repeated what
> Was in the script.
>   Then the theatre was changed
> To something else. Its past was a souvenir.[7]

Published in 1942, "Of Modern Poetry" can be read as a meditation on the divergence of English and American poetry in the twentieth century. It emphasizes the importance of a poetry made out of the "living . . . speech of the place" to which it is addressed. This place, of course, is not simply midcentury America — Stevens's "poem of the mind" takes place in a "theatre" that transcends time and place. But the eternal sphere of English literature still requires the materials of reality to "construct a new stage" (a phrase that puns on the renovation of the spatial and temporal). Stevens's opening lines chime with Gertrude Stein's proposal, in "What is English Literature" (1935), that the difference between English and American literature lay in the transition from a settled, island culture of "daily life" which simply had to be "told" in verse to a new continent where "daily life was not the daily life" in the same way, although the language retained the memory of this life ("its past was a souvenir").[8] For Stevens, poetry is the imaginary recreation of Stein's island condition: a means — as he wrote in his wartime lecture, "The Noble Rider and the Sound of Words" (1942) — of resisting the "pressure of reality" in an international world, where, through broadcast media, "we are intimate with people we have never seen and, unhappily, they are intimate with us."[9] "It has to be living, to learn the speech of the place," continues "Of Modern Poetry," a phrase that Gizzi also pointedly revises: "To learn / the speech of the place is to earn to speak in this place." The existence of "this place," in fact, is not to be distinguished from the living event of two or more people speaking and listening to its language. "You are invented," not "invited," to listen: the speech of this place, that is, does not exist prior to its speakers. The deictic shift is crucial: "the place" of Stevens is out there, the stage on which the poem has "to find" in its own satisfactory act of becoming; "this place" is the poem itself, the place where we already are.

The distinction between "the place" and "this place" is an important moment of transition in "Ding Repair"'s poetic nomadism too, shifting its allusive lodestar from Stevens's wartime "poem of the mind" to the postwar lyricism of W. S. Graham. In Graham's work — which Gizzi discovered on his first visit to England in 1994 — "this place" recurs as a reflexive gesture toward the imaginative space that is being made in words. The phrase occurs nine times in Graham's major long poem, *The Nightfishing* (1955), where it signifies both the place of being ("When I fell down into this place") and the place of reading ("At this place / The eye reads forward as the memory reads back"), until, in the final part of the poem, "Home becomes this place."[10] To allude to Graham in this way is to invoke a poet for whom poetry is always — as the title of a later poem has it — "The Constructed Space," an "abstract scene" in which the life of language may be experienced as the communication "between us two whoever / We are":

> [. . .] Anyhow here we are and never
> Before have we two faced each other who face
> Each other now across this abstract scene
> Stretching between us. This is a public place
> Achieved against subjective odds and then
> Mainly an obstacle to what I mean.[11]

"Ding Repair" echoes this important passage from Graham twice. Its invocation of "this place" is followed by a scene in which two people are presented "facing each other at breakfast." Then, in its final lines, it urges the reader: "Now when you go to your job, your table or your bed / can you remember this place, a piece / of space left behind" (*AH*, 78; 81).

Gizzi's rerouting of Stevens's line on learning "the speech of the place"— as immigrants to real places are commonly expected to do — into Graham's displaced poetic notion of "this place" affirms, therefore, his own notion that "home is established only in the act of singing, in the moment of song"[12] ("The Constructed Space": "The times continually disclose our home"). The politics of this are against colonial sentiments of destiny and settlement, as expressed by a poem such as Robert Frost's "The Gift Outright," with its opening line, "The land was ours before we were the land's."[13] Gizzi's imagined home "far from here / not from where we have come but where we imagine" exists only in a present oriented toward the future — or, as he has put it in interview, in the simultaneously "spoken and present and . . . posthumous time" of poetry.[14]

"Ding Repair" is one of the poems in *Artificial Heart* that Gizzi's "An Open Letter on Poetics" classifies as "a meditation on the 'long road' (the *lungo drom*)." The concept of the *lungo drom* is derived from Isabel Fonseca's study of Roma culture, *Bury Me Standing* (1995), where it denotes "a nostalgia for utopia or (as she translates it) 'a return to nowhere,'" which inspires much of the traditional song of Roma travelers.[15] "Perhaps uniquely among peoples," Fonseca observes, "they have no dream of a homeland."[16] This is an idea that resonates with the treatment of nationhood in Gizzi's work, which repeatedly confronts modern America as a place "that ghosts inhabit," as he says of Jack Spicer's 1960s California: a nostalgically comforting show of cultural imperialism.[17] "Revival," the long poem in the middle of Gizzi's 2003 collection *Some*

Values of Landscape and Weather, begins, "It's good to be dead in America," and is shadowed throughout by its ironic disavowal of European culture. "It's good to be lost among the pillars of grass," asserts the poet, echoing John Ashbery in "They Dream Only of America" ("To be lost among the thirteen million pillars of grass"):[18] "I never once thought of My Last Duchess / or the Pines of Rome." To be "dead" in America is to live immersed — or buried alive — in its culture. As the poem reaches conclusion, Gizzi toys with the poetry of homemaking and the pioneer spirit, "hoping to build a house, part snow, part victory":

> These parts wobble, stitching frames
> to improvise a document:
> all this American life. Strike that.
> All our life, all our American lives gathered
> into an anthem we thought to rescue us,
> over and out. On your way, dust. (*SVLW*, 52)

The self-correcting distinction ("Strike that") between "all this American life" and "all our American lives" is crucial. The single, collective experience of "this" idea of a place is devolved into the plural and individual. We all have "our American lives" even if we are not American — and there is no American who does not also have a European life.

"Revival," writes Cole Swensen, "is about the loss America has made, and about the dangerous way we compensate ourselves for that loss by enjoying it." The politics of such a critique are implicit in what Swensen calls the "longing *for* the self" exhibited by Gizzi's first-person voice, which "can't quite believe in the ideal, consolidated subject and the coherent world that such a subjectivity constructs."[19] Gizzi has spoken about his preoccupation with "the debt of address" incurred by the American Whitmanic mode, which openly "contains multitudes" in its "'throwing' of the voice." This throwing is done partly by projecting the lyric "I" into the lyric "you" in the interpersonal moment of speech: "the amplification of self by standing next to oneself . . . a form of discovery within the baffles of pronominal reality." But it is also achieved by the "vamping" that this voice performs by patching together and improvising on voices from the past: "who Peter Gizzi might be or might have been, through the baffles of tradition."[20]

Among these counter-factual Gizzis, the one whose poetic life takes place among the voices of English poetry is an important presence in *Some Values of Landscape and Weather. "And this is no other / Place than where I am—* W. S. Graham" reads the epigraph to "A History of the Lyric," the sequence that opens the collection (*SVLW*, 3). The lines signal another moment in Graham where the speaker of a poem ("The Dark Dialogues") turns toward the reader on the other side of "this . . . place," the printed page:

> And this is no other
> Place than where I am,
> Here turning between
> This word and the next.[21]

The penultimate section of Gizzi's sequence, also called "A history of the lyric," describes this place as a dark, oral one of synesthesia and longing:

> I lost you to the inky noise
> just offscreen that calls us
>
> and partly we got stuck there
> waving, walking into the Percy grass. (*SVLW*, 11)

"Percy" is not a variety of grass, which leaves readers to speculate over its adjectival usage. In the context of the history of lyric, the Percy Folio is the important collection of ballads discovered by Thomas Percy in the eighteenth century, and published as *Reliques of Ancient English Poetry* (1765). Gizzi's dreamlike image again recalls Ashbery's "pillars of grass," but suggests the exploration of a more arcane cultural landscape: the long grass of the English language (previously figured as the "inky noise/ just offscreen"). "Stuck" in this place of beauty and obscurity — the next lines evoke, with gorgeous, Guest-like abstraction, "A sinking pictorial velvet spray / imagining vermilion dusk"— we remain within reach of each other and yet also separated: "Why can't we or is it / won't you leave your solo ingle // beside the page."[22] "Ingle" is another word (meaning "fireside") that Gizzi gleans from earlier poetry, such as Ezra Pound's "Invern" ("O'er scant-logged ingle blaze").[23] Echoing here out of "inky noise," it also suggests a pun on the paradoxical idea of a private language, or "solo English."

"A History of the Lyric," then, reflects on how poetry incorporates different eras and nationalities into the illusion of a "solo" voice. Gizzi has said of his poem "Château If" that it was written when, in 1999, he visited Marseille in the south of France, the troubadorial "land of Amours," and "wanted to respond to this tradition in some way."[24] The previous year, Gizzi attended the Cambridge Conference of Contemporary Poetry and subsequently published a pamphlet, *Add This to the House* (1999), with the Cambridge-based press Equipage, which contains at least one self-consciously "English" poem: "The Ballad of the Boy with Green Hair." Although not written in ballad stanzas, each of the poem's four parts ends with a refrain-like distich on flesh's proverbial conversion into grass by worms:

> what comes of your vim in the end?
> It feeds the worm, colors the grass. Why ask?
> . . . .
> your punch when all's said, done,
> only fuels worms, adds luster to the grass.
> . . . .
> your very best effort when they find you dead
> is only food for the worms and green for the grass.

The last part reads, in full:

> And now that you've asked will you please be still
> and accept your fate and that plot on the hill
> above your head a flower spurts, a bee sucks,
> and a bird and a dog are one, grateful you've become
> a meal for the worms, rich peat for the grass.[25]

The poem is uncharacteristic of Gizzi, and has not been reprinted in any of his later collections. It has a jaunty rhythm and parodic exuberance reminiscent of W. H. Auden's sinister chattiness when evoking his creepy England of the 1930s (for example, "The Witnesses": "For I'm afraid in that case you'll have a fall; / We've been watching you over the garden wall").[26] The poem culminates in a swift one-two of jokey allusions to the pastoral poetry of Shakespeare (Ariel's song, which begins "Where the bee sucks" in *The Tempest*, Act V.i) and the final line of T. S. Eliot's most resonantly "English" poem, "Little Gidding" (1942): "And the fire and the rose are one."[27]

The American tongue fairly bulges in the cheek as it reaches this conclusion, especially if one hears the informal pun on the poet's own first name ("peat") in the final phrase. There may also be an autobiographical joke hidden in the poem's title. *The Boy with Green Hair* (1948), directed by Joseph Losey, is a film about an American orphan called Peter whose parents have been killed in the Blitz, who comes to believe he has an important, antiwar message for the world. Here, the American poet is the boy with green hair, a punk interloper reincarnated from the organic matter of the Old World. In its *jeu d'esprit* way, "The Ballad of the Boy with Green Hair" adumbrates a deeper and more complex statement of the same theme a decade later in *Threshold Songs* (2011), the book that was completed during Gizzi's tenure in Cambridge, England, as Judith E. Wilson Fellow in Poetry. The title of Gizzi's poem "Tradition & the Indivisible Talent" announces its intention to engage again with the example of Eliot, the American who became an English poet. But it does so via Jack Spicer, whose lectures Gizzi edited and published as *The House That Jack Built* (1998). In his afterword, "Jack Spicer and the Practice of Reading," Gizzi offers a definition of the "tradition" of Spicer's poetry:

> His poems create a space that both the living and the dead share in the act of reading. What Spicer calls time mechanics is essentially a kind of quantum poetics through which different poets are patiently writing the same poem in different times and places. Hence the poem is always in the present; its time is outside time. The poem is not immortal because it endures through the ages but because it exists in all ages at once. For Spicer this constitutes "tradition."[28]

Gizzi's metaphysical phrasing here ("the living and the dead") echoes Eliot's famous vision of a transcendent canon in his 1919 essay "Tradition and the Individual Talent."[29] But there is implicit disagreement, too, with the way in which, for Eliot, the present is hierarchically "directed by" the past—a disagreement that Spicer was vocal about. In the third of his Vancouver lectures, Spicer is asked about his notion of "the Outside," a force that dictates poetry to poets, and whether this has "anything to do with former poets." He replies, equivocally:

> I think in some senses it can [. . .] I think it's more a tradition of the past. I've never gotten any poet but Lorca, which was just a direct connection like on the telephone. Which wasn't the poets of the past but was Mr. Lorca talkin' directly [. . .] I think when you pay attention to tradition like Eliot does,

> you get into all sorts of the most soupy static that you can possibly have, so that you don't know what is your reading of English literature and what is ghosts.[30]

Spicer's notion of "soupy static" alludes to his belief that "the poet is a radio," receiving signals from the Outside ("Sporting Life," *The Collected Poetry of Jack Spicer*: 373). By concentrating too consciously on what he supposes or desires to be the source of poetic inspiration — dead European poets — Eliot is in danger of tuning out the live (dead) voices, not least those that emanate from the American tradition that he excludes from his Anglocentric literary "order."

The spirit of this argument against the omission of the living informs Gizzi's diction of "Tradition & the Indivisible Talent," which is sprinkled with American vernacular quirks just as "A history of the lyric" was punctuated with Old World curios such as "Percy" and "ingle." The first stanza introduces the poem's American voice as a kind of vaudeville bickering with vatic wisdom:

> If all the world says something
> we think then we know something
> don't we? And then the blank screen
> or memory again. You crazy.
> No, you crazy. (*TS*, 46)

The Romantic lyric "I" that haunts so much of Gizzi's writing recovers its poise sufficiently following this interlude to make an elegant statement about its own organic and inspired nature: "I am rooted but alive. / I am flowering and dying. / I am you the wind says, the wind." But the next stanza wobbles off immediately into the diction of Dumb America again: "The embiggened afternoon / was just getting started." "Embiggen" is a neologism from the TV comedy *The Simpsons*, where it sends up the ersatz historical pomp of the American dream as embodied by the small town of Springfield. The motto of Springfield is "A noble spirit embiggens the smallest man," and the Springfield Song includes the lines "That a people might embiggen America, / That a man might embiggen his soul."[31]

The word is comically clumsy, but Gizzi delivers it with a straight face, as just one more particle of a whole that is "all atomic anyhow"— all bound together, that is, by the fundamental "electron / part of being," however divided life may appear at the higher levels of "human or digital, vegetable, / mineral." The "indivisible talent," then, is not the individual poet but the life force that moves through all things seen and sounded in a poem:

> birdsong caught in the inner ear
> even the curios seem animated
> in their dusty shelves —
> the song is alive.
> That part of tradition. (*TS*, 47)

Like "The Ballad of the Boy with Green Hair," "Tradition & the Indivisible Talent" is ultimately about life as inspired matter, mysteriously dedicated to its own continuation. The penultimate stanza concludes on the thought that "fire" is "seemingly the only element / to get gilded up in song"— another glance, perhaps, at Eliot's "Little Gidding" and its triumphant fire symbolism. Gizzi, instead, asks,

> How about dirt? I love you
> like dirt. I miss you dirty mouth,
> dirty smile, oh, and my dirt
> is your dirt is nice also.
> Closer to the ground, perhaps,
> on the ground, that's real enough
> and those goddam spuggies
> are fledged and it's spring
> and the books in my shelves
> in my head have all turned. Nothing
> but earth and peat and mold
> and rich soft living manna
> you can breathe. The must
> at the root of it all, desire
> and wanting, must know. (*TS*, 48)

The switchbacking eloquence and rhetorical urgency of the passage — which is a tour de force of enjambment and grammatical surprise — suggests the influence of another postwar English poet: J. H. Prynne. Prynne's writing is distinguished by its uncompromising modernist commitment to lyric verse as a polyphonic art. As Gizzi writes in his introduction to the American reissue of Prynne's early collection, *The White Stones* (1969),

> The work is full of necessary and productive restlessness in the service of discovery, you can feel the breath driving the poem [. . .] This massing of clauses and perspectives creates an effect whereby any given singularity of personhood is defined and perhaps generated by a multiplicity of larger structural forces.[32]

"Star Damage at Home" in *The White Stones*, for example, is concerned with the apocalyptic "song" of a universal motivation, a desiring and emphatic "must" that yokes the individual subject into the first-person plural: "we must mean the / entire force of what we shall come to say," "we desire what we mean / & we must mean that." It concludes: "We live here / and must mean it, the last person we are."[33]

Wavering between noun and verb, Gizzi's repeated "must" is a softer collective imperative than Prynne's: it is the musty smell of the earth itself, the soil that gives rise to all culture, including the eroticism of "dirty" talk — a passage that sees the return of the poem's disruptively unsophisticated vernacular American voice. A bold allusion in the first half of the stanza complicates any dichotomy here between high modernism and low Americana. "And those goddam spuggies / are fledged" identifies one of the "books in my shelves / in my head" as *Briggflatts* (1966), the late masterpiece of the English poet Basil Bunting. This long, autobiographical poem has as one of its epigraphs the single line "The spuggies are fledged," a dialect word that Bunting glosses as "little sparrows."[34] Despite the gloss, this is not in itself an obscure allusion for an American poet to make. Bunting's friendship with Pound and Louis Zukofsky saw his work well received in postwar America, where he accepted invitations to read and teach in the 1960s, and where *Briggflatts* became a familiar reference point for readers of modernist poetry. Ron Silliman's *Woundwood*, for example, garbles the second line of *Briggflatts* ("descant on Rawthey's madrigal") for its epigraph — "*discount on Rawthey's mudra gal*" — announcing itself as a minor American echo of Bunting's poem of memory.[35]

Silliman's ironic nod may be contrasted with Gizzi's wholehearted admiration. Writing on his blog in 2005, Silliman recalled how "As much as I loved Zukofsky's *'A,'* Bunting's *Briggflatts* and Oppen's *Discrete Series*, I couldn't quite see how to directly employ in any present sense a poetics that had evolved among folks who were — let's face it — considerably older than my parents."[36] Gizzi's poetry has never evinced the programmatic, Poundian formal emphasis on the "new" that Silliman expresses in a statement such as this. His more Eliotic sympathies come to the fore in another interview given after the publication of *Threshold Songs*, in which he speaks about the personal, elegiac nature of the volume, but also "the borderless nature of selfhood and tradition":

> My bibliography is, all the books I've read, is a huge part of my autobiography. So when I say the borderless nature of selfhood and tradition, what I'm saying is that it's not only the people I've lost who are called back through the book, but so are all these other poets that I've read throughout my life. They're here in the language, in the layering of the voice.[37]

This layering may be heard, again, in what Gizzi introduces into Bunting's line: "And those goddam spuggies / have fledged" interjects the American vernacular of the poem into Bunting's Northern English voice, but in a way that is itself allusive, this time to Pound's refrain "sing goddam" from his parody of Middle English lyricism, "Ancient Music," which vents spleen at the British winter: "Skiddeth bus and sloppeth us, / An ague hath my ham. / Freezeth river, turneth liver, / Damn you, sing: Goddamm."[38]

There remains room on the shelves of this passage for at least one more poet compelled by the "must" of British soil, and whose vision of the lyric tradition arguably provides the passage's ideational dynamo. It is, again, W. S. Graham, and a poem from his third collection, *The White Threshold* (1949). "Listen. Put on Morning" is a Yeatsian aubade in praise of the moment when "A man's imagining / Suddenly may inherit / The handclapping centuries / Of his one minute on earth":

> The centuries turn their locks
> And open under the hill
> Their inherited books and doors
> All gathered to distil
> Like happy berry pickers
> One voice to talk to us.[39]

When "the books in my shelves / in my head have all turned" for Gizzi, as he writes in "Tradition & the Indivisible Talent," it is these lines from Graham that lie on top of the pile. With its layered echolalia of *The Simpsons*, Eliot, Pound, Prynne, Bunting, and Graham, the poem conjures in one lyric burst what William Wootten calls the "synchronic" temporality of the modernist long poem, which, like "nationalist consciousness," expresses "the present as suffused with the past."[40] The time shared by the ancient and modern people mentioned in *Briggflatts*, for example, "is like the heroic age of the nation," because it locates them all within the Anglo-Saxon kingdom of Northumbria—the landscape in which Bunting took a fierce native pride when he used a word such as "spuggies" or wrote that "Southrons [that is, the Southern English] would maul the music of many lines in *Briggflatts*."[41] But what Gizzi has called his "homespun amerikun version of the [ancient Greek] aorist tense—a sonic blurring in time"—that is, an atemporal effect created by "singing one's self in time as a rhetorical figure, disembodied and refigured as an embodied line of verse"[42]—ultimately aligns itself with W. S. Graham and his egalitarian vision of the English language as "scored and impressed by the commotion of all of us since its birth."[43]

The "inherited books" of Graham's lines are "like happy berry pickers" when they come together in a new song because they represent the immediate, chance fruit of the literary tradition, not its wholesale uprooting. Similarly, in "Tradition & the Indivisible Talent" we are told that "Twigs torn from brambles / nest and house this cooing thing" (*TS*, 47). All castled kingdoms and canons of tradition are constructed spaces here. As Gizzi writes in his note on the cento form of *Ode: Salute to the New York School*, "literary movements survive primarily in the ruins of the texts they leave behind rather than the unified literary histories we create for them after the fact."[44] It is with this feeling for the life of ruins that Gizzi's poetic sensibility has gravitated toward the English lyric tradition, seeding his works with allusions to the reading and travel that has cultivated them. *Threshold Songs*, for example, obliquely reflects Gizzi's 2010 to 2011 residence in England when it mentions "this bridge of sighs" ("Tiny Blast")—the famous Victorian ornament of Cambridge college architecture that spans the river at St. John's College—and includes, in "Apocrypha," a postcard note from the Europe of Rimbaud and Pound: "6. I've seen the Eurostar, the drunken boat [. . .] and the H.S. Mauberley covered in brine" (*TS*, 41; 53).

Even more obliquely, the lines from "Analemma" that state "I am *quelque chose* / something with birds in it" (*TS*, 16) echo the English poet R. F. Langley and his poem "To a Nightingale," which posthumously won the Forward Prize for Best Single Poem in 2011 ("I say none of this for love [. . .] It / is anyone's quelque chose"[45]). In addressing itself to the nightingale, of course, Langley's poem conjures up the ghosts of Keats and Coleridge. Allusions nest within allusions in English poetry, the product of Stein's "daily island life" where "these things birds beasts woods flowers, roses, violets and fishes were all there [. . .] just telling that they were all there made poetry for any one."[46] The appeal of such a place to Gizzi's pluralist, "rich peat" poetics is clear: as he has observed in interview, "for me the space of the page is crowded."[47]

ACKNOWLEDGMENT

Thanks are due to David Nowell Smith and Anthony Caleshu for commenting on an earlier version of this essay.

NOTES

1. Ben Hickman, *John Ashbery and English Poetry* (Edinburgh: Edinburgh University Press, 2012), 8–9.

2. Cole Swensen notes how the "internationalism inherent in early Modernism" informs Gizzi's poetry, particularly after he spent time as a writer-in-residence in France and Spain ("Peter Gizzi's City: The Political Quotidian," in *American Poets in the 21st Century: The New Poetics*, ed. Claudia Rankine and Lisa Sewell [Middletown, CT: Wesleyan University Press, 2007], 108–23 [111]). See also, as editor, his *Exact Change* yearbook (1995), a one-off review of avant-garde verse that included work from America, Canada, Britain, Ireland, China, France, Russia, and the Caribbean.

3. W. S. Graham, "Notes on a Poetry of Release" (1946) in *The Nightfisherman: Selected Letters*, ed. Michael Snow and Margaret Snow (Manchester: Carcanet, 1999), 380.

4. Peter Gizzi, "An Open Letter on Poetics to Steve Farmer (revised for the CIPM newsletter 1999)," www.petergizzi.org/assets/an-open-letter-of-poetics-to-steve-farmer-%281999%29-revised.pdf.

5. "Ding," however, might also point us to German, and Heidegger's 1951 essay "Das Ding" ("The Thing"), which is concerned with the modern problem of "dwelling" in a world where "the frantic abolition of all distances brings no nearness" (Martin Heidegger, *Poetry, Language, Thought*, trans. Albert Hofstadter [New York: Harper and Row, 1971], 163–84).

6. Elizabeth Bishop, *The Complete Poems 1927–1979* (London: Chatto and Windus/Hogarth Press, 1983), 93–94.

7. Wallace Stevens, *Collected Poetry and Prose* (New York: Library of America, 1997), 218.

8. Gertrude Stein, *Look at Me Now and Here I Am: Writings and Lectures 1911–1945*, ed. Patricia Meyerowitz (London: Peter Owen, 1967), 53–54.

9. Stevens, *Collected*, 653–55. Stein's nostalgic vision of "daily island life" for English

poets up to the twentieth century may be compared with Stevens's wistful sketch in "The Noble Rider and the Sound of Words" of the speed of news in the Napoleonic Era: "Coleridge and Wordsworth and Sir Walter Scott and Jane Austen did not have to put up with . . . Europe, Asia and Africa all at one one time. It seems possible to say that they knew of the events of their day much as we know of the bombings in the interior of China and not at all as we know of the bombings of London" (Stevens, *Collected*, 58).

10. W. S. Graham, *New Collected Poems*, ed. Matthew Francis (London: Faber and Faber, 2004), 107, 117, 119.

11. Graham, *New Collected Poems*, 161–62. "The Constructed Space" is a key poem in Graham's fifth collection, *Malcolm Mooney's Land* (1970), which repeatedly casts its speakers as lonely beings lost in "this place." The book opens with its title poem, spoken by a polar explorer, who asks, "Why did you choose this place / For us to meet? Sit / With me between this word / And this" (*New Collected Poems*, 155). It ends with "Clusters Travelling Out," a poem spoken by a prisoner in solitary confinement, who writes, "If this place I write from is real then / I must be allegorical" (193).

12. Gizzi, "Open Letter."

13. Robert Frost, *Collected Poems, Prose and Plays* (New York: Library of America, 1995), 316. Like Stevens's "Of Modern Poetry," Frost's poem first appeared in the war year of 1942.

14. Ben Lerner, "Poetry at the Threshold: Peter Gizzi on Lyric Selfhood and the Perils of Singing," www.poetryfoundation.org/article/243686.

15. Gizzi, "Open Letter."

16. Isobel Fonseca, *Bury Me Standing: The Gypsies and Their Journey* (London: Chatto and Windus, 1995), 5.

17. Jack Spicer, *The House That Jack Built: The Collected Lectures of Jack Spicer*, ed. Peter Gizzi (Middletown, CT: Wesleyan University Press, 1998), 201.

18. John Ashbery, *The Tennis Court Oath* (Middletown, CT: Wesleyan University Press, 1962), 13.

19. Swensen, "Peter Gizzi's City," 111.

20. Lerner, "Poetry at the Threshold."

21. Graham, *New Collected Poems*, 168.

22. Compare the end of W. S. Graham's "To My Wife at Midnight": "Maybe from my sleep / . . . / I'll see you here asleep // In your lonely place" (*New Collected Poems*, 59).

23. Ezra Pound, *Poems and Translations*, ed. Richard Sieburth (New York: Library of America, 2003), 46.

24. Daniel Kane, "Interview with Daniel Kane for *Teachers and Writers* (2000)," www.petergizzi.org/assets/interview-with-daniel-kane-for-teachers-and-writers-%282000%29.pdf.

25. Peter Gizzi, *Add This to the House* (Cambridge: Equipage, 1999), 18–19.

26. W. H. Auden, *The English Auden*, ed. Edward Mendelson (London: Faber and Faber, 1977), 130.

27. Eliot, *Complete Poems*, 198.

28. Gizzi, Spicer, *House*, 182.

29. Eliot's essay concludes that the poet must be conscious "not of what is dead, but of what is already living" (*The Sacred Wood* [London: Methuen, 1920], 59).

30. Gizzi, Spicer, *House*, 138–39.

31. Dave Sweatt, "The Jebediah Springfield File," *The Simpsons Archive*, www.snpp.com/guides/jebediah.html, accessed Sept. 5, 2014.

32. Peter Gizzi, introduction to *The White Stones*, by J. H. Prynne (New York: NYRB Poets, 2016), ix–x.

33. Prynne, J. H., *Poems* (Newcastle upon Tyne: Bloodaxe, 1999), 108–9.

34. Basil Bunting, *Collected Poems*, 2nd ed. (London: Fulcrum Press, 1970), 50.

35. Ron Silliman, *Woundwood* (Buffalo, NY: Cuneiform Press, 2004), n.p. Another Language poet, Charles Bernstein, quotes the opening section of *Briggflatts* in a similarly ludic, non-sequiturial way in "Of Time and the Line": "'Take a chisel to write,' but for an / actor a line's got to be cued" (*Rough Trades* [Los Angeles: Sun and Moon Press, 1991], 43).

36. Ron Silliman, *Silliman's Blog*, Nov. 9, 2005, ronsilliman.blogspot.co.uk/2005/11/william-carlos-williams-dorn-if-we.html.

37. Anthony Caleshu, "In Conversation with Peter Gizzi," *PN Review* 39.3 (2013), 50–51 (50).

38. Pound, *Poems and Translations*, 293. Gizzi speaks in the Caleshu interview of his use of another idiom —"there's nothing in it"— as "reminiscent of Pound's admonitory language." Compare the words of "Mr. Nixon" in *Hugh Selwyn Mauberley*, another poem of discontent with life in England: "And give up verse, my boy, / There's nothing in it" (*Poems and Translations*, 554).

39. Graham, *New Collected Poems*, 59–60.

40. William Wootten, "Basil Bunting, British Modernism and the Time of the Nation," in *The Star You Steer By*, ed. James McGonigal and Richard Price (Amsterdam: Rodopi, 2000), 27–29.

41. Bunting, *Collected Poems*, 156.

42. Lerner, "Poetry at the Threshold."

43. Graham, "Notes on a Poetry of Release," 380. In the same essay, the lines quoted from "Listen. Put on Morning"—"A man's imagining / Suddenly may inherit / The handclapping centuries / Of his one minute on earth"— appear as a prose sentence.

44. Peter Gizzi, *Ode: Salute to the New York School* (Tucson, AZ: Letter Machine, 2012), 43.

45. R. F. Langley, "To a Nightingale," *London Review of Books* 32.22 (2010): 25.

46. Stein, *Look at Me*, 54.

47. Caleshu, Gizzi, "In Conversation," 51.

PART II | LYRICS AND ETHICS

8 | OLIVIER BROSSARD

Peter Gizzi's Hypothetical Lyricism

Introduction: "A History of the Lyric"

Opening a book by Peter Gizzi is venturing into *lyrical* territory, the reader is told. Writing about his first book, Chris Stoffolino tells us, "The poems of *Periplum* have a philosophical lyricism which invites the reader to participate in a world that falls between (and in some cases immolates) the poles of ego and language."[1] Gizzi's subsequent collection of poems, *Artificial Heart* (1998), is said by Andrew McCord to be "on the quixotic mission of recovering the lyric."[2] In his review of *Some Values of Landscape and Weather*, Tim Peterson refers to Gizzi's "reinvention of the lyric."[3] While Adrienne Rich, on the back cover of *The Outernationale*, has it thus: "Peter Gizzi's disturbing lyricism is like no other — the innermost whir of the daily curtain rising on outer catastrophe."[4] Regarding Gizzi's most recent collection, *Threshold Songs* (2011), Dan Chiasson tells us, "Gizzi's innovation has been to treat the lyric like a big radio antenna, simultaneously transmitting and receiving eerie broadcasts from the air."[5] In the short space afforded the blurb or review, where "lyric" appears in different guises (the adjective "lyric," the nouns "lyric" and "lyricism"), it's difficult to say just what is meant by Gizzi's lyricism. This essay focuses on Gizzi's middle volumes, *Some Values of Landscape and Weather* and *The Outernationale*, as a way of exploring what seemingly appears most obvious about Peter Gizzi's work, but which begs to be defined.

Continuing the experimental tradition of American poetry, Peter Gizzi himself seems to be puzzled by the term "lyric" when it is applied to his poetry:

"at a reading someone said, 'You're really a lyric poet.' When I asked her what she meant, she said, 'Well you're not a narrative poet.' To which I responded by saying that I think I am a narrative poet — I'm just narrating my bewilderment as a citizen."[6] Although Peter Gizzi insists on the narrative dimension of his work, he does not deny that he is a "lyric poet"; he simply casts aside its restrictive definition as someone who does not relate stories. Revealing the difficulty to agree on the meaning of lyric writing, this anecdote also shows that Peter Gizzi's conception of lyricism goes beyond the traditional opposition between lyric and narrative. In *The Architext: An Introduction*, Gérard Genette has shown that classical theoreticians falsely attributed to the ancients (Plato and Aristotle) the mapping out of the literary space into three genres: the lyric, the epic and the dramatic. The lyric came to be considered as a potpourri of any writing that did not belong to the narrative or dramatic category.[7] However, Genette shows that the initial definition of the purely narrative mode (the dithyramb) had a common point with lyric poetry: the poet was the only subject of the enunciation, the only person speaking in the poem.[8] When Peter Gizzi says that he's "just narrating his bewilderment," he is offering a personal definition of his lyric mode of writing, bypassing the generic opposition between lyric and narrative. What matters, in terms of both the narration and the emotion felt (being bewildered), is the lyric subject as the subject of the enunciation of the poem: he (or "I") feels and he (or "I") tells. In that sense, it is true to state that Peter Gizzi aims at renegotiating the lyric tradition.

In the 1980s, Marjorie Perloff considered that such a renegotiation and its correlative attempts at defining (or practicing) the lyric were becoming urgent. Commenting on the publication of *Lyric Poetry: Beyond New Criticism*, she wrote,

> The [lyric] genre continues to be defined normatively — it is this situation that bedevils current discourse about poetry. For nowhere in *Lyric Poetry* do we find discussion of the following questions: (1) Is "lyric" merely another word for "poetry," as the interchangeable use of the word in the collection would suggest? If so, why talk about "lyric poetry;" if not, what other kinds of poetry are there and what is their relationship to lyric? (2) How has lyric poetry changed over the centuries? [. . .] How and why is lyric more prominent in some periods than in ours? And (3) since the etymology of the word *lyric* points to its musical derivation, what does it mean to write of

> lyric poetry as if its sound structure were wholly irrelevant, a mere externality? What, for example, does the choice of a particular meter mean? Or the choice of a particular set of linguistic strategies?[9]

For Marjorie Perloff, the transparency of the term "lyric," its thinness and lack of substance in critical discourse, was the result of the still prevailing conceptions of New Criticism: the poem was meant to be an impersonal, unhistorical, autotelic object.[10]

In the steps of poets such as Frank O'Hara, Jack Spicer, and John Ashbery, Peter Gizzi brings answers to Marjorie Perloff's essential questions about the nature of the "lyric." Although his book *Some Values of Landscape and Weather* opens on the long poem "A History of the Lyric," Peter Gizzi does not elaborate a systematic theory of lyric poetry; instead, he develops a practice of lyricism from which the meaning(s) of the lyric can be reconstructed. Poetry can succeed where theory fails:

> If we ask that every song touch its origin
> just once and the years engulfed
>
> If problems of identity confound sages,
> derelict philosophers, administrators
>   who can say I am found
> ("A Panic That Can Still Come Upon Me," *OUT*, 2)

To the multiplicity of the terms (lyric, lyrical, lyricality, lyricism) and of their uses, Peter Gizzi's history of the lyric can be said to focus on the lyric subject, on the problematic tension between its grammatical and syntactical appearance in the line ("I am," "me," "myself") and its presence, within the folds of the poem, as the voice who utters the line (the subject of the enunciation).[11] "Who can say I am found": the original loss of the self leads to a proliferation of relations. The poet pretends to be looking for two persons, "I" and the person who might be capable of "say[ing] I am found." But the poet might also be daring anyone to say "I am found," thus inviting the reader to read himself or herself into the poem. And one may ponder the different directions the line points to: indeed, it is difficult to know whether the last line is a relative proposition connected to "derelict philosophers, administrators" or whether it is a genuine question asked by the speaker, voiced by the poem. Peter Gizzi's lyricism is about "problems of identity," although not in a confessional way, which would demand that language translate his inner feelings onto the page. The poet's "problems of identity" are grammatical and syntactical: having no existence prior to their verbal expression, they do not exist outside of language. "I am far and I am an animal and I am just another I-am poem, a we-see poem, a they-love poem. / The green. All the different windows." ("It Was Raining in Delft," *SVLW*, 81)

In confessing that "I am just another I-am poem," the poet (or the voice of the poem) is staging his awareness that the literary ground he is exploring—that of the lyric—has been downtrodden for centuries, to the risk of being exhausted by incessant passage: "Things that have already been said many times" ("It Was Raining in Delft," *SVLW*, 81). Instead of offering a one-way ticket to poetry, from life to the page, the poet insists on maintaining "different windows," opening multiple vistas on the self.

> "Peter Gizzi" steer[s] clear of writing "I am" poems that make his inner life our roommate—which is no surprise, since today such stuff is as plentiful and wearisome as skateboards. [. . .] Gizzi is well acquainted with lyric poetry's potential for linguistic bravura, but he is not entirely in thrall to it. His poems manage to be [. . .] free of the occupational hazards of contemporary lyric poetry: presumptuous egotism, grating allusiveness, treacly insouciance.[12]

As the blurbs quoted at the beginning reveal (his lyricism is either "recovered" or "disturbing"), Gizzi's poetry goes against the grain of conventional "lyric" writing today. The main question is to know how the poet manages to keep writing in a lyrical vein when so many others fail, when so many poets are not even aware that they fail.

Peter Gizzi's poetry addresses Marjorie Perloff's concerns quoted earlier. (1) No, lyric poetry does not go "without saying": "'lyric' is [not] merely another word for 'poetry,'" but has its own quality and specificity. (2) Peter Gizzi's history of the lyric is not linear; however, the essential historical issue he raises is the question of its possibility today, in times of pain and war.

> If enumerations of the fall
> and if falling, cities rocked
> with gas fires at dawn
> . . . .

> if children, soldiers, children
> taken down in schools
> if burning fuel
>
> Who can't say they have seen this
> and can we sing this
> . . . .
> Too bad for you, beautiful singer
> unadorned by laurel
> child of thunder and scapegoat alike
> ("A Panic That Can Still Come Upon Me," *OUT*, 2–3)

The model of the lyric singer of yore proves inadequate. (3) Yet Peter Gizzi also renews with lyric poetry's aspiration to song. To find a space where singing will not feel out of tune with the world, such is the poet's quest. "Can I still say 'I' or 'myself?'" and "Can I still sing?" are the two sides of the same question. In 1951, in a talk given at the Museum of Modern Art in New York, Wallace Stevens said that

> in an age in which disbelief is profoundly prevalent or, if not disbelief, indifference to questions of belief, [. . .] men feel that the imagination is the next greatest power to faith: the reigning prince. Consequently their interest in the imagination and its work is to be regarded not as a phase of humanism but as a vital self-assertion in a world in which nothing but the self remains, *if that remains*.[13]

As if a faint echo of Stevens's lecture were reaching us today, the last few words, "if that remains," give a new import to contemporary doubts about subjectivity. "If the self remains" could be an apt password into the lyric territory Peter Gizzi invites his readers to explore, the land of his conditional lyricism.

Absence without Leave

"The self is farther than it appears": such could be the secret subtitle to Peter Gizzi's lyric adventure. In "A History of the Lyric," the "I" is indeed conspicuously absent from the first "chapter," titled "*Objects in mirror are closer than they appear*" (*SVLW*, 3). The pronoun "you" is its only distant presence, a grammatical stand-in, a mere prop that soon collapses and gives way to a long enumeration of objects.[14] In the very first pages of *Some Values of Landscape and Weather*, the self is shown to be receding into its own absence, defecting to the material world. Perhaps this is the only possible way to begin — and to keep on — writing the self in modern poetry, bearing in mind the lessons taught by such poets as Rimbaud and Ponge. Things, shapes, sounds, and colors fill the void left by the self: "Where am I in this thing called morning / with a ricochet of boys in the street, / the walls lemon with olive shutters" ("Etudes, Evidence, or a Working Definition of the Sun Gear," *SVLW*, 72). The objective world flies to the rescue of the self who has lost its bearings: "So things come together, one / and one. And if one, and if // an overwhelming sense of rescue: / fallen leaf. Broken acorn. Schoolyard tears" ("*In the garden*," "A History of the Lyric," *SVLW*, 9).

Not only has the lyric subject forgotten its own whereabouts in the world, it also seems to have lost all relation with itself. In spite of the grammatical presence of the lyric "I" in the poems, absence prevails and morphs into an absence from oneself, a form of absentmindedness: "Sometimes I am so far from myself / the stumble above only makes it worse. // . . . The distance is keening and sharp with tears. / This distance is loose wire free of its mooring" ("Take the 5:10 to Dreamland," *SVLW*, 36). From losing to loosening oneself, the "I" seems to have shed all hopes of ontological unity; the proliferation and outpouring of distance ("loose," "free of its mooring") expresses the vanishing of any coherent sense of authority: it's all "stumble above," all stutter. Lyric presence in Peter Gizzi's poetry does not rely on unabashed lines of "I-me-myself" but rather on the exposure of grammatical manifestations of the self to doubt and erasure. In "Beginning with a Phrase from Simone Weil," the last poem of *Some Values of Landscape and Weather*, the philosopher's phrase, "There is no better time than the present when we have lost everything," expands and transforms itself in the final stanza: "Is there no better presence than loss? / A grace opening to air. / No better time than the present." (*SVLW*, 96) There is indeed no better presence of the self than what its initial loss allows for; it is striking that the last line of the poem repeats Simone Weil's sentence, only taking out the idea of loss itself, as if loss could also be finally left out; as if what mattered and happened between "presence as loss" and "the present" was "a grace opening to air." In these final lines of the book, the lyric "I" and "we" have disappeared only to listen to (a) grace opening to the lyric air of the poem. The absent presence of the lyric self is none other than the voicing of its absence in the air as poem, as song.

Inside Out

In Peter Gizzi's poetry, the presence of the self comes in the shape of a doubt, of a question: "A child I became a question / sitting on the grass. / To be told how lucky I am. / An open field" ("Stung," *OUT*, 13). The autobiographical impulse of the first two words soon peters out into the progressive abstraction of the "I." The final line quoted here can be read as a strange metaphor for the lyric self: an image giving a shape to the "I," yet grudging it any specific contents — besides the possible allusion to Charles Olson's poetics.[15] The metaphor of the open field can also be understood against a conception of the lyric subject as a self-contained entity, precisely defined and closed upon itself. The self can survive only by opening itself up to questions, thus writing its own ontology as methodical doubt:

> I would like
> to expose doubt itself
> to open up
> the mechanics of want
> -ivorous, -etic, -esque, so
> someone can feel it ("The Outernationale [2]," *OUT*, 99–100)

The poet's "mechanics of want" aims at elaborating a critique of contents and substance. At the same time as words are gutted, hollowed out, and reduced to a litany of suffixes, making for a constant verbal stumbling in the poem, the lyric "I" repudiates the idea of interiority, a mere illusion. "The difficulty of being here is what do we transmit of ourselves that we can ever really know? / The single benefit of food is that we recognize it is food. / Can you spot the decoy?" ("Imitation of Life: A Memoir," *SVLW*, 33) There is no psychological or confessional food to be passed onto the reader in his poetry: the decoy is precisely the "inner" experience the poet is supposed to "ex-press" on the page. Writing with one's "guts" or "heart" makes no sense if one considers such organs as containers of emotions to be exported into literature. The lyric subject is more of an outsider than an insider.

When interiority, perceived as a threat, reveals the possibility of enclosure, the self steps out:

I was beside me as architecture,
solid as a house, a hovel made of sticks,
a shack whose chimney is a cloud at dusk,
a broken shack stove in by a single vista,
a room where countenance continues to fall,
a retinue of hair. ("Masters of the Cante Jondo," *SVLW*, 57–58)

This portrait stages a degradation of the metaphors chosen to define the self, from a solid house to a ramshackle shed, to a more abstract room. In the same way as the shack and its chimney seem to evaporate in the third line, the face collapses in the next-to-last line. "De la vaporisation et de la centralisation du Moi. Tout est là."[16] Gizzi's "centralisation" of the self functions through a critique of the notion of countenance both as "face" and as *contenance* (from the Latin *continere*, to hold together). "No amount of cable will connect this structure" ("Imitation of Life: A Memoir," *SVLW*, 33): Peter Gizzi's lyric subject cannot keep its composure nor can it hold itself together, and it is defined as architecture (house, hovel, shack) only to step aside and to contemplate the illusion of interiority from the outside. The disfigurement of the self is enacted in the text by the multiplicity of images defining it: the face does not "hold together" because the poet willfully suffers from metaphorical incontinence. Metaphors do not hold or keep; contents are emptied out as soon as they are proposed: the lyrical subject cannot be ascribed any specific ontological substance. It is at best a "retinue of hair"—a perverse expression as it both expresses motion (a group of attendants who travel with someone of importance) and containment ("retinue" comes from the French *retenir*).

Perhaps, then, escaping is the only way for the self to avoid being immobilized by a precise image, description, or definition. The first poem of *The Outernationale*, "A Panic That Can Still Come Upon Me," ends on the following lines:

If the crowd in the mind becoming
crowded in streets and villages, and trains
run next to the freeway

If exit is merely a sign (*OUT*, 3)

Running will not do: the last line shows that the escape hatch is but an illusion; it does not lead anywhere. If the poem is indeed the song of an illusory escape, it should nonetheless be added that the exit sign points to the only possible route: the only way "out" is not to be found in so-called reality but in the land of signs, in language.

Reaching "m-y-s-e-l-f": Zeno's Arrow

Peter Gizzi's poetry is animated by two seemingly contradictory impulses: a desire to escape from the self in its traditional sense and a will to come as close as possible to the "I" in the poem. His work thus seems in keeping with a philosophical and literary tradition analyzed by Karl Malkoff in his study of American poetry:

> It is important to realize that the loss of a potent self, which has often been characterized as *the* contemporary illness, does not necessarily lead to terror and despair. Some of our most influential thinkers have not only welcomed this loss of self, they have advocated it with an urgency that derives from their conviction that many of the horrors of the modern world spring precisely from the traditional definition of the self. For them it is probably more accurate to describe the phenomenon under consideration not as the *loss* of the self, but the *escape* from the self.[17]

Malkoff's analysis is based on close readings of the work of poets such as Ezra Pound, William Carlos Williams, Charles Olson, the Confessional poets, and some of the Beat poets and "members" of the New York School. Since his study was published at the end of the 1970s, the critic did not go on to mention the critique of subjectivity undertaken by the L=A=N=G=U=A=G=E poets. One may read Peter Gizzi's work in the wake of this critique initiated before the 1980s—although in no theoretical way—by poets such as Frank O'Hara and John Ashbery. However, it is important to note that Peter Gizzi rings changes on the poetic approach of the self. Yes, there are instances in his work when the lyric subject seems to be on the run,[18] as if fleeing its own shadow or about to do away with itself:

> If I am a bridge I am standing on, thinking,
> saying goodbye to myself

when I stood by the water in life
thinking of my life, pine boughs
the hill next to water ("A Panic That Can Still Come Upon Me," *OUT*, 9)

But rather than the theme of escape of or from the self, what should be noted is the paradoxical way the self is treated formally and poetically: at the same time the self is shown to be on the run, the poet tries new ways to get closer to it. As if, taking stock of the critique of traditional subjectivity of the past decades, the poet were now ready to say "I" again—or at least to attempt to do so. This paradoxical approach to the self is here revealed in the tension between the marks of subjectivity ("I am" repeated twice, "myself," "my life") and their preemption by the initial hypothesis "if," which qualifies the subsequent statement. This is all fictional, the poet says, all conditional: so much depends on "if." The impossible morphology of the lyric "I" in those lines (it is standing on itself) is symbolic of Peter Gizzi's aesthetic: he only says "I" when the self, suspended in the void by the initial conjunction "if," is about to jump off into the water, the poet knowing he can drop the pronoun at any time.

The opening pages of *The Outernationale* display the range of what one may call Peter Gizzi's hypothetical lyricism. From the very first line of the book, the authority of the lyric "I" is sapped, its expression undermined:

If today and today I am calling aloud

If I break into pieces of glitter on asphalt
bits of sun, the din

if tires whine on wet pavement
everything humming

If we find we are still in motion
and have arrived in Zeno's thoughts, like

if sunshine hits marble and the sea lights up
we might know we were loved, are loved
if flames and harvest, the enchanted plain
("A Panic That Can Still Come Upon Me," *OUT*, 1)

The lyric space of love, the locus of "the enchanted plain," and the cry of the poet, seer and singer, are all preempted by the litany of hypotheses. "I am" does not mark the origins of Gizzi's poetic world; the conjunction "if" does. The condition "if" applies both to a somewhat exalted vision of the lyric "I," "calling aloud" to the world, and to a chaotic portrait of the self collapsing, breaking "into pieces." "If" is the instrument of a methodical doubt applied to subjectivity, regardless of the qualities thus undermined. In such a context, the presence of Zeno of Elea may allow us to establish a parallel between the paradox of the "arrow" and Peter Gizzi's approach of the lyric "I." According to Zeno's paradox related by Aristotle, the flying arrow is a mere illusion: one has the impression that it flies when it is really at rest. The line "If we . . . have arrived in Zeno's thought, like" is inconsequential, it does not move; like most of the poet's hypothetical clauses, it does not lead anywhere but to the word "like" left dangling at the end of the line. If we still thought the poet was leading us to some specific place, we have the confirmation here that he wants to leave us (and himself and his self) hanging in language. One never reaches one's final destination or the object one aims at, "because of [one] having to reach the half way point before one reaches the end."[19] Always at one remove, objects and persons maintain a distance, the intermediary space of "like": such is the poetic territory inspired by Zeno. The irreducible space that keeps the arrow from reaching its target is akin to the unbridgeable distance Peter Gizzi maintains around the lyric "I."

The only architecture that may finally suit the self is the fictional space of "Château If," the first section of the poem "Fin Amor":

> If love if then if now if the flowers of if the conditional if of arrows the condition of if
>
> . . . .
>
> if I say myself am I saying myself (if in this instant) as if the object of your gaze if in a sentence about love you might write if one day if you would, so
>
> if to say myself if in this instance if to speak as another––
>
> if only to render if in time and accept if to live now as if disembodied from the actual handwritten letters m-y-s-e-l-f (*SVLW*, 82–83)

One could read the endless chain of "ifs," the "conditional if of arrows," as the laborious movement toward the self, a progress that can never quite reach its destination, thus missing its mark in the end.[20] The proliferation of conjunctions as arrows even dissects the self when the pronoun "m-y-s-e-l-f" expands accordion-like, as if the hammering of inconsequential hypotheses were bound to lead to its breaking down and thinning out. Each hyphen finding its way into the pronoun can be read as the typographical materialization of an "if," of an arrow: instead of having flown out, aimed at the world, "the conditional if of arrows" is suspended within the self, disrupting its structure. "If I say myself am I saying myself": the poet is not only aware of the lack of coincidence between being and saying myself, he is also concerned by the discontinuous experience of saying myself from one moment to the next. Avoiding aporia and motionlessness, Peter Gizzi continues to say, to speak, to write without shirking the consequences of his methodical doubt: "To live now as if disembodied" is precisely what happens to the self in his poetry, the only way for the "I" to maintain itself without lying or lapsing into indecency. To say "if" is therefore the only way for Peter Gizzi to voice a lyric "I," the only way to say and sing the world. "If I," "if the world" are the two axes of his poetic universe: it is then tempting to read his title as *Some Values of Landscape and "Whether."*

"Nobody came before"

The disembodiment wished for in "Fin Amor" could pass for a mere literary pose, a metaphor of contemporary angst, if it were not a poetic principle of the poet's work. Peter Gizzi elaborates an aesthetic of disembodiment that contributes to salvage the lyric self exhausted by ages of overexposure. Disembodiment should then be understood as abstraction from "the actual . . . letters m-y-s-e-l-f," to quote the poet's line in full. The tension at stake is between the verbal incarnations of the self in the text ("I, me, myself, we, ourselves") and its withdrawal in the folds of the lines as the subject of the enunciation of the poem, the invisible speaker. Such is the variable morphology of the lyric "I" in Peter Gizzi's poems. "*The ethics of dust*," the second part of "A History of the Lyric," opens on the following lines:

> to think I have written this poem before
> to think to say the reason I came here
> sound of yardbird, clinking lightbulb
>
> to think the world has lasted this long (*SVLW*, 6)

Gizzi's history of the lyric bids farewell to the conception of poetry as "the spontaneous overflow of powerful feelings" (Wordsworth 266). These lines stage the first appearances of the "I" in *Some Values of Landscape and Weather*: far from taking the lyric "I" for granted, the poet denies it any immediacy by rhetorically delaying its entrance in the poem. In the first line, "I" is preceded by "to think," and in the second line, the rhetorical layer triples: "to think to say the reason." The self does not go without saying, without someone — or the poem — voicing it. Peter Gizzi reveals the mechanics of his ontology: "I am" always implies "To think I am" or "To think to say the reason I am." These are not merely rhetorical niceties but the expression of the moving relationship between the "I" in the poem and the subject of the enunciation:

> The "I" of the enunciation is in a mobile relationship with the "I" of the text: it is both destination and source, both effect and cause. This tension, no mere dialectics, emphasizes the instability of the subject: the lyric subject *in question*, that is to say the subject as question, as restlessness, as a force of displacement.[21]

"To think I" is the literary space of doubt opened up by the poet, the buffer zone between the subject of the enunciation (the voice of the poem) and the many grammatical shapes the self assumes. As soon as the subject presents itself in the lines just quoted, it is sent back into the past ("I have written," "I came") as if the lyric "I" could not manifest itself grammatically without risking petrifaction. Instead of being located in nouns and pronouns, "the lyric subject . . . as a force of displacement" should be understood as the tense movement from the infinitive verb "to think"— waiting to be conjugated or uttered as an exclamation — to the past tenses attributed to the two grammatical subjects in the poem. "To think I": the self in Gizzi's poetry is dependent on breathing and enunciative assistance. The lyrical "I am" is summoned to wager its presence and existence at each reading of the poem.

"To think I have written this poem before," the first line of "*The ethics of dust*," plays with the illusory idea of a lost original poem. There is no "before" to the poem we are reading: "*this* poem before" is none other than the poem we are reading each time we are reading it. In the same way, the lyric poem is not meant to reveal the original identity of the self. "[N]o there is no precedent of history no history nobody came before / nobody will ever come before and nobody ever was that man," Frank O'Hara wrote in "For the Chinese New Year & for Bill Berkson."[22] Similarly, in Peter Gizzi's poetry, the lyric self is not a given substance, a constituted identity the words should serve and translate as accurately as possible: there is no ontological precedent to the poem. "The lyric subject should therefore not be understood as a given which expresses itself in a certain language, the language made song, but as a process, a quest for identity."[23] Such a process is revealed in the fifth movement of "A Panic That Can Still Come Upon Me" when the poet writes,

> if I wanted to go all over a word
> and live inside its name, so be it
>
> There is my body and the idea of my body
> the surf breaking and the picture of a wave (*OUT*, 11)

The variable geometry of the lyric self appears here in its complexity: the poem bears the marks of its presence, whether hypothetical ("if I") or plainly stated ("there is my body"). However, what should be noted is the general movement toward abstraction, when the body gives way to "the idea of my body" before being washed away by "the surf," itself replaced by a mere image. This abstract movement is the lyric process at work: as in the naïve imagery of Épinal, the lyric subject is not where one thinks it is. The self is not to be found in the first three words, "If I wanted," which are at best a hypothetical prop, a mere decoy. The self is hidden in the folds of the performative expression "so be it," one of the rare consequential clauses in the book. Although in the second line quoted here, the "I" has disappeared, the lyric self is more than ever present in its engagement as the subject of the enunciation of the phrase "so be it," replacing the more traditional and static "I am." When the poet says "I am," his identity is limited to the attributes of the grammatical subject. Here, by withdrawing into the enunciation of the poem, the self fulfills its desire to live inside the name of a word, inside language. Its identity is no longer limited to one specific proposition, "I am x or y," but expands into a correspondence between the self as speaker and language as it is spoken: the "I" no longer cuts a clear and specific figure in the text; its body becomes the poem itself.

The desire for disembodiment marked by metaphors of fragmentation and disfigurement leads to the erasure of subjective contents from the poem, to the retreat of the lyric "I" to its abstract position as the subject of the enunciation. Paradoxically, this self-abstraction allows the lyric "I" to have greater pretensions and to embrace the entire poem as its own body, as its new self. Lyricism in Peter Gizzi's poetry does not rest on a conception of the poem as a receptacle for the poet's feelings: this would imply that there is something "before" or "outside" the writing, whereas lyric interiority for the poet is the inside of the poem and of language. In "Saturday and Its Festooned Potential," the call of the outside is canceled at the end by the absorption of all space and temporal dimensions "inside the poem":

> When the mind is opened forth
> by a gentle tink tink
> or light speckled
> and whooping in the periphery
> . . . .
> When twigs swaying
> just outside
> the library's large glass
> signal, scratch, and join
> to an idea of history
>
> When twigs scratching
> join to an idea of time
> to a picture of being
>
> Like to be beside and becoming
> to be another and oneself
> to be complete inside the poem
>
> To be oneself becoming a poem (*OUT*, 59–60)

Peter Gizzi's lyricism could be summed up by the final line, "To be oneself becoming the poem," a new equation for the traditional "I am." When one reads the end of this poem, one has already become the poem. One has already become a lyric subject without having uttered "I am" (the verb "to be" is not conjugated): one has become the voice of the poem. Peter Gizzi does not so much say "I am" as his poem does it for him, animated by the readers' voices:

> By the time of this speech
> the original has vanished
>
> without promising emancipation
> The sound is a body
>
> This sound is my body ("*(song)*," "Masters of the Cante Jondo," *SVLW*, 61)

The issue raised here is whether there ever was an original, a self preceding the poem. "By the time of this speech / the original has vanished": these lines are reminiscent of spy movies where secret messages are meant to self-destruct once read. Only the opposite situation happens in Peter Gizzi's poetry: the lyric subject self-constructs only when the reader as special agent completes his reading of the poem.[24] "This sound is my body," the sound of the poem, the sound of language is "my" body: the body of the self, the body of the poem voicing the self, the body of the reader reading the poem. "My voice in what you say" (*SVLW*, 6): in other words, "I" am what you say "I" am, "I" do not exist before "your" voice breathes life into "me." As in much of Gizzi's poetry, the "you" can here be simultaneously understood as the "you" of the poem — or, more generally, of language — and the "you" of the reader. Gizzi adds,

> at this moment you say
> wind through stone, through teeth
> through falling sheets, flapping geese
> everything is poetry here
> ("*The ethics of dust*," "A History of the Lyric," *SVLW*, 6)

Although the "I" is absent from this section of the poem, one can say that this is a moment when the lyric subject is expressed most powerfully. The self is not grammatically present, and therefore it is not limited in the poem. Lyric expression here is the exact coincidence between what the words say and the words themselves, between what is enunciated and the process of enunciation, between meaning and voice. When one reads "at this moment you say / wind through stone, through teeth," one is saying "wind through stone, through teeth," one is going through the poem as Peter Gizzi's lyric subject, one is singing and saying "every thing is poetry here" on behalf of the poet. Lyricism, then, is the perfect correspondence between the words "this moment," "here" as they are written down and as they are voiced, between what is written and what happens, between the poem as possibility and the poem as performance.

Conclusion: Alone Together

If "I" am what you say "I" am, there is the possibility that the nature of the lyric self changes according to the reader who breathes life into the lines. To the question "who is the 'I' in your poems," Peter Gizzi answers,

> Well, it's me and not me. When I write, it's something just next to me — the observing I. To speak with an honest interplay of knowing and not-knowing. For me if a poem is a closed, contained vessel, it's dead on arrival; instead, I want to leave some part of the poem open so that I or another reader can enter it again and again. In a poem the I is always the reader as well as the poet. (Gizzi 2008, 61)

The risk for the lyric self to lose its identity because of its abstraction and openness is welcome rather than feared. The notion of identity is not contained in the poem; it depends on the interaction of the reader with the lyric subject as a variable in the poetic equation:

> So many strangers
> alive in a larynx.
> So much depends on *x*
> so much more
> on the book in your hand.
> Start from nothing
> and let the sound reach you. ("The Outernationale (2)," *OUT*, 93)

The final "you" here applies indistinctly to the reader and the lyric self as they are becoming one in the process of reading the poem: let the sound of the poem reach you as it constitutes you — the self, the reader, and the poem. "You" have started from nothing in the first line, but by the end of the poem, "you" have undergone a change:

> I love the opening to Beckett's late novel *Company* [. . .]: "A voice comes to one in the dark. Imagine." That the book is titled *Company* but the voice comes to "one." It's a wonderful description of how it is to be in a cinema, an inherently public experience — to be alone together connected by images and phantasms of light and shadow, dreams. But it's also a wonderful correlative to being alone in one's room in one's library, memory, alone together in one's books and a voice comes to one and then a poem begins. A world comes to one. And for a moment you are your self and another becoming another thing, a poem.[25]

These comments hint at two related dimensions of Peter Gizzi's lyric project that would require further scrutiny: the reflection on the possibility of a common language capable of uniting myself and "company"; and the dream and need of singing in a war-ridden world.[26]

The title *The Outernationale* sums up what is at stake in Peter Gizzi's poetry: a negative of the "Internationale," *the book* seems to be a modern symphony, the movement of which is centrifugal, rejecting individuals away from the center (of power, of civilization) to the margins, thus excluding them. The neologism "outernationale" turns the idea of nation inside out: what is questioned is the very possibility of relating (a story, a feeling) to someone. In a time when the public sphere is shrinking, what is at stake is "our" ability to be and speak together in a world that mass-produces isolation. In that case, the renegotiation of the lyric self is a way to adjust to this new situation and to find new bearings in the world:

> This is winter where childhood lanterns skate in the distance
> where what we take is what we are given.
>
> Some call it self-reliance. *Ça va?*
> To understand our portion, our bright portion.
> ("Last Century Thoughts in Snow Tonight," OUT, 55)

Peter Gizzi's own version of self-reliance is not satisfied with "what we are given," as the ironic "*Ça va?*" hints. The self's lot can be improved if one turns away from solipsism, "if speech can free us" (OUT, 6), if poetry offers hope for the creation of a collective "we." "[The] dangerous state [we are in] feels metaphorically 'out-of-doors' to me, outside the discourse of power and this out-of-doors (or outer) position or voice has proved useful to imagine selfhood or to make a voice that is at once neglected and empowered because of it."[27]

The prefix "outer" is therefore not exclusively negative, as it also hints at a vantage point from which the lyric self can speak, hoping that its voice will be joined by others:

> o say, can you see?
> What does it mean to wait for a song
> to sit and wait for a story?
> For want of a sound to call my own
> coming in over the barricades,
> to collect rubble at the perimeter
> hoping to build a house, part snow, part victory,

ice and sun balancing the untrained shafts,
part sheet music, part dust, sings often––
the parts open, flake, break open, let go.
. . . .
These parts wobble, stitching frames
to improvise a document;
all this American life. Strike that.
All our life, all our American lives gathered
into an anthem we thought to rescue us,
over and out. On your way, dust. ("Revival," *SVLW*, 51–52)

The long-awaited song, which the poet begins to write in his poetry against a perverse version of the national anthem, comes from the margins where everything crumbles, "flakes, breaks open and lets go." But isn't this space the limbo-like region inhabited by Orpheus, who, torn apart by the Maenads, began to sing? Perhaps this is one of the oldest ideas hinted at in "The Outernationale (2)":

[. . .] writing along the edge
which is of course
writing about hope
. . . .
Have you a single
new idea? Yes,
I carry the oldest ones.

Who will live
inside the song? (*OUT*, 94–95)

The answer does not come from the name of Orpheus but from the invitation issued in the third part of "A History of the Lyric":

If the dark speaks what does it say
in a dark time. As words choose me

are they mine, and the counterpointing wind.
If a catalog inserted here, your name here.

If the road turned, if your erratum
came to naught (for *with* read wick,

for *tear,* read torn), if you found me.
("*In the garden*," "A History of the Lyric," *SVLW*, 8)

"Your name here": no one is invited in particular, no one has exclusive rights to "live / inside the song," all are welcome. In the margins of the dominant discourse of power, outside of the language of social, economic, and political oppression, Peter Gizzi is inviting any reader to inscribe his name within the poem and join forces with "me" in "dark times." "Your name here": the invitation sent to the reader is above all sent to language itself. It is the name of language the poet calls upon in "A History of the Lyric": it is up to the reader to accept the invitation on behalf of language itself and to embrace this "outer" idiom, both personal and collective, in the momentary experience of reading.

One may also remember that *Your Name Here* is the title of a collection of poems published by John Ashbery in 2000. Peter Gizzi is using another poet's title to extend an invitation that is not only his but also one of his personal and poetic friends', thus sketching the beginning of a poetic community in the act of reading. Peter Gizzi's lyricism is a poetic system based on generosity and exchange, as the last few words just quoted show: "if you found me." The semantic and temporal ambiguity of the verb allows for different interpretations: you have found me, you are constructing me (*fundare*), you are melting me (*fundere*). Finding, building, pouring myself into a new mold: all this is implied in Peter Gizzi's "offrande lyrique"; all this, of course, provided we accept the poet's invitation. Then and only then will we be able to say "we found each other" in the poem.

NOTES

This essay was originally published as follows: Olivier Brossard, "Peter Gizzi's Hypothetical Lyricism: *Some Values of Landscape and Weather* (2003) and *The Outernationale* (2007)," *Études Anglaises* 61 (2008): 146–63.

1. Chris Stroffoliono, *To Magazine*, Apr. 1, 2004, www.petergizzi.org/assets/peri plum-(1992), accessed Apr. 1, 2016.

2. Andrew McCord, *New York Review of Books, Reader's Catalog.*

3. Tim Peterson, *Harvard Review* 26 (Apr. 1, 2004), harvardreview.fas.harvard .edu/?q=authors/tim-peterson, accessed Apr. 1, 2016.

4. Adrienne Rich, back cover blurb, *SVLW.*

5. Dan Chiasson, "The Higher Frequences: Peter Gizzi's *Threshold Songs* and D. A.

Powell's *Useless Landscape*," *New Yorker*, Feb. 6, 2012, www.newyorker.com/magazine/2012/02/06/the-higher-frequencies, accessed Jan. 15, 2015.

6. Peter Gizzi, "An Interview with Robert N. Casper," Jubilat 14 (2007): 49.

7. Gérard Genette, *Introduction à l'architexte* (Paris: Seuil, 1979), 39–40.

8. Ibid., 38–39.

9. Marjorie Perloff, "Can(n)on to the Right of Us, Can(n)on to the Left of Us: A Plea for Difference," in *Essays on Modernist and Postmodernist Lyric* (Evanston, IL: Northwestern University Press, 1990), 17.

10. Ibid.

11. Dominique Rabaté, ed., "Énonciation poétique, énonciation lyrique," in *Figures du sujet lyrique* (Paris: PUF, 1996), 65–66.

12. John Palattella, "A Delicate Balance: Peter Gizzi's Some Values of Landscape and Weather," *Los Angeles Times Book Review* (Mar. 21, 2004): R16.

13. Wallace Stevens, "The Relation Between Poetry and Painting," in *The Necessary Angel: Essays on Reality and the Imagination* (New York: Knopf, 1951), 170.

14. In that section of the poem, "you" finds itself in no glorious position: "they [the objects] are right next to you / in the lanes, hugging a shoulder // they twitter in rafters / calling down to your mess" (*SVLW*, 3).

15. Charles Olson, "Projective Verse," "Statements on Poetics" in *The New American Poetry*, ed. Donald Allen (New York, London: Grove Press, Evergreen Books, 1960), 386–87.

16. Charles Baudelaire, *Mon cœur mis à nu. Œuvres complètes*, vol. 1, ed. Claude Pichois (Paris: Gallimard, Bibliothèque de la Pléiade, 1975), 676.

17. Karl Malkoff, *Escape from the Self: A Study in Contemporary American Poetry and Poetics* (New York: Columbia University Press, 1977), 2–3.

18. "I ran away. I ran / away. Above everything / I held one true thing. / This scene moved through me, / a seesaw" ("Stung," *OUT*, 13).

19. Aristotle, "Zeno's Arguments on Motion Present No Difficulty for Us," in *Physics*, VI.9, trans. Robin Waterfield (Oxford, New York: Oxford University Press, 1999), 239b9, 161.

20. Although these lines are excerpted from *Some Values of Landscape and Weather* and not from *The Outernationale*, where the presence of Zeno is summoned, one may say that "the conditional if of arrows" looks forward to the presence of the philosopher in the opening pages of *The Outernationale*.

21. Rabaté, "Énonciation poétique, énonciation lyrique." The English is the author's translation of the original by Rabaté: "Le 'je' de l'énonciation est dans un rapport mouvant avec le 'je' de l'énoncé, à la fois but et source, effet et cause. Cette tension, qui ne se résout pas en une dialectique, fait ainsi porter l'accent sur l'instabilité de ce sujet: le sujet lyrique *en question*, c'est-à-dire ce sujet comme question, comme inquiétude, comme force de déplacement" (Rabaté 66). The "I" of the enunciation is a concept that's also used by Lacan, translated as such on www.lacanonline.com/index/2011/05/three-ways-to-understand-the-subject-of-the-statement-and-the-subject-of-the-enunciation.

22. Frank O'Hara, *The Collected Poems of Frank O'Hara*, ed. Donald M. Allen (New York: Knopf, 1971; Berkeley, Los Angeles: University of California Press, 1995, rev. ed.), 393.

23. Rabaté, "Énonciation poétique, énonciation lyrique." The English is the author's translation of the original by Rabaté: "Le sujet lyrique n'est donc pas à entendre comme un donné qui s'exprime selon un certain langage, la langue changée en chant, mais comme un procès, une quête d'identité."

24. "Consider this as an address / of an agent to his operative. / Hello you, if that's okay" ("The Deep End," *SVLW*, 28).

25. Gizzi, "An Interview with Robert N. Casper," 58.

26. "if children, soldiers, children / taken down in schools / if burning fuel / Who can't say they have seen this / and can we sing this" ("A Panic That Can Still Come Upon Me," *OUT*, 2–3).

27. Gizzi, "An Interview with Robert N. Casper," 57.

9 | DAVID HERD

The Lyric Voice as Ethical Medium

Peter Gizzi and the Contemporary Polis

The Voice as Medium

More than with any other contemporary poet in the avant-garde tradition, when I read the poetry of Peter Gizzi I hear the poet's voice. In saying so, I do not mean that when I read a Gizzi poem I hear his performance of it. What I am pointing to, rather, is the way that his language is shaped by the act of voicing, framed by the process of achieving voice.[1] I take this quality of the writing to be axiomatic. In attending as closely as he does to the way voice forms in language, Gizzi, I want to propose, is engaged in a profoundly ethical inquiry. Drawing on the historical function of the lyric, to present the relation between singular human consciousness and shared linguistic structure, he re-situates this ancient mode to articulate contemporary ethical pressures. At times that articulation is discursive, with the poetry addressing itself straightforwardly to issues of conduct. As the conclusion of "Modern Adventures at Sea" has it, the question is "How to live. / What to do." (*TS*, 85). Crucially, however, it is as the voice itself is formed in the process of writing that the poetry is tuned most closely to ethical concerns. Voice, this is to claim, and the act of voicing, has a centrality to Gizzi's work that makes it appropriate to describe it as his medium.

I mean medium here in the sense that Jasper Johns works with paint and newspaper, or in the sense that David Smith worked with recycled iron. More specifically to poetry, I mean the term in the sense that Susan Howe works with the documents of the archive or in the sense that Charles Olson developed meaning through the dimensions of the page. For Gizzi, the medium of poetic inquiry is voice itself, the complex dynamics of the act of voicing being the material through which the work's larger meanings are made. This is not to suggest that, against the prevailing tendency of modernist poetics, Gizzi's poetry should be identified as expressionism. Rather, just as Howe uses the archive (and its exclusions) to think poetically, so voicing in Gizzi, the process of arriving at a voice, should be understood both as actual subjective process and also as conceptual act. As the voice is heard to form in his writing, so do the real and painful questions that come of human separation and interaction. It is in his intimate and affective tracing of the elusive act of voicing that Gizzi's poetry establishes its contemporary ethical ground.

Saying

To argue that the voice, or the act of voicing, is the medium of Gizzi's poetry is not to make an unproblematic claim. How, it should be asked, can the qualities of voice be taken to be the basis for an aesthetic inquiry? How can such qualities compare to the properties of stone or paint such that one might think of voice not as mode but as medium? To start to answer this question, one has to be clear about the degree to which voicing frames the work. This is not poetry in which voice features as a discrete element within a ruminative process, as sometimes in Ashbery, nor in which after its initial appearance it can recede from view, as in *The Maximus Poems*. In Gizzi, by contrast, the poem is close against the ear, calling constantly for that discriminating listening that enables it to assume its shape.

One way this is signaled is by the prominence of the act of questioning. "Does that help?" the voice asks seven lines into "Saturday and its Festooned Potential," confirming that whatever the poem's potential, the reader must be invoked if it is to be made good (*OUT*, 59). This is always true: poems need readers. What distinguishes Gizzi is that in his poetry, this relation of invocation is fundamentally to the fore, the frequency of questioning being such that the relation between voicing and listening becomes not just the basis of articulation but its primary subject. "Caption," for example, follows an epigraphical question ("But where are the snows of yester-year?"— François Villon) with a question of its own: "One less body is lost in snow / The dying one (in time) becomes a landscape, / do you remember how it came about?" (*AH*, 30). Such is the prominence of the question in Gizzi's work that it functions metonymically, indicating a poetry in which the implied relations of voice constitute the inner architecture of the whole work.

Gizzi's word for this aspect of writing, as he observes a similar disposition in Jack Spicer, is "reception." Reception is a governing term in Spicer, stretching from his commitment to coterie as reading community to his image of the poet as radio and therefore receiver of the culture's meanings. As Gizzi puts it in the afterword to *The Collected Lectures*, "it would be almost impossible to overestimate the importance of reception within his practice."[2] One does not need to posit influence to observe a significant intersection between Gizzi and Spicer on this question of reception. The composition of the poem, as Gizzi proposes it, is a tuning to contemporary language that in turn calls for a heightened act of listening on the part of the reader. As in Spicer, then, "reception" is critical to Gizzi's practice—except if anything more so, or at least, to a degree that short-circuits Spicer's model of readership and his metaphor of composition. In Gizzi, this is to say, the question of reception is right there on the page, invoked without interval at the moment of utterance. Witness the first poem of *Threshold Songs*, "The Growing Edge," where the threshold in question lies at the emergence of the voice:

> a distant thrum
> you call singing
> and how many nights
> this giganto, torn
> tuned, I wonder if
> you hear me
> I mean I talk
> to myself through you
> hectoring air (*TS*, 1)

In a way that such intensification of the issue of reception dramatizes, the act of voicing is the fabric of Gizzi's poetry, its medium, as I have suggested, by analogy with stone or paint.

Still, greater specification is required, because if it is clear how an artist might work with a given medium, it is less clear how voice might be similarly worked. Voice, this is simply to point out, is not like paint, nor even like the documents one finds in an archive. What is it, therefore, one can point to in the act of voicing that Gizzi as poetic maker can be said to *work*? This, I want to propose, is something like the primary question in his poetry, one the writing itself repeatedly takes us toward. As "Modern Adventures at Sea" (the final poem of *Threshold Songs*) has it,

> And where does
> the voice
> come from?
> What life
> was attached
> to its lift,
> to its feint,
> its gift of sight. (*TS*, 84–85)

In a way that does not entirely destabilize its capacity for statement or observation — for the provisional truths that are core to the work — what defines the voice of Gizzi's poetry is its readiness to inquire after its own source. This is in no sense a contradiction; it is because the voice is plainly audible in the writing that the basis of that audibility can become the subject of the inquiry. The material of Gizzi's poetry, this is to argue, is the array of differentiations and dispositions that come of inquiring seriously into the act of voicing, the forms of thought and expression on which an ethical appreciation of voice and its agency depends.

To put some meat on the bones: frequently, as the poetry asks after its own basis of expression, where it comes to settle is the speaker's throat. It is a trope present in the poetry from the beginning, as in the early prose poem "Despite Your Notices," the opening of which inquires into the desirability of singular expression: "This is my poem. The one I was afraid to show you. A poem to provide against the voices that will ultimately ensure my failure in this endeavor" (*PEROP*, 36). Where this inquiry leads to is, as aforementioned, the throat, to

> Earth so frozen it came up to you in slags that still get caught in my throat every time you tell me you love me. So don't. I mate with these voices on the other side. Their memos become the mottos my solo walk into emblem. As the torn metal of all industrial accidents flowers in my brain. Yeah, I saw the broadcast. Transmission deceived. (37)

Much of what has been proposed so far is carried by these intellectually supple lines. Here is the voice of the poet contemplating its relation to other voices, catching itself in the moment of reception, and positioning itself in relation to the culture. The luminous detail, though, is the presentation of the throat, both as it mediates landscape and as it articulates affective response. If we are to understand human relations, as the poet sees it, it is to the dynamics of the voice that we should attend, as well as its place of natural delivery: the throat.

This mediating function of the throat in the act of articulation figures in some of Gizzi's most important poetic statements. In "The Outernationale," for instance, one encounters

> One sonic color into
> the egregious public air.
> Start from nothing and be-
> long to it. I guess
> the rosy and bluish streaks
> move counter to the feelings
> exposed beneath them.
> The signal and its noise
> -itsy, -ancy, -oid.
> So many strangers
> alive in a larynx. (*OUT*, 92–93)

The larynx is a necessary medium, this time to the image of linguistic intersubjectivity, as if human community could be located in the actions of the throat. Physiology, however, is in no sense the end of the story in Gizzi. If "The Outernationale" repeats the gesture of nominating the physical source of human sound production, it also seeks to isolate the more evasive quality that identifies writing as voiced. The poem's word for this, a word Gizzi insists on elsewhere, is "saying," the poem setting out to catch what we mean when we observe that language is *said*. The metonym in this case lies in the poem's repeated iteration of suffixes, as in the lines quoted earlier: "-itsy, -ancy, -oid." The point here is not to speak (or imagine speaking) the sounds out loud, not to engage the throat in the production of phonemes, but to refine the reader's sense of the relation between voice and language by observing that in the act of voicing, the language can be thought to be said.[3] The act of saying, then, becomes a central element of the discourse in "The Outernationale":

If we could say
the world has changed,
it has changed. If we say
the world is the same
then so it is. But nothing
changes everything
and we know this. (*OUT*, 101)

What we are called on to contemplate, in this instance, is what occurs in the act of saying, where the difference we are looking for is not so much an alteration in the world as an alteration in the relation between speaker and language.

The same subtle relation is enunciated at the end of "It Was Raining in Delft":

There is so much stone here. And grass. So beautiful each
        translucent electric blade.
And the noise. Cheers folding into traffic. These things.
        Things that have been already said many times:
leaf, zipper, sparrow, lintel, scarf, window shade. (*SVLW*, 81)

What we are to register is not just that "Leaf, zipper, sparrow" are said once more, but that the poem as a whole presents itself as an act of saying. As such, it inhabits another answer to the question, "And where does / the voice / come from?" One possible understanding of voice is that it originates in the saying of language. It is there, in other words, in the act of saying, that the voice becomes audible, the subject emerging in the enunciation of that which has been "already said."

As Mladen Dolar argues in *A Voice and Nothing More*, fundamental as it is to an account of subjectivity, the voice nonetheless lies at the periphery of our capacity for expression. Drawing an analogy with Lacan's notion of the gaze, Dolar observes that "the gaze is not something that could be present in the field of vision, yet it haunts it from the inside."[4] The analogy helps frame the force of Gizzi's primary question: "And where does / the voice / come from?" It is a question, as has been argued, that carries us into the poetry's own medium, to the questions and possibilities by which the intellect sets out to frame the voice. What remains to be observed is how such renderings of voice carry argumentative charge, how by tracing the act of voicing to its limit, Gizzi tunes his medium to questions of ethics.

Voicing Space

For the act of voicing to be an ethical, as opposed simply to an expressive medium, it requires grounds on which individuals, or individuals and collectives, can be understood to interact. Defined as it is, in other words, by temporality, by the ongoing process of its emergence, if the act of lyric voicing is to register an ethical charge, then one way or another it must also carry a sense of space. In the modern tradition, the poet most committed to the articulation of space as the grounds of human interaction was Olson, *The Maximus Poems* being precisely a field on which historical actors are heard to interact. The basis for such a field, however, was established in "Projective Verse," Olson's manifesto concerning itself explicitly with space as a setting for the projection of voice. Thus, on the question of the space of the poem — the poem's field — the critical point is that it enables the expression of relations. As Olson puts it,

> every element in an open poem . . . must be taken up as participants in the kinetic of the poem just as solidly as we are accustomed to take what we call the objects of reality; that these elements are to be seen as creating the tensions of a poem just as totally as do those other objects create what we know as the world.[5]

It is through the space of the projective poem, as Olson presents it, that the relations that constitute the world can be represented. Space is also crucial, however, to Olson's presentation of voice. Referring to the expressive possibilities generated by the typewriter, Olson observes that

> For the first time the poet has the stave and the bar a musician has had. For the first time he can, without the conventions of rime and meter, record the listening he has done to his own speech and by that one act indicate how he would want any reader, silently or otherwise to voice his work. . . . If a contemporary poet leaves a space as long as the phrase before it, he means that space to be held, by the breath, an equal length of time.[6]

In formulating the claims of his manifesto, Olson presents many of the elements that have structured the discussion so far, in particular voice and its physiology (characterized here and elsewhere in the manifesto in terms of breath), and readerly reception expressed as an act of listening. Where Olson adds something, in this context, is in the image of the poem as spatial arrangement. It is there, in that representation of space, that the ethics of Olson's poetic polis reside.

The intention here is not to argue that Gizzi is an Olsonian poet. The list of poets important to his development is well documented and includes, among others, Dickinson, Pound, Oppen, Schuyler, Ashbery, and (not least for his model of poetic inheritance) Eliot.[7] Olson's verbal manner and archival method, by contrast, are wholly absent from Gizzi's writing. Any suggestion of influence firmly disavowed, however, it should equally be acknowledged that Gizzi is hardly unaware of Olson's discourse. In his 2004 talk at the AWP, he discussed his practice by advancing a considered sense of the term "field":

> Rather than thinking in terms of inside & outside, I tend to think of all our work as occurring within a field. A field is a ground. And even though the word seems to suggest openness and freedom, the field is haunted.
>
> In 1863 when Lincoln made his dedicatory remarks at Gettysburg, that field in southern Pennsylvania was first open land, then a homestead and a farm, then a battlefield where 50,000 fell in 3 days, then a graveyard, and now it is a national park surrounded by shopping malls and Jacuzzi motels.[8]

Among the various senses of "field" at play here, Gizzi declines to indicate the geometrical sense of the term that underpins "Projective Verse." In recalling Lincoln's address at Gettysburg, however, what he clearly presents is an image of the voice framed by contested space. Such a sense of contested space is crucial. "Of the 18 definitions of field," he observes, "a third of them have to do with war." It is also, however, "an extended surface, a liberating expanse," one example being a sports field.[9] As poets, he concludes,

> The field we work is a battlefield and at times a garden, the realm of overlooked poets rescued from their apartments, from well-meaning librarians, and from landfill. Writing, editing, and teaching are all ways of working the field, making use of what we see and what we know, reshaping it, making others a part of it.[10]

Both in his elaboration of the term's meaning, and in the claims he derives from it, Gizzi's discussion of the field is striking. The poet, we are to understand, operates on a historic site of conflict, where the voices calling for attention represent lost or occluded cultural possibilities. It is an image of voice and voicing that recalls the seemingly very different project of Susan Howe, where the difference lies precisely in the poets' chosen media, but where the similarity lies in the express intention to recover the historically marginalized voice.

Howe's archival poetic can hardly be reduced to such a position, but equally she signals it as guiding concern, hence the much observed statement in "There Are Not Leaves Enough to Crown to Cover to Crown to Cover": "I wish I could tenderly lift from the dark side of history, voices that are anonymous, slighted — inarticulate."[11]

Howe, even so, is not the primary point of orientation here. As a contemporary American poet, one cannot elaborate on the meanings of the term "field" to the degree that Gizzi does without appreciating the force it had for Olson; without registering that as Olson introduced the term, what it enabled him to achieve was an articulation of human relations. Gizzi registers the value of Olson's discourse without appropriating his procedures. The same was true of Spicer. As Gizzi himself puts it,

> Olsonian field theory is translated by Spicer into a brawling, noisy, beer-drinking field of everyday heroism. Through baseball, Spicer re-writes the Polis, unseating Olson's authoritative poetic agency by grounding it in a populist, even athletic origin. . . . the process is literalized in the imaginary construction of Vancouver from the baselines of a baseball diamond.[12]

My suggestion here is that to understand how Gizzi's writing carries its ethical charge, we need to appreciate the sense in which he also rewrites Olson, not through anything as literal as the baseball diamond, but through the contours of the voice itself.[13]

What these references to the New American Poetry help us to understand are the ways poetry in that tradition moves between an understanding of the poem as a spatial medium to engagement with civic and political space. Building on this framework, there are two ways in particular that Gizzi draws civic and political space into his presentation of voice. The first is by repeatedly depicting what we might think of as a postindustrial polis, a degraded civic space in which communication struggles to occur. It is this space one glimpses in the transmutations of the field at Gettysburg: the compromised site of the poem's own vocal performance. The volume in which such sites are most carefully dwelt on is *Some Values of Landscape and Weather*, the title registering the writing's concern both with the immediacy of the present (the weather) and with the historically structured space it plays across (landscape). "To Be Written in No Other Country," for example, depicts the arena of what it calls the "body electorate":

It is a sorry day for the pollster and body electorate
for the mildewed pages of a wound dresser.
And when and whenever past Saturdays
of adolescents in faded Kodak
enter the discourse of politicians
know you are not alone and your scrapbook
will be enough in talk of resolutions
and what you plan to do this weekend
to the garage and to the porch. (*SVLW*, 46)

The lines are framed by various kinds of nostalgia: the nostalgia produced by politicians through simplified cultural discourse; the nostalgia of the contemporary poet for the image of Whitman addressing his writing to the urgencies of the Civil War. Really what emerges, though, is the restricted sense of civic space that the poem exists to counter, a public sphere determined by pollsters in which agency is restricted to plans for the garage and for the porch. Not that Gizzi is dismissive of those plans; he is too committed to the American vernacular to travesty the citizen's domestic projects. Still, what the poem sets out to trace is a landscape in which other values have been, and might still be, articulated. The poem's voice is rendered spatial therefore, in that as it situates itself, what it depicts is the vestige of a polis.

For the richest depiction of the postindustrial civic environment, however, one has to turn to the title poem itself, the fifth section of "Some Values of Landscape and Weather" providing a brilliantly eloquent presentation of contemporary social space:

We fought in a war, looking for a sound,
some frequency
a human animal could field
beyond the other registers of everyday
and fancy, a tuning perhaps,
to focus for this instant, the effort
towards dotted archipelagoes was a part of it,
documentary hydroelectric facilities,
sno-cone mountain views, certainly
the unruly assembly of public space
is essentialism, there can be pigeons,

statehouses and prisons, freeways
etcetera. There were big chords,
a piece of the total score, the trajectory
(not facts, but hands) is this further sound,
scratch of pen to parchment
in a flight of democracy. (*SVLW*, 23)

For a poet who has tended to resist the temptations of the statement of poetics, this passage constitutes one of Gizzi's most finely honed articulations of his aesthetic stance. Here, as in the previous example, what he depicts is the field of the contemporary poem, where what characterizes that field is the "flight of democracy," and where what the poem would seem to desire above all is an adequate expression of the "unruly assembly of public space." What really distinguishes the writing, however, is not the spatialized image of a democratic deficit, but the way that image is keyed to Gizzi's language of "frequency" and "tuning." What we have here, then, is an image of political geography (with its troubling archipelagos) carried by a poetic medium governed by the possibilities of the poetic voice.

It is in this sense, I suggest, that Gizzi can be heard to rewrite Olson. Thus, whereas in Olson, and notably in "Projective Verse," one is presented with voice and space as if they existed in the poem as separate elements, in Gizzi, as "Some Values of Landscape and Weather" proposes, space in the poem is folded into voice. Both positions are sustainable. Olson can hold the elements apart because of the way he depicts the page; there is, in his practice, a space on which the voice occurs. In Gizzi, however, such is his commitment to lyric utterance that space cannot be rendered as if it were outside the writing's primary medium.

Stating this understanding of voice as an ambition for writing, what Gizzi's poetry consciously seeks is "some frequency / a human animal could find / beyond the other registers of everyday and fancy." Taking the "archipelagoes" the poem subsequently mentions in a literal sense, I read the "beyond" of this statement as primarily spatial, and I take the process by which the voice tunes to such distances to be primarily syntactical; the key element in that syntax being the gesture the passage identifies as "etcetera," but which elsewhere is referred to by the adverb "also." Take, for instance, the short lyric "In Defense of Nothing":

I guess these trailers lined up in the lot off the highway will do.
I guess that crooked eucalyptus tree also.
I guess this highway will have to do and the cars
        and the people in them on their way.
The present is always coming up to us, surrounding us.
It's hard to imagine atoms, hard to imagine
        hydrogen & oxygen binding, it'll have to do.
This sky with its macular clouds also
        and that electric tower to the left, one line broken free. (*SVLW*, 53)

Placed twice, emphatically, at the end of the line, "also" is where the weight of the voice of this anti-manifesto poem falls. In carrying that weight, it recalls another structuring term in Gizzi's poetry: the term "item," as in the poem "Pierced," the last lines of which read

here is my instrument
last will and testament

Item: 1 locket, broken, its vowels stolen

Item: to give up loneliness, give up happiness
(poor *maudit*)

Item: 1 cock, 1 comb, another evening
a predictable event

two cars race to the horizon. (*AH*, 71–72)

It is true that "item" and itemization are Gizzi's "instrument," the poetry frequently building itself by registering singularities. "Item," we should therefore notice, derives from the Latin for "also." One can hear a silent itemizing, then, in "In Defense of Nothing": "I guess that crooked eucalyptus tree also."

It is by repeatedly vocalizing this sense of "also" that Gizzi voices space. This is apparent in the conclusion to "Pierced," in the fact that after the poet has performed the act of itemizing, "two cars race towards the horizon." The poem proposes a link. It is through the process of itemizing that which is also present that the voice of the poem is carried out spatially, able to register that which is removed from the site of utterance. This is a lyric poetry, in other words, that has a capacity to address what Olson called "The Distances," but without departing from the exploration of voice that is its primary medium. What this means, in terms of ethics, is that the voice of Gizzi's poetry has a determinate sense of what occupies its periphery, a sense of the contested archipelagoes and the battlefields that constitute its outlying sites, the conflict that is its outlying condition:

> A nervous moon and winter branches
> all that needs be recorded for now
> and the value of gunmetal
> fading to midnight all around.
> The chill is real, that much
> can be said in early November. (*SVLW*, 22)

These lines, again, are from "Some Values of Landscape and Weather." As they voice the peripheral violence that is a condition of contemporary lyric utterance, they can be sung to the tune of Gizzi's next book, *The Outernationale*.

Lyric's Appeal

To restate the claim: the argument of this essay is that in the care with which Peter Gizzi explores the possibility and potential of the contemporary lyric, he makes the voice of that poetry an ethical medium. That it is ethical, and not simply expressive, owes partly to the fact that it communicates a sense of space, that it registers both the compromised civic environment and the fraught periphery that are the conditions of contemporary lyric utterance. This is not, however, a complete statement of the way the exploration of voice in Gizzi's poetry constitutes an ethical inquiry. Two further aspects of the writing require consideration: the fragility of its utterance and, by way of conclusion, its articulation of shared subjectivity.

Fragility is a defining quality of the voice of Gizzi's poetry: always struggling to establish itself and also always, as it emerges, contemplating the prospect at any moment of being cut off. "A Panic That Can Still Come Upon Me," the first poem of *The Outernationale*, is among the most carefully poised articulations of this framing condition; witness the opening passage:

> If today and today I am calling aloud
>
> If I break into pieces of glitter on asphalt
> bits of sun, the din

if tires whine on wet pavement
everything humming

If we find we are still in motion
and have arrived in Zeno's thought, like

if sunshine hits marble and the sea lights up
we might know we were loved, are loved
if flames and harvest, the enchanted plain

If our wishes are met with dirt
and thyme, thistle, oil,
heirloom, and basil

or the end result is worry, chaos
and if "I should know better"

If our loves are anointed with missiles
Apache fire, Tomahawks
did we follow the tablets the pilgrims suggested

If we ask that every song touch its origin
just once and the years engulfed (*OUT*, 1–2)

The fragilities in evidence here are various and exemplary. In characteristic fashion, the poem's voice announces itself by the gesture of struggling to make itself heard. Voicing, this is to say, as Gizzi's poetry presents it, is defined by difficulty, by the kind of difficulty indicated here by the stuttering syntax of the opening line: "If today and today I am calling out loud." To stutter or stammer is to experience a series of breaks against the language, the stuttering voice not readily able to establish fluency. Gizzi has spoken in interview about the fact that he was himself "a stutterer, a stammerer" as a child, and has drawn attention to a similar disposition in the poetry itself.[14] As he told Robert Casper in an interview for *Jubilat*, he hears the repetition of suffixes that recurs through *The Outernationale* "as a stutter or a stammer . . . like the skipping of a damaged CD."[15] It is a tendency in the writing that critics have drawn attention to, not primarily as biographical fact but as an aspect of Gizzi's presentation of the lyric voice itself.[16] What marks that voice out, in other words, is the difficulty of getting going, a need to start over captured in "A Panic That Can Still Come Upon Me" by the repetition of clauses beginning "If."

The linguistic break carried by the tendency to stutter is replicated across the poem's performance. One hears it in the provisionality of the line openings, in the repeated "If" that declares the poetry's vulnerability to circumstance. One hears it also at the end of the line, as the poetry proceeds by enumerating a series of only partially connected things. One hears it crucially, as well, in the fact that presence in the poem is determined constantly by the prospect of absence, dramatized here by the military hardware, "Apache fire, Tomahawks" that threaten to cut the enunciator off. At every turn of its performance, in other words, the voice of the poem is determined by its vulnerability, by the breaks in transmission that condition its emergence and convey the constant prospect that it might be curtailed.

The way such breaks carry ethical charge can be variously articulated. In his interview with Casper, Gizzi suggests that the precarious quality of "A Panic That Can Still Come Upon Me" is partly prepared for by the last poem of *Some Values of Landscape and Weather*, "Beginning with a Phrase from Simone Weil."[17] The phrase in question ("There is no better time than the present when we have / lost everything") comes from Weil's investigation of human fragility, *Gravity and Grace*. To understand the phrase's value in poetic terms, however, one can turn to Weil's brilliant essay on Homer, "*The Iliad*, or The Poem of Force." Written during World War II, Weil's reading of *The Iliad* emphasizes precisely the clarity with which the poem communicates the fact that at any moment a life might be cut off: "Somebody was here, and the next minute there is nobody here at all; this is a spectacle *The Iliad* never wearies of showing us."[18] For Weil, this repeated expression of exposure to force makes Homer's poem a defining articulation of the value of presence, and also therefore of the counter fact that "this indefinable influence that the presence of another human being has on us is not exercised by men whom a moment of impatience can deprive of life."[19] *The Iliad*, in other words, is the great poem of limits, of beginnings and endings, it being by the constant play of presence and absence that the poem communicates its ethical charge. It is there, in that sense of limit, that Weil helps frame Gizzi's concerns in "A Panic That Still Comes Upon Me," the crucial distinction being that in his lyric medium, it is in voice itself, not narrative action, that the sense of human limit is conveyed. It is through the beginnings and endings of the voice, not the depictions of action, that lyric communicates the fragile presence of another human being; that "indefinable influence" that constitutes what Mladen Dolar calls the voice's primary "appeal."

Such vocal appeal, as Dolar presents it, is most vividly communicated when the voice is least voice-like, when it is engaged in one of a number of actions a linguist might designate nonvocal: coughing, babbling, hiccoughing, screaming. Dolar's interest in such limit cases lies in the way they disclose the underlying features of vocal performance, in the fact that babbling, for instance, for all the absence of meaning, "[d]isplays the structure of address."[20] Screaming, on the other hand, communicates appeal: "The scream becomes an appeal to the other; it needs an interpretation and an answer, it demands satisfaction."[21] My suggestion here is that we might add the stutter to Dolar's list, or at least that we might read the periodic syntactical stutter of Gizzi's poetry as a further limit case of vocal appeal. As the voice of the poem struggles to emerge, as it halts and starts again, it communicates the difficulty and the value of the process of being heard. This is not at all to argue that the stutter is Gizzi's defining trope, nor that the poetry is always marked by that expressive difficulty. It is to argue, however, that Gizzi's poetry is acutely attentive to beginnings and endings, not least as they define the line itself; to the silences out of which the lyric voice emerges and the breaks in transmission to which it is always threatening to succumb. It is in part in that acute sense of limit that Gizzi's lyric carries its ethical charge, communicating the vulnerabilities of voice upon which human appeal depends.

Threshold Songs

To address the vulnerable appeal of Gizzi's lyric voice is to arrive at what he has come to call the "threshold." It is a term that has many meanings in his poetry, and which has, arguably, been axiomatic to him all along. In his preoccupation with elegy, in his sense of the difficulty of expression, in the image of tuning that constitutes his image of composition and reception, Gizzi has always been at or close to the threshold. It is only with his most recent work, however, that he has been explicit about this relation, making the threshold the site for the song itself. That he has situated his work in this way, located it at the threshold, requires us to consider the term itself.

To start with the dictionary, a threshold, according to the *Oxford English Dictionary*, is

> 1. a strip of wood or stone forming the bottom of a doorway and crossed in entering a house or room; 2. a level or point at which something starts or ceases to happen or come into effect; from the Old English thresh, meaning "tread."

In the context of this discussion, the implications here are rich, at both the level of literal meaning and the level of metaphor. In one sense, the definition is a reminder that the threshold is a primary scene of American poetry, Whitman having located its themes and established its authority in the dooryard. It is also a site of beginnings and endings, the point where something "starts or ceases to . . . come into effect," a proper setting, therefore, for the voice as it struggles to emerge and sustain itself. As the dictionary defines it, in other words, the threshold is an entirely natural focus for Gizzi's concerns.

It is not only meaning we should consider, however, but also recent usage. Addressing himself to the question "What is the Contemporary?" Giorgio Agamben has fixed on the threshold as a way of orienting his discourse. As he put it at the beginning of his discussion, "The question that I would like to inscribe on the threshold of this seminar is: 'Of whom and of what are we contemporaries?'"[22] To inscribe the threshold at the beginning of a seminar on the subject of the contemporary is to make the term itself a marker of contemporariness. What the contemporary calls for, in other words, as Agamben's essay goes on to propose, is a style of thought that understands itself as operating at a crossing. Such thinking will necessarily be supple, but crucially, as Agamben sees it, it will involve an appreciation of what he terms an era's obscurity:

> The contemporary is he who firmly holds his gaze on his own time so as to perceive not its light, but rather its darkness. All eras, for those who experience contemporariness, are obscure. The contemporary is precisely the person who knows how to see this obscurity, who is able to write by dipping his pen in the obscurity of the present.[23]

The real interest of both terms in Agamben, however, both "threshold" and "contemporary," is how they function and cross over from his political discourse. As he describes the "state of exception," therefore, with particular reference to its most recent manifestations, Agamben identifies such acts of legal suspension thus:

> This transformation of a provisional and exceptional measure into a technique of government threatens radically to alter — in fact, has already palpably altered — the structure and meaning of the traditional distinction between constitutional forms. Indeed, from this perspective, the state of exception appears as a threshold of indeterminacy between democracy and absolutism.[24]

A different argument would pursue the link between Agamben's essay on the contemporary and his devastating inquiry into the state of exception. What such an argument would flesh out is the way "obscurity" functions in both discussions, the fact that, as Agamben sees it, the reemergence of the state of exception as a tactic of liberal regimes constitutes the peripheral darkness of our own period. What matters here, however (even as Agamben's argument chimes with Gizzi's sense of "the flight from democracy"), is not precisely the obscure settings of contemporary politics, but the image of the "threshold" that Agamben uses to approach it. If, as he proposes, the threshold we find ourselves on in the contemporary moment is between democracy and absolutism, then one way or another this takes us back to the voice.

That the contemporary threshold, the indeterminate zone between democracy and absolutism, returns us to the voice is not just because voice and democracy are intimately linked. It is also because to consider the act of voicing brings the threshold into view. As Dolar argues,

> We are social beings by the voice and through the voice; it seems that the voice stands at the axis of our social bonds, and that voices are the texture of the social, as the intimate kernel of subjectivity.[25]

The purpose of Dolar's argument, in *A Voice and Nothing More*, is to answer the question Gizzi is heard to articulate in the closing pages of *Threshold Songs*: "And where does the voice come from?" Like Gizzi, what this involves Dolar in is a series of explorations of the different possibilities a concerted inquiry into the voice produces. If he can be said to settle anywhere, however, it is on the axis he has just described. Where the voice comes from, in other words, as Dolar wants us to understand it, is that zone of intersecting subjectivity where the self tunes to the frequencies of the other. The voice, by this account, is quite properly a function of the threshold, from which it can be thought to follow that the fullest form of song is the threshold song.

The argument, then, is this: that in the contemporary moment, when the defining threshold is the zone of exception between democracy and absolutism, what that threshold calls for not least are presentations of voice that appreciate its dynamics, capable of registering its origin between self and other. Gizzi, it will be recalled, puts it this way, in "The Growing Edge" (the opening statement of *Threshold Songs*):

I wonder if
you hear me
I mean I talk
to myself through you
hectoring air
you're out there
tonight and so am I
for as long as
I remember
I talk to the air
what is it
to be tough
what ever
do you mean (*TS*, 1)

It is there, in the act of listening, that Gizzi's lyric voice establishes itself most fully as ethical medium. What Dolar proposes, as theorist, is that in the contemporary moment, what we need is an account of voice that understands its relation to the axis of social bonds. What Gizzi provides, as poet, is a rendering of voice formed out of that social axis, an ongoing act of voicing understood as tuning and listening: a threshold song keyed to the urgencies of the polis.

NOTES

1. Gizzi is, in fact, a memorable reader of his own work. Enunciating each word as if the line might break, what he provides is not a recital but a reassembling of the poem's materials, a public reconstitution of the poem as spoken artifact. For online examples of Gizzi reading, see his performance at "Poetry International in Rotterdam," June 14, 2014, www.youtube.com/watch?v=J9OL3192ZoQ, viewed July 11, 2014, and

his reading of "The Quest" accompanied by kinetic typography, www.youtube.com /watch?v=u-ow_NSEjMw, viewed July 11, 2014. In both readings Gizzi makes characteristic use of caesura to give the impression that the poem is being recomposed.

2. Jack Spicer, *The House That Jack Built: The Collected Lectures of Jack Spicer*, ed. with an afterword by Peter Gizzi (Middletown, CT: Wesleyan University Press, 1998), 174.

3. In drawing attention to the enunciation of the phoneme in this way, Gizzi echoes both Spicer (as discussed) and James Schuyler. For an excellent discussion of Spicer's interest in linguistics, see Daniel Katz, *The Poetry of Jack Spicer* (Edinburgh: Edinburgh University Press, 2013), 140–73. For a discussion of Schuyler's acts of enunciation, see David Herd, *Enthusiast! Essays on Modern American Literature* (Manchester: Manchester University Press, 2007), 168–96.

4. Mladen Dolar, *A Voice and Nothing More* (Cambridge, MA, and London: MIT Press, 2006), 41.

5. Charles Olson, *Collected Prose*, ed. Donald Allen and Benjamin Friedlander (Berkeley and London: University of California Press, 1997), 243.

6. Ibid., 245.

7. To sketch Gizzi's presentation of his influences, one clearly hears the following poets in the following poems: Dickinson in "Speck," Pound in "Periplum," Oppen in "Psalm," Schuyler in "Wintry Mix," Ashbery in "Vincent, Homesick for the Land of Pictures," and Eliot in "Tradition & the Indivisible Talent." This last title indicates the self-consciousness with which Gizzi relates to other voices, a relation that can be understood (in the terms developed here) as an act of *saying*.

8. Gizzi, "Inside/Outside: Poets in the Academy," *Revista canarai des estudios ingleses* 52 (April 2006), 20.

9. Ibid., 20–21.

10. Ibid.

11. Susan Howe, *The Europe of Trusts* (New York: New Directions, 1990), 14.

12. Spicer, *The House That Jack Built*, 194.

13. For a careful unknotting of Spicer's complicated relationship with Olson, see Daniel Katz, "From Olson's Breath to Spicer's Gait: Spacing, Pacing, Phonemes," in David Herd (ed.), *Contemporary Olson* (Manchester: Manchester University Press, 2015), 77–88.

14. Robert N. Casper, "An Interview with Peter Gizzi," *Jubilat* 14, reissued in *Poetry Daily*, poems.com/special_features/prose/essay_gizzi.php, viewed July 21, 2014, n.p.

15. Ibid.

16. Steve Collis opened his review of *The Outernationale* by noting, "Every time I think the lyric is dead, it lifts itself up again, it whispers 'you' at me, stuttering its sonic stuff." Steve Collis, "Review of *The Outernationale*," *Poetic Front* 1.1, journals.sfu.ca/poetic front/index.php/pf/article/viewFile/6/4, viewed July 21, 2014. Writing about the same volume, Olivier Brossard observed "the vanishing of any coherent sense of authority: it's all 'stumble above,' all stutter." Olivier Brossard, "Peter Gizzi's Hypothetical Lyricism:

Some Values of Landscape and Weather (2003) and *The Outernationale* (2007)," *Etudes Anglaises* 2008/2, vol. 61, 154.

17. Casper, "Interview," n.p.

18. Simone Weil, "*The Iliad*, or The Poem of Force," trans. Mary McCarthy, *Chicago Review* 18.2 (1965): 5.

19. Ibid., 9.

20. Dolar, *Voice*, 28.

21. Ibid.

22. Giorgio Agamben, *What Is an Apparatus?* (Stanford: Stanford University Press, 2009), 39.

23. Ibid., 44.

24. Giorgio Agamben, *State of Exception* (Chicago: University of Chicago Press, 2005), 3

25. Dolar, *Voice*, 14.

10 | RUTH JENNISON

The Outernationale

Only Transition! or, the Poetics of Unfreedom

What is the opposite of Peter Gizzi's neologism "Outernationale"? Though certainly it palimpsests the nineteenth-century Communist anthem "The Internationale," its true antonym is something like "the Innernationale." "The Outernationale," then, presents a negation of arid interiority as we might find a supplement to projects uncompleted by century's prehistory of revolutionary struggles. Gizzi's volume, I want to show, charts a Bush-era path of no redemption: neither in a collective project nor in the lyric cry of the individual hived off, seeking impotently its own freedom. *There is no third way.* To attempt to find one in *The Outernationale*, whether in a worn velvet of affect, or in deracinated particulars, however luminous, or in a lyric somehow made adequate to a present that has condemned the house of lyric as uninhabitable, or in the fantasies of so many ghosts of the great democratic (Whitman; Williams) is to think about Gizzi's poetics from within a superannuated Cold War frame, in which the aesthetic trips its way between, or even finds a way beyond, the two antipodes of individual and collective, of US and USSR. At the heart of *The Outernationale* is a neo-nihilism, rendered in language whose frequent beauties issue forth by way of a tremulous occupation of at least three intersecting historical developments: the end of the Cold War; the rise of a system of financialization whose overthrow is not apparent; and the dominance of the visual registers, whose revolutionary potential is as much of the distant past as are the modernist utopias. In what follows, we trace Gizzi's tracks through each of these conjunctures, paying special attention to the *The Outernationale*'s formal mediation of profound unfreedom.

The Outernationale's Eulogy to Modernism and Democracy

The collection begins with an epigraph from George Oppen, written in 1981. In response to a request for a one-line poem to read at the Cambridge Poetry Festival, Oppen wrote, in defiance of the requested single-line form:

The Poem

A poetry of the meaning of words
And a bond with the universe

I think there is no light in the world
but the world

And I think there is light.[1]

Gizzi shaves the first two lines from the poem, excising its assertion of the interdependence between our suturing to a vast unseen totality and the very meaning of language itself. What remains are three lines dedicated to inhabiting what first appears to be two simultaneous and contradictory thoughts: that there is no light in the world and that there is light in the world. On closer inspection, the statements are in fact noncontradictory. When the speaker thinks alone, then "there is no light in the world." When the speaker "and the world" think together ("the world / And I think there is light"), light is restored. What happens when Gizzi editorializes this poem, and what does it mean for practices, forms, and ideologies of the broader collected volume? We have lost the context of *why* the presence of light depends on whether the subject is singular or plural: because the very meaning of words depends upon a "bond with" (not, significantly, "to") the world without. Without this opening assertion that does nothing less than aphorize the entire action and meaning of "poetry," we are left with an assertion of what appear to be two equal perspectives: the individual who can find no light, and the collective that can. Without the first three lines, we fail to see that the perspective of the individual alone is *untrue* and *meaningless* in its unbonded form. The omission of these lines preserves the possibility of the lyric as a source of meaning and value, but affirms the blindness and hopelessness of its perspective.

For Oppen, the singular cannot confer meaning; it cannot make a "poem." I want to suggest here, then, that Gizzi's shave marks his point of departure, however melancholic, with the traditions of radical democracy that energized the late practitioners of high modernism. Two historical coordinates underwrite this departure from Oppen and that tradition. One is meridian and world historical, the other punctual and national. Gizzi writes *The Outernationale* eighteen years after the end of the Cold War (or, the end of the antipodal imperial powers, whose co-presence provided the ambient politics for most of the poet's life) and from within the rise of the Bush-era marriage of neoconservative imperialist war and neoliberal austerity measures. In the first of two poems entitled "The Outernationale" in the volume, we find "democracy" transferred to the realm of nature, from the real of human action; the populist enthusiasms of the participants in W. C. Williams's "The Crowd at the Ball Game" reprised as "a crowd / that too quickly invested / and then discarded power" (*OUT*, 22); and the "I" asking "what happened to us?" The architecture of Greco-democracy finds its legacy not in human institutions but in "leaves" that "arch over everything / they are so democratic." But even this is a pathetic fallacy that the poem undoes as but a likeness thrice-removed by receding figurations, where "the sand here *seems* coli*seum-like*" (emphasis added) (*OUT*, 20). Two "seems," the second embedded in the coli*seum* itself, and a simile mark even the idea that nature is the original democracy as a projection and a fantasy: neither blades of grass nor motes of sand speak democratic. The poem searches for a name for this historical moment:

> Something is something
> when the administration
> of money flows backward. (*OUT*, 21)

Here we find Gizzi finding the limits to the poem, which is finding the limits to capital. Austerity and dispossession give the lie to the façade of a neutral technocratic "administration of money"; accumulation does not accumulate and instead, money "flows backward." When money, or the social representation of the capital relation, meets a crisis in valorization, another crisis unfurls in the figural representation more broadly: "something is something." Neither the vehicle nor the tenor illuminate the real ground of things; they each point, unproductively, to searching, but opaque abstractions. The turn to negation in protest of these bad abstractions is swift: "before we were happy / we were unhappy. / Such is the dialectical / awakening everyone / is hankering to embrace" (*OUT*, 21). Recalling Hegel's "unhappy consciousness," a stage in the "dialectic" in which self-consciousness recognizes painfully the alienation upon which it is predicated, Gizzi's "dialectic" counterintuitively travels backward, much like the flow of money in a time of crisis, when it can no longer exchange in the service of accumulation, but rather is saved and horded, anything but reinvested. This dialectic is an entirely negative one, not one of sublation but the rediscovery of alienation beneath the patina of happiness. Thus alienated, the poem turns to the Williamsian ballgame, a respite from the self-reflection of "the blinking reflection / in a darkened window glass." Instead of populist enthusiasms, though, we find "a crowd / that too quickly invested / and then discarded power" (*OUT*, 21–22). The enjambment suggests a population hastily turning to the sparkling hegemonies of finance capital ("too quickly invested") as it also abandons its own "power." The circuits of communication and exchange mark the "days" as they "gallop into grass rushing wind / into miles of cable." When time is scored by the rapid failures of bad investments and the unfurling of cable wires, Gizzi asks:

> When the pistons call,
> when I was a wedge of sun
> over steel mills,
> when I asked what happened
> I meant what happened to us? (*OUT*, 22)

Through these cables "call" the pistons, but to whom? A tense shift after the call suggests we can find an answer only from a previous historical subject, one that was as universal as the sun glittering over a modernist past of manufacture and factories. "What happened" is a searching phrase uttered by a speaker condemned to hear the authoritarian call of dead labor, the "pistons" of constant capital, a call detectable only to those who both know and find irretrievably lost, modernism; and the by turns utopian and productivist dreams that energized it.

The Revolution; Flows of Capital; and Tragic Nontransformations

Gizzi notes that the title of the poem "Bolshevescent" "comes from Osip Mandelstam's poem 'Stanzas'" (*OUT*, 110). In keeping with my attempt here to give historical coordinates to what many will describe as Gizzi's filigreed melancholy, or affectful lyricism, I want to ask the following question: What does it mean to write about the modernist revolutions after the decisive defeat of the antipode, the victory of finance over state capitalism?

The choice of "Stanzas" is an interesting one. Written while in exile in Voronezh, the poem of eight stanzas moves rhythmically, dynamically, between national encomium, critique of Stalinist repression, socialist realism, praise for the sartorial habits of the Soviet overcoat, and importantly for Gizzi, hymn to a life lived as a bolshevescent:

> I have to live, breathing and bolshevescent,
> laboring with language, disobeying, I and one other.
> I hear the Arctic throbbing with Soviet pistons.[2]

Attention is usually paid to Mandelstam's fate at the hands of the Stalinist state: exile; camps; death. Gizzi's point of departure is a poem of great complexity. It is a tribute to revolutionary enthusiasm and the insurgent character of the Russian revolution; a decidedly left modernist alignment of the factories of the workers' state and the labor of the poet. But it is also a poem of the defeat of that same revolution:

> Once my country talked with me,
> indulged me, scolded me a little, never read me.
> But when I grew up and was a witness
> she noticed me all at once, and like a lens
> set me alight with one flash from the Admiralty.[3]

I want to suggest here that the choice of "Stanzas" is a choice opened up by the end of the Cold War; it is both *safe* and *dangerous* to return to the figure of the Boshevik. Safe because it is consigned to the relics of history, dangerous because it threatens the received history of modernism as formally avant-garde and politically reactionary, and in doing so, opens back up the content of communism. Gizzi's poem mediates both of these recuperative models. The poem is in second person, after the second world. It begins:

> You stand far from the crowd, adjacent to power.
> You consider the edge as well as the frame.
> You consider beauty, depth of field, lighting
> to understand the field, the crowd. (*OUT*, 79)

"You" are neither of nor in the crowd; you are also not oppositional, preferring adjacency to negation. Instead, the addressee is removed, a photographer or Kino-director with an adjacent, rather than subordinate, relationship to power. A contemplative ("you consider"), compositional perspective provides the condition of possibility for "understanding" the crowd. Revolution disrupts the removed inspection:

> Late into the day, the atmosphere explodes
> and revolution, well, revolution is everything.
> You begin to see for the first time
> everything is just like the last thing
> only its opposite and only for a moment. (*OUT*, 79)

"Atmosphere explodes" but the revolution is actionless; it simply dilates to a universal. What is the nature of that universal "everything"? That it negates everything, including itself. The absence of a revolutionary subject gives the revolution an ambient, nonhistorical character. Under the pall of the neoliberal present, the rewriting of an early twentieth-century revolution is at once *safe* and *dangerous*. It is safe because the revolution has no prehistory or evolution, it is not part of any available action one might take, and it promises its own extinguishing; it is dangerous because it is ecological and also because as the proletariat has become nonparticularized, expanding, along with late capitalism into a universal that is everywhere and everything, so has revolution. But what interests Gizzi most is what he finds compelling about Mandelstam: the effect on consciousness that exceeds the time of inevitable defeat. Note, in the following, that while the revolution lacks subjects, it possesses "objects":

> When a revolution completes its orbit
> the objects return only different

for having stayed the same throughout.
To continue is not what you imagined.
But what you imagined was to change
and so you have and so has the crowd. (*OUT*, 79)

The objects are "different" because they stayed the same; their acquisition of immutability is, paradoxically, the only change they have born. The poem continues to assert the self-negating character of revolution, both as an inherent, self-limiting property, and as a property of "your" inability to "imagine" its continuation. The change incurred by the addressee is not necessarily the same as that of "the crowd," and neither change is necessarily that of the abstracted object, which attained, we noted, the character of immutability. These three terms, the "object," "you," and "the crowd," emerge as swappable, segmented remains of the revolutionary process, now shorn of its subject and its telos. Rereading Mandelstam after the Cold War, and after the short-lived marriage of democracy and capitalism, Gizzi delivers to us a triptych of moving parts. When revolution is abstracted from history, and indeed, from possibility, we are left with objects, spectators, and crowds, none of whom can muster a verb (make | follow | support) in their relationship to transformation. It will further not surprise the reader to note that the subjectlessness of the revolution bears a strong resemblance to the apparent subjectlessness of the movement of capital itself. As Marx reminded us, the capitalist is merely "capital personified"; "the valorization of value . . . is the sole driving force behind his operations."[4] By this Marx means that capital, in order to remain capital, must be engaged in the process of valorization and accumulation; humans are, in effect, the "objects" of a subjectless process. Marx, like Gizzi, also uses the centrifugal movement to understand the circulation of commodities:

> [T]he exchange of commodities implies contradictory and mutually exclusive conditions. The differentiation of commodities into commodities and money does not sweep away these inconsistencies, but develops a *modus vivendi*, a form in which they can exist side by side. This is generally the way in which real contradictions are reconciled. For instance, it is a contradiction to depict one body as constantly falling towards another, and as, at the same time, constantly flying away from it. The ellipse is a form of motion which, while allowing this contradiction to go on, at the same time reconciles it.[5]

The "orbit" of the commodity form also allows for the appearance of fantastical changelessness, a direct obfuscation of contradiction within the form itself. Money intercedes in the process of commodity production and allows for (1) commodities with wildly differing use values to gain equivalence in exchange and (2) this process to appear as an endless series of equivalence swaps, where money and commodity swap endlessly and surplus value extraction and profit are obscured from view. Might this curious orbit of the commodity, whose appearance of endless circulation and exchange hides the change it experiences as the object of labor, be also captured thus: "the objects return only different for having stayed the same throughout"?

Mandelstam ingeniously transforms the Bolshevik insurgency into an adjective ("escent"), where it might be preserved as an enthusiastic comportment, safe from the desiccating winds of history. In "Bolshevescent" we find that Mandelstam's signature movement, from history to language, turned out not to be a prophylactic against the further undoing of the revolutionary impulse, but rather the necessary precondition for Gizzi's formal disarticulation of transformation from below: where a revolution without a subject arrests itself, orbits without overthrow, and "you" are changed, but without consequence to history.

Only Transition

Although history may decide that the Bolsheviks and the revolutionary poetics that accompanied those first social rebellions against capital will no longer be with us, that other legacy of modernist energies, cinema, has had an altogether different fate. What does *The Outernationale* do with this contemporaneous visual pressure? If "The Outernationale" addressed itself to the contraction of political possibility whose form was "democracy," and "Bolshevesence" wrote the prehistory of that contraction in the dissolution of the revolutionary subject, then "Lumière" sublates the problem of transformation into one of transition, between frames, between lines, between now and what we cannot have. "Lumière" is one of many poems in *The Outernationale* that takes cinema as inspiration: from the suburban "cineramas" of "Dead Air" to the imagistic reveries of "Phantascope (1895)," Gizzi's poems reckon with the cultural and technological history of moving pictures. "Lumière," Gizzi notes, "takes its title from the early pioneers of film and was inspired by David Lynch's one-minute film using their original camera." (*OUT*, 110) This film, "Premonitions of an Evil Deed" (1995), is a fifty-two-second montage that responded to the challenge of Lumière et Co. to not only use the original Lumière camera, but to also refrain from edits or synchronized sound; and to use only one reel of film, which would necessarily permit only films of around a minute in length. Lynch's film consists of five different scenes: (1) three police officers advancing on the body of a woman in a field; (2) a concerned woman in her living room; (3) a pastoral scene with two women, dishabille, lying on an outdoor divan; (4) male aliens administering electric shocks to a nude woman trapped in a tank of water; and (5) the return of the woman in the living room, accompanied by a man, rising to greet a police officer. A dark figure hovers behind the living room window.

There is much to say about this short film that will not be said here, including Lynch's preoccupation with the saturated culture of the 1950s, with its fantastical science fictions and perverse domestic intensities; or Lynch's meditations on the structuring of a specifically American cinematic genre-field by violence. What interests us, and Gizzi, are the *transitions* between scenes. In order to present such a varied selection of scenes, Lynch sacrificed some of his time by closing the lens, and physically moving the camera at great speed. Paper set ablaze after the alien scene provides visual distraction for another scene change. It's useful to quote Gizzi's "Lumière" without stopping, so as to obey the ekphrastic compulsion of imagining we might move through the poem as we might move through Lynch's piece:

> 2 shots fired off screen
>
> 3 peace officers in the field
>
> a body of a young woman
>
> some moviola music
>
> the ticking of a clock
>
> den with worried housewife
>
> the image fades its borders
>
> image pulsing with the clock

cut to bed of lilies

arbor and vine, swing, nymphs

black screen

smoke, the sound of beating wings

fire dissolves the frame white

it's spring (*OUT*, 72–73)

The poem excises the last two scenes of the film, notably the alien torture scene, which appears between the two transitions that the poem describes as "smoke, the sound of beating wings" and "fire dissolves the frame white" as well as the last scene, where the policeman arrives, presumably to deliver bad news to the couple. In place of this final scene we are told, "it's spring."

We are interested here in how Gizzi embodies the problem of transition, between genres and scenes. The first method uses sound: between the first scene, and its ironically rendered "peace officers," and the second scene "with worried housewife," we find "moviola music" and "the ticking of a clock." (The transubstantiation of what, in the film, is surely the sound of a phonograph record, having reached its end and skipping scratchily into "a clock" is of note.) In the second transition, verbs begin to well up for the first time, and the first actant appears, albeit with an intransitive verb: "the image fades its borders," followed quickly by a verb with no subject, "cut." By the end, all that appears are the transitions, now with Malevichian simplicity: "black screen"; "smoke, the sound of beating wings"; and "fire dissolves the frame white." "Fire dissolves the frame" brings us the first s-v-o of the poem, and the first agent is also the last: fire destroys itself in the process of destroying the "frame." This reminds us of Gizzi's relationship to the orbit of revolution as well: transformation undoes the change it seeks. In the final three lines of the poem, transition and then destruction sublate the torture-horror and the fateful domestic scene. In the film, the narrative lurches forward by way of antiedits that "solve" the technological limitations of the archaic motion picture machine. In contrast, "Lumière"'s transitions bridge nothing to nothing, but they make possible what is not in history, or in film: for transition to follow transition, with no actors, epochs, shifts, or transformations in between. This perpetual transition stands as a formal cognate to the ceaseless movement of the commodity form, where exchange proceeds without care for use value, or for labor enkerneled, or for content of any kind. What is excised in the process of exchange is labor, and the grinding violence of surplus value extraction, or, in the case of Gizzi's adaptation of Lynch's film, the scene of torture and electrocution by aliens.

In Conclusion

In these proceedings, I have offered a series of historical coordinates by which we might trace *The Outernationale*'s complex engagement with not only modernism, but the revolutionary enthusiasms of the modernist moment. Not content to reprise Gizzi as a mournful lyricist whose occasional, panging delight in particulars lubricates the time from now until the apocalypse, we instead found a poetics that unflinchingly forged *no way out* of the current conjuncture. In the place of escape, we discovered a post-antipodal occupation of unbending historical fact (the splitting off of democracy from capitalism; the alienation from revolutionary movements that the end of the Cold War managed to imprint on certain generational imaginations) and recalcitrant contradictions (the temporality of the fantasmic exchange cycle). In our opening, we wondered about the title *The Outernationale*, noting its negation of interiority and its curiously affiliational relationship to the song of solidarity and universal emancipation. If the volume has done anything in service of the latter, it is that it dwells in forms that offer no inauthentic resolution. Gizzi's *Outernationale* is a work of resolute unfreedom; capital accumulation and social and political authoritarianism underwrite a lyric finally unindexed by emancipation.

NOTES

1. George Oppen, *New Collected Poems*, ed. Michael Davidson (New York: New Directions, 2002), 309.
2. Osip Mandelstam, *The Selected Poems of Osip Mandelstam*, trans. Clarence Brown and W. S. Merwin (New York: New York Review of Books, 1973), 80.
3. Ibid.
4. Karl Marx, *Capital: Volume 1*, trans. Ben Fowkes (London: Penguin, 1976), 254.
5. Ibid., 198.

11 | LYTTON SMITH

The Bewilderment of Peter Gizzi's "Plural Noises"

Toward a Poetics of Citizenship

> This is the city, and I am one of the citizens;
> Whatever interests the rest interests me—politics, wars, markets,
> newspapers, schools,
> Benevolent societies, improvements, banks, tariffs, steamships, factories,
> stocks, stores, real estate, and personal estate.
> —Walt Whitman, *Leaves of Grass*[1]

The Wild in the Citizen

"Let me begin by saying that I have often characterized my voice as, simply, an ongoing narration of my bewilderment as a citizen in the world," Peter Gizzi has said.[2] This essay explores how such bewilderment recognizes behavior that exceeds limits and so invites a reassessment of human domesticity and citizenship. *Threshold Songs* (2011), and Gizzi's work more widely, locates citizen status not in rights and responsibilities but in our responsiveness to the world around us: to be open to bewilderment is to be open to accidence and transformation, and transformation is what constitutes a poetics of citizenship within Gizzi's oeuvre. His work embodies what Melanie White calls "creative acts of citizenship"[3] and thus refocuses attention from traditional definitions of the citizen, linked to habitual activities such as voting or jury duty, and toward an awareness of the publicly oriented, unexpected agency of citizens.

At stake is a poem's ability to speak to and reimagine the conditions of being a citizen. Speaking as Maximus, Charles Olson wondered, "Who / can say who are citizens?"[4] His implication was that the act of speaking out as a citizen grounds citizenship itself.[5] More than simply being a "world citizen," Gizzi's bewildered narrator is "in" the world: amid it, inextricable from it. The ghost of "word" in "world" implies language is indivisible from social space within Gizzi's poems.[6] They exist at the faultline between expression and experience: "If we could say / the world has changed, / it has changed" (*OUT*, 101). This essay seeks to answer Olson's question through Gizzi's work, to show how the poem might articulate the citizen through exploring transformative subject positions.

I through You

Underpinning my reading of Gizzi is a sense that his work concerns itself with more than interior expression entering the world and encountering others; rather, Gizzi explores how others' words and acts affect and compose our own individual subjectivity, and vice versa. *Some Values of Landscape and Weather* (2003), for instance, records the workings of vast external systems on what the book terms "just another I-am poem, a we-see poem, a they-love poem" (81). Although Gizzi's work is frequently discussed in terms of its lyric dimensions, this line slips from singular "I" to plural "we."[7] Such moments provide the ground for this essay's argument that Gizzi's exploration of citizenly behavior takes as its methodology the deployment of an "I" that is rarely a singular human consciousness. Gizzi's "I" speaks with the polyvocal influences of all it has absorbed from the outer world. As Cole Swensen has argued, Gizzi's poems are "cities themselves . . . diverse but synchronized collectivities."[8] Throughout *Threshold Songs,* voice and self emerge through what others have said: books read, sights seen, chance hearings. These poems trace the process of "becoming the thing I see" (7), of "accepting air in a new body" even though "it hurt" (38). Within Gizzi's poems, "the body's seal is broken" (67): the external enters in, transforming the "I."

Gizzi has been lauded for reinventing (American) lyric, yet a plural conception of the lyric "I" is as classical as it is contemporary. Medievalist A. C. Spearing uses the term "subjectless subjectivity" for moments where the "narrating [lyric] 'I' is not constituted as a self or a character at all, but is merely the function of the process of narration."[9] Lyric often confronts us with the ways "I" is spoken, rather than the ways it speaks. We might equate this to Robert Creeley's opening lines to "The Pattern": "As soon as / I speak, I / speaks."[10] These two "I"s share a line but are divided from one another, first by a comma and then by the act of speaking; their co-presence calls into question stable lyric selfhood. Spearing's contention and Creeley's lines alert us to the ways "I" often names the *circumstances* of speaking, the instantaneous temporality of "as soon as," more than delimits a consciousness.

A focus on the inner self as it both speaks to and vibrates in response to the sights and sounds of the external world is key to *Threshold Songs*' "threshold." Gizzi principally explores two linked liminal spaces: first, the transition from life to death, with its concomitant epistemological uncertainty, the dead passing into what the living cannot know; second, the frayed intersection between individual being and the wider world. In suggesting that a song or poem's "smallest syllables // can be sown into the mouth" ("A Note on the Text," *TS*, 59), scattered like seed through air to take root in a part of the body from where they can again be brought forth, Gizzi introduces an image not of poetic inspiration or influence, but of poetic conversation as it crosses liminal spaces.

A grief book, dedicated to three recently deceased figures, *Threshold Songs* eulogizes the dead not through a lament for their absence but by recognizing their continued presence: "now that you're here / and also gone / I am just learning / that threshold" ("Analemma," 17). As Jennifer Jean has noted, "a 'threshold song' is sung by a community before or while one of their members 'crosses over'—usually from life to death but also, possibly, from any one state of being into another"; a number of these Threshold Choirs exist within the United States.[11] Such threshold songs offer an analogy for the composite self: as the individual crosses a boundary, changing in state, they simultaneously inhabit a communal space, their identity defined by that plural body as well as by their individual transformation.

Threshold Songs' opening poem, "The Growing Edge," takes place at such a limit, within the home, at the physical site of death—"what does it mean / to enter that room / the last time" (2)—as it presents an "I" trying to come to terms with itself: "I talk to the air / what is it / to be tough / what ever" (1). The self exists simultaneously within the room and somewhere else, "out there" where others are. The "edge" of the title is both the edge (end) of life, and the edge between self/other: "you're out there tonight / and so am I" (1). It is also the edge of the poetic line as it risks silence yet seeks new meaning; repeatedly within "The Growing Edge" one line reinterprets or complicates another as the poem accumulates down the page. Consider the way the poem traces a moment of temporal and spatial osmosis:

> I've not been here
> before, my voice is
> looking for a door. (*TS*, 2)

Even as these lines indicate a physical room, their lineation unsettles that location. The lineation suggests that "I" has not been "here" at any time, not just "before," even though the "I" is, by dint of speaking, present; the effect is to disembody "I," dissevering speech from speaker. In his "Artist's Statement" in Reginald Shepherd's anthology *Lyric Postmodernisms,* Gizzi explains, "as I listen to a poem unfold in my ear it becomes clear that for every line I hear there are more lines resonating in the same field of meaning."[12] In "The Growing Edge," any sense of identity that "my voice" offers is undercut both by the voice's *prior* emergence, "before," in the previous line and phrase, and by the voice's presentation as incomplete, synesthetically "looking" for something.[13]

The voice's anticipatory reliance on a way out through a door it cannot find recalls Fredric Jameson's naming of the doorframe as "the metonym of human habitation and the social," which "'opens the door' to a host of historical and economic anxieties."[14] Gizzi offers a similarly radical metonymic movement between individual identity and social sphere:

> tuned, I wonder if
> you hear me
> I mean I talk
> to myself through you (*TS*, 1)

The poem's concern here is with its audience, but not for fear of going unheard: the "I" needs a listener to address *itself.* Moreover, the self cannot emerge without speech first going "through you," the addressed other (1). Within these lines the site of subjectivity is repeatedly displaced; both the uttering "I" and the listening, addressed "you" trade positions of hearing and talking, of hosting and inhabiting. The confidence of a line like "you hear me" is undercut by the surrounding lines' uncertainty about the relationship between "I" and "you," between the mourner and the figure he mourns but also knows has composed him. That is, the mourned figure in part owes his or her identity to the thoughts and speech of the mourner, while Gizzi's mourner also recognizes the role of the departed dead in shaping him *through* speech, the mourner unable to know himself without the absent presence of the mourned.

As with the Threshold Choirs, these poem-songs pluralize the experience of death while also complicating its temporality: through death we come "to understand I'll be gone / that the future is already / some where / I'm in that somewhere" (*TS*, 15). If the encounter with death leads to a moment of doubt—"what does it mean / to be tough / or to write a poem"—it also leads to a moment of collectivity: "we carry / within us a body" (3). As Gizzi has suggested elsewhere, "[Death]'s layered just like one's voice is layered";[15] whether personally known to the speaker or part of "my bibliography, all the books I've read," the dead form "a huge part of my autobiography" and so shape the speaker's voice and self as they enter in. *Threshold Songs* documents how we go about "learning / that threshold," understanding ourselves through others—made up, as it were, of others' voices.

Accidental Selves

To "carry / within us a body" is more than just to be affected by those we have loved and by what we've seen: it is to be transformed by the "I" encountering "plural noises," as it does in "Modern Adventures at Sea," where the speaker wonders,

> Can I transform
> this body
> I steward. This
> my biomass.
> My accident. (*TS*, 84)

Here, self and body are not synonymous, and cannot be if the body is to carry others inside it. In identifying the body as an "accident," the poem suggests that it is more than its biological materials: it is the product of its encounters, from whence transformation stems. The pun on "I" and "eye" may be slight, but it is developed through the poem, whose fourth line, "the bluing of all I see," suggests that self and sight are intimately linked. It is a pun, moreover, that haunts the collection, with titles such as "Eye of the Poem." To see is not simply to notice, but to take in the sights that compose the I.

Such paronomasia, a hallmark of Gizzi's work, functions as more than literary technique or poetic wit: paronomasia becomes the means by which we transform, one of the ways the outside world enters us and alters us. "Hypostasis & New Year" tries to find a way beyond the (deceased) body and toward that annual moment of resolution and reflection. The poem opens fearing the sources and horizons of poetic speech:

> For why am I afraid to sing
> the fundamental shape of awe
> should I now begin to sing the silvered back of
>   the winter willow spear
> the sparkling agate blue
> would this blade and this sky free me to speak
>   intransitive lack —
>
> the vowels themselves free (*TS*, 6)

Though the desire to sing might recall epic's cantatory opening, this poem looks not to a Muse but to the natural world for its source. In order to sing, one must be freed by grass and air, "this blade and this sky." Song, and poetry, emerge from the accident of the world around us.

Yet if the vowels are at liberty, why is the "I" so "afraid to sing"? What causes the "I" to hesitate is precisely the experience of death, that "intransitive lack —" (the root of "intransitive," the Latin *intransitivus*, means "not passing over"). "Hypostasis & New Year" stumbles at its outset from a fear that what it sings might not cross over to others. Following the intimate address of "The Growing Edge," with its overlapped "you" and "I," and the poem "Lullaby," in which "Everyone's listening to someone in the air" (*TS*, 4), we can't help but be struck by the absence of a "you" in this poem. Part of the poem's intransitive nature is its lack of addressees. When it does reach out to name a listener, "Hey shadow world" offers little response. Whether this shadow world is a form of Hades or simply the poem's own silhouette, no answer results. The poem's problem lies in how to express both external world and interior being; its unease is rooted in not knowing what to do with return, "when a thing comes back / comes back unseen but felt and no longer itself" (7).

Such uncertainty, though, is less a place of despair than a figure of Gizzian bewilderment. The poem's solution to its own not-knowing—"what then," it asks — lies in accepting "mystery" (*TS*, 7), or, to take a later phrase, how "I love the unknown sound in a word" (8). Like the paronomasiac "eye" of *Threshold Songs,* the idea of "unknown sound in a word" is the idea of accidence, the chance by which a (mis)heard word gives rise to another, as when, in the book's final poem, "Modern Adventures at Sea," the "pitch" of the sea becomes a vocal quality: "When lost at sea / I found a voice" (84). This is what "Hypostasis & New Year" names when the "I" turns to "compel and confess open form / my cracked hinged picture doubled" (8). This is what allows the poem to name, finally, an addressee: to ask, "Mother where from did you leave me on the sleeve / of a dying word" (8). If "leave" calls to mind the natural quality of the opening lines, "blade and sky" (6) it also bodies forth the "sleeve," garment and album cover, behind which the decaying word hides.

Such punning language is not arbitrary, as the end of "Hypostasis & New Year" makes clear:

> on a sidewalk I hear "buy a sweatshirt?" and think
> buy a shirt from the sweat of children
>   hell
> I'm just taking a walk in the sun in a poem
>   and this sound
> caught in the most recent coup (*TS*, 8)

A seemingly innocuous attempt to sell the narrator clothing conjures up a politics of consumerism that disturbs a pseudo-Romantic poetic "walk in the sun." In transcribing this aural phrase, the poem ascribes one interpretation, while also, through breaking and inverting the compound word, reinterpreting it. This act of reworking language offers a distillation of the negotiation between the interior self and external world that Gizzi's work considers. As we move from the figurative, literary "shadow world" of death to the living and working conditions of illegal child labor, the location of "hell" becomes layered. We are caught, also, between hearing speech and re-externalizing it, aural and oral — caught, then, in our own selves' plurality.

This "hell" is also, of course, an idiomatic curse, the poem's reluctance to face up to the situation, its desire to take that walk in the sun uninterrupted. That curse dramatizes what David Herd has identified as the ethical, rather than merely expressive, dimensions of Gizzi's work, the way "the act of lyric voicing" can "register an ethical charge" as it "carr[ies] a sense of space."[16] The speaker, listening to the hawker, is troubled into the dilemma of sweatshops. The reader, who sees and hears the poem, encounters that dilemma, too: though the hawker is not in front of us, the sweatshops he calls to mind exist. Gizzi's punning drift of language raises an ethical problem, and that ethical problem strikes with the force of a "coup" in the poem's final word: not simply an achievement, nor as far off as a *coup d'etat* safely spoken in another language, but, etymologically, a blow to our ears.

The poem's slippage from sweatshirt to the sweat of child labor reminds us that we do not choose what we hear, only how we respond. To privilege such accident, and to place the "I" at the heart of it (which Gizzi literally does in "Modern Adventures at Sea," in the line "accident. I accidentally" [*TS*, 81]) — is to think about the relationship between language's aleatory propensities and the political world we inhabit. "A Note on the Text" depicts a poem-song moving among the populace. Its opening lines reject Plato's conception of transformative poets as dangerous to the populace:

> The good poets defy things
> with their heart
>
> This is how a fragment
> enters the people (*TS*, 59)

Rebutting a priority for conservative, imitative poets, these lines position defiance as the key poetic act, suggesting that we don't respond to texts uncritically, digesting them hook, line, and sinker. Poetic defiance, the poem asserts, aims not to teach or instruct the people, but to "enter" them:

> Don't say beauty say the beautiful
> say the people
>
> Say it is through chants that writing
> entered the people (*TS*, 59)

While Étienne Balibar has pointed out that "whenever *the people* is invoked, most often it is state interest that is speaking,"[17] Gizzi's "say" positions the populace not as a single organism but as a plurality: "they," "we." The oral origin of writing as chant yields a pun on chance, a reference back to the need for poetic accidence. Gizzi's title dispenses with an identifiable canonical "text" around which "the people" might gather. Instead, it invokes the fragmentation of texts as a meaningful dimension of heterogeneous literary and political experience. As in "The Growing Edge" and "Modern Adventures at Sea," the possibility of a transformative reciprocity between speakers and listeners constitutes this complex, composite subjectivity. That reciprocity recalls and surpasses Whitman's "whatever interests you interest me": where Whitman's speaker offers to share others' preoccupations, Gizzi's citizen is altered by such preoccupations, and alters "you" in turn.

Like being lost, like bewilderment, accident emerges in *Threshold Songs* as a space of creative exploration. Whether through homophones, homonyms, paronomasia, mishearings, or the plurality of meanings created across line breaks, language occupies listeners, entering them in unexpected ways, carried within like the bodies of the dead. The aim, "A Note on the Text" claims, is "To stretch the vocal pattern / Its linenlike thread" (*TS*, 60), to spool out a connection through allowing language to pitch and drift not just among people, but also inside them. The demands this pitch places upon us are — hell — not merely pleasurable.

Acts of Citizenship

Within this transformative and reciprocal space of bewilderment and accident, I find a move toward a poetics of citizenship within Gizzi's work, one that extends from the ethical stance Herd identifies. Locating voice within "the compromised civic environment and the fraught periphery that are the conditions of contemporary lyric utterance," Herd reminds us that ethics always exist within the contours of specific social, historical, and geographic moments. His ultimate argument is that "social bonds" depend upon "an ongoing act of voicing understood as tuning and listening: a threshold song keyed to the urgencies of the polis."[18] If the question of what to do, whether in response to the knowledge of sweatshops or when at sea, is an ethical question of how to act, it is also a question of our social obligations and commitments. As such, it concerns how the *citizen* might behave.

I know of only two mentions of "citizen" in Gizzi's poetry, both in *Artificial Heart* (1998). "Decoration Day" depicts "buried there / a citizen there" (56); "Ding Repair" imagines a scene in which "we must behave / as we explain the mess we've made / one note for citizen, soldier, object, history" (80). These citizens might as well be loose synonyms for residents, nationals, inhabitants; the citizen might seem outside Gizzi's purview, a term his poems barely explores.

To think so, however, is to ignore the importance of citizenship as a lived as well as legislative category. Citizenship, Melanie White points out, "constitutes a web of obligatory social beliefs and practices" that emanates from an "impersonal force of pressure or authority."[19] This impersonal force is what Gizzi's "we must behave" registers. Why? According to whom? For what purpose? Such questions go unanswered in the poem, although the lines preceding this statement express a wish to "let the body evolve whole / rising out of the throat and out of the mouth into night" (*AH*, 80). The citizen enters into Gizzi's poetry at the intersection of conditioned behavior and bodily resistance; an urge to communicate with others is what defines Gizzi's citizen. At stake amid the quotidian is the hope of significance: "Even as adults we hope to witness ordinary spectacle / evolve into meaning, ordinary and rare each time" (*AH*, 79). The application of "evolve" both to body and to the phenomenological world suggests that world and individual are inextricable, that the body is a constantly changing site through which sound emerges outward, from internal being to the social world via the threshold of the mouth. Reading beyond the simplistic lexical occurrence of "citizen" as a term, we discover within Gizzi's work the idea that the self needs the outside world as part of its ongoing evolution. The self, for Gizzi, is avowedly a social being; in being so, it must — it cannot not — come to terms with citizenship.

Such moments in Gizzi's poetry offer a poetics of citizenship — a making of citizenship, a reimagining of it — because they focus our attention on the chance, unexpected, and innovative ways citizens might behave despite the pressure of governmental or social codes. Indeed, Gizzi's work offers a poetic manifestation of developing theories in citizenship studies over the last fifteen years by scholars including Engin Isin, Étienne Balibar, and Aiwha Ong. Although citizenship, in its narrowest sense, is a legislative category, designating an individual to whom a state has accorded a set of rights and responsibilities, Engin Isin and Greg Nielsen's edited collection, *Acts of Citizenship* (2008), reorients citizenship studies toward "collective or individual deeds that rupture social-historical patterns." They argue that "acts of citizenship" differ from familiar practices of citizenship in that they are spontaneous, innovative actions with the potential to alter the terms of citizenship through unanticipated and unanticipatable encounters with other citizens, with would-be citizens, and with institutions of state authority. Habitual practices like voting risk being "passive and one-sided in mass democracies," whereas "acts of citizenship break with repetition of the same," [20] manifesting as innovations that constitute new versions of the citizen — and which do so, crucially, in the eyes of other citizens or would-be citizens. A citizen, then, is one who acts with and toward others, rather than participates in predefined processes that affirm an existing hegemonic script. Such conceptions of citizenship move away from a familiar "rights and responsibilities" understanding of the citizen, but they do not ignore the role of the State in sanctioning citizenship, nor do they overlook the unequal experience of citizenship as it is lived. They do, however, seek a distinction between habitual actions and the unpredictable acts by which the citizen can reimagine herself.

Most pertinently for Gizzi's poetry, Melanie White has located within "acts of citizenship" an emphasis on "moments of aleatory possibility [. . .] the emergent, the new, and, ultimately, the creative in becoming political."[21] She offers a Bergsonian reading of acts of citizenship in which both citizenship and creativity are "expressed in terms of an aspiration to change."[22] For White, creativity is marked by a capacity for the transformation of self, others, and the assumptions of social action: "in order to be truly creative, the citizen must overcome the force of habit by provoking a genuine encounter that poses the problem of how to act."[23] Citizenship's network of obligations (and, I would add, rights and protections) work to stabilize but also to neutralize individuals within group identity: "each time we obey, we reinforce the general principle of obligation in society," White claims.[24] The alternative involves "disrupt[ing] the tendency towards closure."[25] Such moments of creative citizenship are reliant on *encounter*, defined as "the meeting or confrontation between people and things." Creative encounters must be unanticipated: if we stage a creative encounter, we prescript a response, precluding the chance for disruption as we ignore the "problem of how to act."[26]

Threshold Songs takes up such confrontations: the overheard language of the sweatshirt seller; the impossible presence of the dead; the fragmentary text entering the people. The "problem of how to act" is, in Gizzi's poetry, the problem of how to reconcile interiority and the external world. Such are the stakes particularly of *Threshold Songs*' "Tradition & the Indivisible Talent," a riposte to Eliot that refuses to place the texts that precede and shape us within a stable notion of the "individual," that Eliotic term removed from Gizzi's title. "If all the world says something / we think then we know something / don't we?": the arch tone of the poem's opening belies its challenging lineation and punctuation, the lines open to several readings, depending on whether "we think" modifies "something" or "then" (*TS*, 46). The poem exists within the pleasures of being shaped by what is seen and heard: "birdsong caught in the inner ear / even the curios seem animated" (47). It also, though, exists within the circumstances of confrontation: "You crazy. / No, you crazy" (46). The same pronoun references different speakers and listeners, that composite tangle of identities *Threshold Songs* engages, and though its accusations are playful, colloquial, they invoke a mode of being with others in the world, a point underscored by the poem's repeated use of imperatives.

"The song is alive," insists the poem, envisioning a choric "part of tradition" that asserts the connections supposed by Eliot's essay while de-emphasizing individuality. The poem's final stanza, however, returns us to the idea of transformation, and locates transformation within language itself:

> How about dirt? I love you
> like dirt. I miss you dirty mouth
> dirty smile, oh, and my dirt
> is your dirt is nice also. (*TS*, 48)

The switch from the cliché of loving someone like crazy, away from the language of "fire in the heart" around which the previous stanza has spun, marks an attempt to sing love in a new register, one that's "closer to the ground, perhaps" (*TS*, 48). This dirt gives rise to "the must / at the root of it all, desire / and wanting, must know," a pun on "must" as both (fetid) smell and modal auxiliary verb. The encounter *Threshold Songs* ultimately considers, its epistemological pursuit, resides in the will to transform language, to suggest an alternative way of expressing desire to one another: "my dirt / is your dirt is nice also."

Gizzi's "threshold song" is not sung from or to a particular consciousness, but instead reveals liminal zones among us, possibilities for alteration: "it's transformation / not transportation / that's needed," as "Modern Adventures at Sea" puts it (*TS*, 83). Attentive to "plural noises" that complicate, as they constitute, lyric subjectivity, these poems foreground encounters with our fellow humans and the environments we inhabit — encounters that construct our experiences as citizens. *Threshold Songs* ends by reminding us that its project has been to try

> To understand
> oneself. With-
> out oneself.
> How to live.
> What to do. (*TS*, 85)

We arrive at self-knowledge, *Threshold Songs* suggests, through letting the outside world enter in: through song, through books, through light. As we experience being "out oneself" and also "with- / out oneself," seeing ourselves from outside and learning to leave ourselves behind, we come "to understand" (85). The body's acts — its doings — provide the last word in this epistemological circuit, as if to suggest that what we say and hear matters to the extent that it alters how we act.

More than ethical questions, then, these are questions of citizenship. As Cole Swensen has argued, the rapprochement between self and city is predicated upon the ways "the world, then, walks into the person, rather than the other way around."[27] She shows how the poem emerges from political spaces and heterogeneous communities that predate it — how, in turn, the poem, threshold song, can shape its listeners, reimagining citizenship by showing how the ways we collectively share civic space might alter the basis of identity itself.

Throughout *Threshold Songs*, *t*ransformation in both individual subjectivity and the relationship between the self and the social world stems from external sounds entering into interior space, shaping a composite speaking identity, and in turn giving rise to song and poem. The challenge is both to allow the outer world to enter in across the body's threshold and to "Say it then or / sing it out" in response (81), not simply to express ourselves, but because a poem, a song, or a sight can enter and transform a person. *Threshold Songs* doesn't just take place "in this city" ("Deus Ex Machina," *SP*, 17); these poems are bound up with modes of activity that might allow us to see ourselves as citizens.

When Gizzi speaks of narrating his bewilderment as a citizen, he aims to do more than dispute the ways the individual is shaped by governmental authority or express dismay at partisan politics. His poems elaborate a poetics of being and acting as a citizen in the world, one that does not consist in claiming citizenship status, nor in behaving according to hegemonic script, but in being open to transformation and alteration. *Threshold Songs* seeks the moment "when bodies inside spin and change shape" (29). Such metamorphosis is communal — and, in establishing the public sphere as its horizon, offers a version of citizenship dependent on unpredictable future encounters. Such a citizenship offers us a chance to "negotiate the present intensities / in the world and its apostrophes" (66): socially, transformatively, perpetually bewildered.

NOTES

1. Walt Whitman, *Leaves of Grass, 1860: The 150th Anniversary Facsimile Edition* (Iowa City: University of Iowa Press, 2011).

2. In a 2007 interview, Gizzi sources this formulation to a reading: an audience member described him as "really a lyric poet," to which he replied, "I think I am a narrative poet — I'm just narrating my bewilderment as a citizen [. . .] that spontaneous answer seemed true and has weirdly stuck with me." Rob Casper, "Interview with Peter Gizzi," *Jubilat* 14 (2007): 47–61 (47).

3. Melanie White, "Can an Act of Citizenship Be Creative?," in Engin Isin and Greg Nielsen, eds., *Acts of Citizenship* (London: Zed Books, 2008), 49.

4. Charles Olson, *The Maximus Poems*, ed. George Butterick (Berkeley: University of California Press, 1983), 3.

5. For a reading of *Maximus* and citizenship, see Lytton Smith, "Projective Citizenship — The Reimagining of the Citizen in Post-War American Poetry" (unpublished doctoral dissertation, Columbia University, New York, 2012).

6. In "Bardo," "word" and "world" end the first lines of the final stanzas: "and if I say the words / will you know them? // Is there world? / Are they still calling it that?" (*SP*, 77). Interviewed by Ben Lerner, Gizzi makes a similar pun, recuperating his poetic syntax from chronicling "the dehumanizing financialization of the world (word)" to instead pursue "the beloved, to other languages and marvels, other art forms, other heights of the imagination." Ben Lerner, "Poetry at the Threshold. Peter Gizzi Interview by Ben Lerner," March 15, 2012, www.poetryfoundation.org/article/243686.

7. Lisa Sewell has argued that Gizzi's "ease with personal self-revelation in poems that meditate on classical Romantic subjects such as nature and loss, allow[s] for a more expansive politicized understanding of [lyric] tradition." Introduction to *American Poets of the 21st Century: The New Poetics*, ed. Claudia Rankine and Lisa Sewell (Middletown, CT: Wesleyan University Press, 2007), 6. Agreeing with the latter part of this claim, my essay questions whether we should read Gizzi's poetry as "*personal* self-revelation."

8. Cole Swensen, "Peter Gizzi's City: The Political Quotidian," in Claudia Rankine and Lisa Sewell, eds., *American Poets of the 21st Century*, 109.

9. A. C. Spearing, *Textual Subjectivity: The Encoding of Subjectivity in Medieval Nar-*

ratives and Lyrics (Oxford: Oxford University Press, 2005), 154. For the idea that a "chorus of public voices or multiple narratorial voices" might result from individual bodies, I am grateful to Jessica Fenn's article "Apostrophe, Devotion, and Anti-Semitism: Rhetorical Community in the *Prioress's Prologue and Tale*," *Studies in Philology* 110, no. 3 (Summer 2013): 434.

10. Robert Creeley, *The Collected Poems of Robert Creeley, 1945–1975* (Berkeley: University of California Press, 1982), 294.

11. Jennifer Jean, "'Grief Is an Undersong': on Peter Gizzi's *Threshold Songs*," *Drunken Boat* 17 (Summer 2011): n.p., www.drunkenboat.com/db17/threshold-songs.

12. Reginald Shepherd, *Lyric Postmodernisms* (Denver: Counterpath Press, 2008), 85.

13. Gizzi's statement on the plurality of listening immediately prefaces, in Shepherd's anthology, the "Periplum" poem, which names "bewilderment," and links bewilderment to plural sound.

14. Fredric Jameson, *Postmodernism, or, The Cultural Logic of Late Capitalism* (Durham: Duke University Press, 1991), 170.

15. Anthony Caleshu, "In Conversation with Peter Gizzi," *PN Review* 209, vol. 39, no. 3 (Jan.–Feb. 2013): 50.

16. See David Herd's chapter in this volume.

17. Étienne Balibar, *We the People of Europe? Reflections on Transnational Citizenship*, trans. James Swenson (Princeton: Princeton University Press, 2003), 134.

18. See David Herd's chapter in this volume.

19. Isin and Nielsen, *Acts of Citizenship*, 49.

20. Ibid., 2. Judith Shklar has identified "social standing," a category related to the ways citizens have regard for one another, as particular to American citizenship; she considers it alongside "nationality," "active participation," and "ideal republican citizenship" as key markers of citizenship (3). David Ricci has argued that "the United States is an association of citizens" (15) in which "no one [. . .] should automatically be excluded from membership in the community because of ethnic origin" (101). Such models of citizenship recognize its social dimension but ultimately locate the citizen in legal or governmental frameworks.

21. Ibid., 44.

22. Ibid., 45.

23. Ibid., 46.

24. Ibid., 48.

25. Ibid., 57.

26. Ibid., 53.

27. Swensen, "Peter Gizzi's City," 112.

12 | NERYS WILLIAMS

"This further sound, scratch of pen to parchment in a flight of democracy"

Reading Peter Gizzi's "Some Values of Landscape and Weather"

It is tempting, in the decades following the publication of the double issue of *New Coast Writing* (from Peter Gizzi's *o-blék* imprint)[1] to gesture to the evolution of a "new" form of lyricism in American poetry, as responding to the early anti-lyricism of early Language writing.[2] This new lyric practice might be viewed as formulating a discursive poetic, while remaining skeptical toward any claim of innate lyric subjectivity. Gizzi (along with others such as Jennifer Moxley and Juliana Spahr) has been given the somewhat dubious honor of reinventing, or reconfiguring lyric practice in recent American poetry. Reflecting on Gizzi's *Some Values of Landscape and Weather*, John Kinsella proposes that his work "has weathered the rearrangements of textual responsibility and *ostranenie* (genuine strangeness) of Language poetry" while retaining "the 'need' to be self critical about the conviction of this lyrical self."[3] Kinsella asserts that "American critics have claimed that Gizzi has re-invented the lyric. What he has done is test its flexibility, and found it as durable in the post-millennium as ever. Innovative post-Language lyric poets have largely hidden behind irony. Gizzi can be extremely ironic, street-savvy but he's also sincere."[4]

In this discussion, I examine how Gizzi's title poem "Some Values of Landscape and Weather" provides a sustained examination of the encounters between private and public spaces, as well as a complex reflection on war. Although it initially might not read as a war poem, I will suggest the ways in which Gizzi offers his lyric as an enquiring force and avoids what Michael Palmer has identified as an American tendency to read "our politics out of these distant events and then to write some almost self-congratulatory oppositional work."[5] Key poems by Palmer, John Ashbery, and George Oppen are used as intertextual resonances to steer the poem away from the temptations of self-reflection and the problems of generalizing statement associated with more explicit antiwar poetry. The citational texture of the work enables a sense of community, however fragile, to emerge and depart at key points.

Considering the fraught relationship between poetry and politics, Gizzi comments, "I have always been wary that 'political' poetry could ever be meaningful in any way regarding the conditions of the state."[6] Gizzi refutes poetry's political role as an easy oppositional sloganeering associated with more "mainstream" political writing. Equally he is suspicious of Language writing's veneration of the materiality of language in the 1970s as laying an abstract claim to political agency.[7] Reflecting on 9/11 and the entry into the Iraq War, Gizzi states, "There were many 'political' poems appearing in journals and flying about on line. I could understand the social aspect of poets banding together to show their numbers and be counted as dissenters from the Bush Doctrine."[8] Gizzi is skeptical of any attempt to harness poetry to overt political statement:

> I felt that what I could add was a simple quiet reversal of many of the claims being made for poetry at that time. I was hoping to return the form and occasion of the poem to poetry itself, that is, the beauty of expression and form, plaintiveness, clarity, and song as its primary estate of resistance.[9]

The opening citation for "Some Values of Landscape and Weather" prepares us for a consideration of whether poetry has any purchase on political thought. Taken from the "Cutty Sark" (third section) of Hart Crane's *The Bridge*, the poem begins with the quotation "Democrat — I know what time it is — ." Spoken by a burned-out sailor, whose words are framed by a nickel-slot pianola, the anecdotes of journeying serve as a prelude to the speaker's walk across the Brooklyn Bridge. The first of the six sections places us also mid-journey, framed by architectural ruin. Throughout these sections the lyric "I" retains a flickering presence, as a mobilized reference point through different landscapes.

Gizzi initially evokes the space of a commemorative public event where a collective "we" walk "single file into winter's steely pavilion" (*SVLW*, 20). While the shadow of Bush's war on terror permeates the sequence, this first section gives an imprint of a ruin with the threat of "a distant rumble like a bulldozer" (20). Reading Gizzi's poetry, one has to remain vigilant about turning evocations into concrete propositions; on closer scrutiny, one realizes that the description addresses "Bits of refrain dovetailing / into a distant rumble like a bulldozer / from memory" (20). This space morphs into the proposition of a chorus, "The song built with the populism of a mural" (20). Gizzi's poetry is densely musical, incorporating citation, digression, meditation, and a provisional self-reflexive testing of the lyric. It also exhibits a fear of being seduced by melody, because the speaker is placed "at the farther edge / of beauty" (20) beyond a shared chorus or song. The centerpiece to this opening reflects on how an embodied "Liberty" mesmerizes and threatens with "her bright flash stinging" (20). Strategically placed adverbs insist on emphasizing a musical phrasing; the speaker walks through the "moss's greening, winningly" and "follows willingly" while Liberty herself sings "haltingly" (20).

Musicality in this opening is viewed with considerable suspicion. Gizzi deconstructs the concept of lyric as song, enabling us to focus on component parts. Throughout the poem there are tensions between ideals of aesthetic beauty, artistic wholeness or completion, and disorder. Roland Barthes's "The Grain of the Voice"[10] enables a further way of reconsidering these conflicts, or the lyric aporia that propels the enquiry of "Some Values of Landscape and Weather." Barthes draws our attention to music and its performance. His two key terms are *pheno-song* and the *geno-song*; the former becoming the impulse toward articulation, expression, and performance, and the latter delighting in the *jouissance* of linguistic materiality. The geno-song has "nothing to do with communication." Instead, it is

> [t]hat apex (or that depth) of production where the melody really works at the language — not at what it says, but the voluptuousness of its sound — signifiers, of its letters — where melody explores how the language works and identifies with that work. It is, in a very simple word but which must be taken seriously, the *diction* of the language.[11]

Barthes places a particular emphasis on the display of the geno-song in the recital, as a form of writing and the recital through its heightened performance of the geno-song becomes in turn a text. Barthes is categorical because he states, "The song must speak, must *write*—for what is produced at the level of the geno-song is finally writing."[12] The emphasis on the "grain" asks us to consider how one applies the analogy of music to poetry; as an element of resistance in the recital, the grain raises a challenge to the idealization of completion and good forms. Turning to the close of this first section in Gizzi's poem, Liberty's "coo and whisper" initially seduces, only to become "a mockingbird's gravelly clank" (*SVLW*, 20). In the fifth section, the speaker directs to a collective who "fought in a war" and the search for "a sound" that might become a "focus for this instant" (23). While there might be attempts at a majestic orchestral chorus—"There were big chords, / a piece of the total score"—the song that is rendered is a "further sound," a documentation or recording of writing as a "scratch of pen to parchment / in a flight of democracy" (23). Returning to the act of writing, or signature in this case, Gizzi emphasizes the fateful bureaucratization of war. The hand that signs the paper also signs for the fate of the people it represents.

"Some Values of Landscape and Weather" projects a considered anxiety over speaking on behalf of others. Doubt pervades the second section of the poem. Ideals of mobility and travel are often frustrated, as in "We've stalled," "I need to stay rutted," and "falling down dark" (*SVLW*, 21). This second section reminds one of the play between privacy and the public sphere that informs Ashbery's poetry, particularly his poem "The One Thing That Can Save America."[13] Ashbery's search for what is "central" expresses an anxiety about the way we identify with generic ideas of political, cultural, and historical continuity. The poem moves peripatetically, between descriptions of domestic intimacy, to reflections on the role of poetry as commanding rhetorical power. Ashbery's speaker asks, "Where then are the private turns of event / Destined to boom later like golden chimes / Released over a city from the highest tower?"[14] Similarly, Gizzi recreates an intimate scene of how we were "having a smoke / after a day in bed" (*SVLW*, 21), which is later challenged by the more abstract need to work "on hands to field / other hoists of rescue" (21). Throughout this section, Gizzi attempts to find the origin of differentiated color in the skyscape: "Odd oranges / and blue velvet outline the roofs" which shift to the dissemination of a more emotive "something / particular to blue has begun" (21). Gizzi appeals to ideas of solitude as enabling focus. "I need stay rutted in my own / long enough to swerve outside this collision of particles / that dogs my view" (21) is almost a rewriting of Ashbery's much cited self-criticism in "The One Thing That Can Save America": "I know that I braid too much my own, / Snapped-off perceptions of things as they come to me."[15] Ashbery's poem offers a conversation on the relationship between being in the world and poetry's ability to activate experiences of relation on the page. Gizzi equally projects a desired intimacy with his reader—"I need you" (21)—as well as a will to abandon poetry as a mediator of thought. This sentiment recalls Ashbery's call to an idealized intersubjective space of the lyric: "I tell you, / And you instantly know what I mean?"[16] In gesturing to the intertextual tenor of Gizzi's lyric, one might consider this degree of self-reflexivity as indicative of an absence of agency. Peter Hühn suggests that the foregrounding of poetic strategies and devices is a protective strategy, creating an opaque smokescreen. He poses that "[w]hen self observation [is] extended to the speaker's capacity as a writer and to his poetic creativity and its sources," the result is "self-doubt, self-paralysis and literary sterility."[17]

Gizzi's poem also evokes Oppen's "Of Being Numerous." Customarily read in Marxist terms as dissecting the relationship of the individual to the masses, Oppen's poem also examines the dilemma of asserting individuality while retaining an obligation to the social contract. This dilemma is articulated in the poem as "the shipwreck / Of the singular."[18] Marjorie Perloff proposes that Oppen's is primarily a poem "about exile—specifically, the acute sense of pain and disorientation attendant upon the exiled American poet's attempt to relearn 'a language of New York' to make his way through the new 'city of the corporations.'"[19] Similarly, the speaker in Gizzi's poem exhibits a degree of displacement; while impressions of a cityscape are gestured to, no direct or identifiable topography is given. The routine sound of a train is defamiliarized, any idealization of cross-country travel is dismissed: "oompahs of dented brass / yesteryear calling on the road" (*SVLW*, 21). Extending this cartoonlike impression, Gizzi combines a more sinister narrative from children's fairy tales with holocaust imagery, as his protagonists attempt to track a passage to safety: "cloth, hair and a string to guide us" (21). What Oppen refers to as the possibility inherent in "the bright light of shipwreck"[20] becomes for Gizzi a threat to selfhood. Following the plaintive "I need you," we are told that "all the ropes thrown overboard / wouldn't find me" (*SVLW*, 21). The comparative that the speaker makes "like sun once / dripping into basement punkdom" (21) emphasizes that the space inhabited is one of self-imposed exile, as the inhabitant of a subculture.

Gizzi states that "though I have always been fascinated by the relationship between poetry and national ideology, the political is always implicit to real writing. It runs through the entire fabric of its meaning and sound."[21] Leslie Scalapino and Judith Goldman's important anthologies *War and Peace* emerged as a response to the Iraq War the year following the publication of Gizzi's *Some Values of Landscape and Weather.*[22] In her essay "Poetry, Intelligence and the Temporality of Crisis," Jennifer Scappettone reflects on the status of representation and public discourse during a period of war:

> A critique of representation that might also have political heft has to take the constructed quality and mediation of discourse as premise, yet must also formulate criteria for fidelity to experience and rationality. Responsibility to social relations and experience demands that we register and foreground contradictions. Poetry's role is to decrease people's capacity to absorb contradictions quiescently.[23]

Gizzi's fourth section interweaves the language of warfare with psychological portraiture and skepticism toward musical harmony. This tension between impressions of combat hardware and abstract expression informs the spine of the poem. Transmuting Tiresias's evocation of the "violet hour" in *The Waste Land* to "the pixel hour," the speaker prepares us for the surveillance imaging techniques of "a witching pre-code silver industry" (*SVLW*, 22). A sensation of extreme psychic pressure is conveyed in the image of "a steely chamber / overhead" with "Ball bearings glide along / making it *ting*" (22). The overall effect is the imagining of a ballistic missile testing run. Gizzi returns a focus on the sonic because the sound created by the "steely chamber" is one that "many are bent to hear" (22).

The section proposes that sound is a document of human experience "as though music were a condition / of all our endeavor here" (*SVLW*, 22). The relationship between musical harmony, science, and social order has an extensive conceptual figuration in Western history. John Hollander draws attention to the connection between the early Pythagorean science of "perfect consonances"[24] and a cosmological order. In this configuration, the music of the spheres could also be reinterpreted "as a metaphysical notion, characterizing not only the order of the universe but the relation of human lives to this cosmological order."[25] Jacques Attali extends this view, suggesting that the preponderance of scientific thought during the eighteenth century appropriated harmony as a powerful instrument to establish a link between social well-being and science. He stresses that far from imposing a concept of uniformed order, harmony relies on an articulation of differences and rule-governed hierarchies within the scale system:

> The harmonic system functions through rules and prohibitions: in particular, what is prohibited are repeated dissonances, in other words critiques of differences and thus the essential violence. Harmony lives by differences alone, for when they become blurred there is a potential for violence. Difference is the principle of order. [26]

The close of this section delights in the ambiguities of sensory readings; we are told that "the value of gunmetal" fades "to midnight all around" (*SVLW*, 22), and we remain unsure whether this is a description of metallic sounds or an attempt to chronicle the color patterns of the sky. Gizzi plays on the tension between stark imagistic renditions such as "A nervous moon and winter branches" (22) and his earlier synesthetic impressions. Though it might be tempting to frame this "strangeness" in terms of Language writing's processes of *ostranenie* or defamiliarization, Gizzi's rendition of dailiness and perception is less dependent on paratactic formations. Instead, his evocative reflections create an impression of musical accretion and saturation, during which the poem delineates a responsiveness to an analogy of the lyric as song.

One might associate war poetry with the recounting of spectacle and event, however we are reminded that "Some Values of Landscape and Weather" is the work of a noncombatant poet. Philip Metres states that the danger for any contemporary poet is that "with nothing to reflect on, and little to witness, the noncombatant lyric poet has recourse only to a kind of guilt-suffused documentation of one's own distance from the scene of war."[27] Rather than focusing on retelling specific mediatized events, Gizzi's poem renders the impact of war on everyday life and chronicles how war informs the texture of the quotidian. In the fifth section, the speaker searches for a sound that serves as a sign for violence:

> We fought in a war, looking for a sound,
> some frequency
> a human animal could field
> beyond the other registers of everyday
> and fancy (*SVLW*, 23)

This desire for a human ultrasonic cue is reiterated by the search for a "focus for this instant" (23). Gizzi resolutely refuses to entertain nostalgia, retelling, or remembrance. The poem's journey is a phenomenological one, attempting to document a present scene of writing, of being *in* landscape and weather. Gizzi's reluctance to memorialize in this poem is indicative of the poet's attempt to avoid a direct protest poem. Scappettone notes that the contemporary war poem has often become a sanitized space of memorialization:

> In times of crisis, poetry's task is thereby restricted to the purview of the elegy. Poetry is of use in encompassing the fossilized past or in embalming and thereby taming recent disturbances of the narcotic chronicle. Conservative culture regards the poem as a monument and documentary writing as ephemera.[28]

Gizzi is intent on trying to find correspondence between the public sphere and private enquiry. Hence we have a reference to a private "tuning" of frequency counterbalanced by an inventory of seemingly random generic public spaces: "hydroelectric facilities," "statehouses and prisons, freeways etcetera" (*SVLW*, 23). The score created in this text is not an anthemic blast of nationalism. Gizzi's text veers instead to chronicle a narrative of making and creation, a "trajectory" composed not of "facts, but hands" (23).

Gizzi's lyric draws from Palmer's proposition of what he calls "the analytic lyric." The "analytic lyric," in Palmer's words, addresses "the problematics of purely private utterance" by "taking over the condensation of lyric emotion and focusing it then on the mechanics of language."[29] Gizzi's lyric, like Palmer's, provides an analysis of utterance and becomes a site for intersecting discourses. Earlier in the poem, we witness a search for a language that may be sufficient to quantify the political landscape:

> Courage! carrots?,
> "Charity," the word says in a notebook
> — to accept the ink of the possible,
> "this proves I have dreamed." (*SVLW*, 22)

The notebook is a site of both the possible and the nonsensical; Gizzi suggests that the values of "courage" and "charity" are mutable, not eternal and susceptible to recontextualization. Here one has only to reflect on the appropriation of terms such as "liberty" and "freedom" under the Bush administration. The text forms an echo chamber of Palmer's fascination with the erasure and censorship of writing in the final "Sun" section of his 1988 volume *Sun*.[30] The parallels are striking:

> A word is beside itself. Here the poem is called What Speaking means
> to Say
>
> . . . .
>
> Pages which accept no ink
> Pages we've never seen[31]

Palmer's poetry exhibits a nostalgia for the book as a site of knowledge. But because access to this idealized work remains untenable, contradiction and opposition is the texture of Palmer's lyric. It might therefore seem fitting that at *Sun*'s close, we are presented with both the destruction and the symbolic renewal of the book: "Pages torn from their spines and added to the pyre, so that they will resemble thought."[32] Equally in "Some Values of Landscape and Weather," the poem, or the book, as a site of possibility is always threatened by erasure or silencing.

Gizzi states, "What I want a poetry to do is to make a space free of location, a rest which exists (like Zeno's arrow) in transport."[33] The final section of "Some Values of Landscape and Weather" reinforces a sense of journey as well as a refusal to memorialize. The poem is marked by its responsiveness to action, patterns of movement, and perception. Its final scene is of a generic city with "Night coming on, goings to and fro" (*SVLW*, 23). The poem asks whether democracy is capable of being defined "Here beneath / the shadow of branch and ballot" (23). Gizzi's configuration of democratic participation is remarkably simple when he questions: "Where else can you say / that to love the questions / you have to love the answers" (23). However, ideas of political possibility could also be read as being under threat, if one entertains the easy slippage of "ballot" to "bullet." Images of hardware and mechanized production persist in Gizzi's night sky, which is described as "a canopy of burning discs" (23).

Gizzi notes that it is precisely poetry's inability to orchestrate and direct explicit political efforts that make its presence a compelling space of possibility:

> W. H. Auden's famous statement that "Poetry makes nothing happen," always seems an apt perspective from which to consider poetry's inability to shape policy. But perhaps this is too narrow a reading of this famous line.

> Perhaps poetry is much more effective as it does in fact precisely make "nothing" happen.[34]

The final section of the poem asserts, "It was all the time / happening" (*SVLW*, 23). The "happening" of Gizzi's poem is not the recording of large events framed by reflection, but the duration of their impact upon dailiness and perception. The poem's process of composition, as well as the impetus toward movement, travel, and interruption, causes the reader to consider the network of associations that make the poem; how any poem must be read as retaining a degree of mobility and momentum at the time of its reading. Gizzi's poetics in "Some Values of Landscape and Weather" finds a shared understanding with Palmer's reflection on poetry's response to what the poet calls "a moment of Barbarism." Palmer seeks to establish the relevance of the contemporary poet's ongoing engagement with society:

> The poem is altered by events that it cannot possibly foresee . . . The point is not simply how work responds to current events, but how previous work is altered by and alters those events . . . Poetry as something happening among other things happening. As something happening in language, and to language under siege. Poetry as memory, sometimes memory of the future. Poetry as both fixed and in process, ever a paradox.[35]

Gizzi's poetry bears the trace of other poets, be it explicit as in the direct citation of Crane's *The Bridge*, or as a form of rewriting such as his responses to Ashbery's periphrasis, Oppen's participant poetics, or Palmer's analytic lyric. Reflecting on the poetics of his generation, Gizzi proposes that their shared connection is an interest in modernity: "we share common texts. Whether it be the writings of Emily Dickinson or Jack Spicer. Ezra Pound or H. D. Gertrude Stein or John Cage, George Oppen or Lorine Niedecker. It is about listening to a tradition that provides method and ground in our present."[36] This sense of a simultaneous writerly community is crucial to Gizzi's consideration of the lyric. At the poem's close, the speaker asserts that the poem itself must create a mutable space that favors "digression" over a distinct linear trajectory. We may desire the epiphanic moment of insight, the lyric spot of time, or what Gizzi gestures to as "the shiny spot's decoy" (*SVLW*, 24); but we are reminded that such moments are fragile and easily displaced. In spite of the assertion that "our gaze / had been altered," Gizzi refutes a finalizing statement in "Some Values of Landscape and Weather," by adding the phrase "and constantly" (24). The spaces conceived in "Some Values of Landscape and Weather" are dependent on acts of transition and displacement, concomitant with Gizzi's proposition that "[p]oems alter our reading of the present . . . Lyric history is a site of perception, of duration and play."[37] The "value" inherent to this poem is that there can be no judgment or totalizing position, or to close with Gizzi's own assessment, "There is no ethical discourse that can contain the indifference that a poem's knowledge contains."[38]

NOTES

1. Peter Gizzi and Juliana Spahr, *Writing from the New Coast: Technique* (Providence, RI: *o-blék*, 1993). The range of poets included in the *Writing from the New Coast: Technique* anthology is impressive, as indicated by the following short profile of a much longer contents listing: Lisa Jarnot, Laynie Brown, Benjamin Friedlander, Cole Swensen, Stacy Doris, Jena Osman, Myung Mi Kim, Kristin Prevallet, Lisa Robertson, Juliana Spahr, and Jennifer Moxley (as well as Peter Gizzi).

2. The relationship between lyricism and Language writing is of course a complex one, and it would be very reductive to read lyric as it is antagonistically formulated (as the straw man) in the debates of the late 1970s and 1980s. I explore the conceptualization and relationship of lyricism and Language writing in some depth, as it relates to the poetry of Charles Bernstein, Michael Palmer, and Lyn Hejinian, in my study *Reading Error: The Lyric in Contemporary American Poetry* (Oxford: Peter Lang, 2007).

3. John Kinsella, "Pastoral Metaphysics" in *Cross/Cultures 161, Spatial Relations Volume One: Essays, Reviews, Commentaries, and Chorography* (Amsterdam: Rodopi, 2013), 439–42 (439).

4. Ibid., 440.

5. Michael Palmer, "Interview: Conducted by Peter Gizzi," in *Exact Change Yearbook no. 1*, ed. Peter Gizzi (Boston: Exact Change, 1995), 161–79 (167).

6. Peter Gizzi, "Statement" in *The New American Poetry of Engagement: A 21st Century Anthology*, ed. Anne Keniston and Geoffrey Gray (Jefferson, NC: McFarland, 2012), 218–19 (218).

7. In this snapshot of the poetics of the late 1970s to early 1990s, I am guilty of rehearsing the well-worn binary between mainstream and avant-garde practices regarding the political efficacy of poetry. However, on reflection, the pronouncements by key manifesto writers affiliated with Language writing concerning the "materiality of the signifier" and "liberation" of the reader appear rather pedagogical (if not utopic) through twenty-first-century eyes. See, for example, Ron Silliman's pivotal essay "Disappearance of the Word, Appearance of the World," in *The L=A=N=G=U=A=G=E Book*, ed. Bruce Andrews and Charles Bernstein (Carbondale: Southern Illinois University Press, 1984), 121–32.

It should be noted that this didacticism is tempered in later writings, where Silliman for example admits that in Language writing, there is a danger that "[t]he idealized, absent author of the New Critical Canon has here been replaced by an equally idealized, absent reader." "Who Speaks," in *Close Listening: Poetry and the Performed Word*, ed. Charles Bernstein (New York and Oxford: Oxford University Press, 1998), 360–78 (365). Gizzi's poetry (as with the diverse body of work that is represented in *New Coast Writing*) is more doubtful of poetry's political agency. He is more intent on performing a discursive analysis of social problems than a thinking of politics in the abstract.

8. Gizzi, "Statement," 218.

9. Ibid.

10. Roland Barthes, "The Grain of the Voice," in *Music Image Text*, trans. Stephen Heath (New York: Noonday Press, 1977), 179–89.

11. Ibid., 182–83.

12. Ibid., 185.

13. John Ashbery, "The One Thing That Can Save America," in *Self-Portrait in a Convex Mirror* (Manchester: Carcanet, 1977), 44–45.

14. Ibid.

15. Ibid.

16. Ibid.

17. Peter Hühn, "Watching the Speaker Speak: Self-Observation and Self-Intransparency in Lyric Poetry," in *New Definitions of the Lyric: Theory Technology and Culture*, ed. Mark Jeffreys (New York and London: Garland, 1998), 215–44 (220).

18. George Oppen, "Of Being Numerous," in *Collected Poems* (New York: New Directions, 1975), 147–79 (151).

19. Marjorie Perloff, "The Shipwreck of the Singular: George Oppen's 'Of Being Numerous,'" originally published in *Ironwood* 26 (Fall 1985), www.bigbridge.org/BB14/Perloff Shipwreck.pdf, accessed Dec. 2, 2015.

20. Oppen, "Of Being Numerous," 152.

21. Gizzi, "Statement," 218–19.

22. The four anthologies spanning 2004 to 2009 were published by Oakland's O Books. Their titles in chronological order: *War and Peace*; *War and Peace 2: Poetry and Essays*; *War and Peace 3: The Future*; and *War and Peace 4: Vision and Text*.

23. Jennifer Scappettone, "Poetry, Intelligence and the Temporality of Crisis," in *War and Peace 2* (Oakland, CA: O Books, 2005), 56.

24. John Hollander, *The Untuning of the Sky: Ideas of Music in English Poetry 1500–1700* (Princeton: Princeton University Press, 1961), 28.

25. Ibid.

26. Jacques Attali, *Noise: The Political Economy of Music* (Manchester: Manchester University Press, 1985), 62.

27. Philip Metres, *Behind the Lines: War Resistance Poetry of the American Home Front Since 1941* (Iowa City: Iowa Press, 2007), 224.

28. Scappettone, "Poetry, Intelligence and the Temporality of Crisis," 58.
29. Michael Palmer, "Interview," in *Regions of Unlikeness: Explaining Contemporary Poetry*, by Thomas Gardner (Lincoln: University of Nebraska Press, 1999), 238.
30. Michael Palmer, *Sun* (San Francisco: North Point Press, 1988).
31. Ibid., 84–85.
32. Ibid., 85.
33. Peter Gizzi, "For the Time Being," in *Writing from the New Coast*, 167–68 (167).
34. Gizzi, "Statement," 219.
35. Michael Palmer, "Poetry and Contingency: Within a Timeless Moment of Barbaric Thought," *Chicago Review* 49.2 (2003): 65–76 (75–76).
36. Peter Gizzi, "After Language Poetry," *OEI* 7, no. 8 (2001), *UbuWeb*, accessed Dec. 2, 2015, www.ubu.com/papers/oei/gizzi.html.
37. Gizzi, "For the Time Being," 168.
38. Ibid., 168.

13 | PETER MIDDLETON

Peter Gizzi's Radical Irony

Apophasis has been a powerful counter current to the affirmative projectivism and diminished self-ascription of the more radical American poetries. Its darkening stain can be seen in Peter Gizzi's "Protest Song," which uses the reflexivity instigated by its opening "This" to offer a list of most genres of poetry — the love poem, the battle chant, the didactic poem, the epic, the confession, the anthem, the elegy, the lyric, the ode — and a disavowal of any aim to rouse patriotic sentiments, memorialize the dead, console, or offer catharsis. In one of many negations, the poem tells us that it itself is "not a garden of earthly delights" (*OUT*, 88), not that paradoxical vision of a heaven built on hell that Bosch painted, not in other words a prophetic vision.

"Protest Song" is even more troubled by the challenge of our divided world and its conflicts, as well as the more local tensions between poetry and politics. Gizzi might seem to be saying that poetry is ineffective when he writes poignantly, "This won't help when the children are dying / no answer on the way to dust" (*OUT*, 88). His poetry certainly can be read as a principled radical's refusal to agitprop his poetry for the many worthwhile political causes of today, but if we read these lines about the apparent powerlessness of poetry when children are shown dying in one war or another alongside an earlier, well-known poem by George Oppen, "Street," we will notice a more complex meditation on poetry's apparent powerlessness to alter the world. Oppen's poem considers difficult ethical paradoxes with which the sight of poverty confronts poetry. Poverty is also a concern of Gizzi. In the second of the title poems, "The

Outernationale," he ponders the disorienting realization that one's previously well-grounded vocation as a poet may require a revolution in some realm — but where and how? — outside the material history of internationalism, given the dawning awareness that "the new poverty is just / like the old poverty" (*OUT*, 100).

Oppen longed for the "end of poverty," new and old, along with an end to the damage it does to us all, while being acutely aware that such a desire was inextricably bound up with his own privileged perspective as a poet making poetry from his feelings about such deprivation. He writes, "It is terrible to see the children, // The righteous little girls; / So good, they expect to be so good."[1] The repetition of "good" does something extraordinary. It connects the author's feeling of approval for them (*good* little children) that he feels when he watches them, with their own self-confidence (they themselves try hard to be *good* children) and bluntly confronts both attitudes with the social values of goodness (what the social norms say a *good* citizen should do), values that the children may well have to violate in order to be good enough to survive. It is these seemingly ineradicable connections between the modes of the good that the poem's irony about the good compels to our attention. Our disenchanted knowledge of the difficulty the children will face being "good" calls into question any confidence we might have in our own other ethical and aesthetic concepts of the good. Are we, are our poems, good? Can they change anything? Can they alter those social norms and roles that enforce the lack that is poverty?

At first glance it could seem that Gizzi's "Protest Song" is nodding to Auden's prewar disillusion that "poetry makes nothing happen." In his collection of poems offered in risky mimetic homage to poets, *Hours of the Book*, his "Poem for John Wieners" accrues images of despair on the street as signs of the poet's helplessness, which is baldly announced in an opening refrain: "I am not a poet / but a witness."[2] In this early poem the intertextual music slips revealingly from the romantic agonies of early Wieners to the more maudlin cynicism of Eliot's "Prufrock," and the poem hangs onto the life-raft belief that whatever the writer's failings, poetry is "real." "Protest Song" avoids any such risk of wounded narcissism. In fact, the poem goes much further than offering a cynical shrug at poetry's ineptitude faced with our nations' barbarisms solicited in their gardens of earthly delights. To begin with, the poem winks at us as it alludes to the modernist exposé (think Magritte, perhaps) of the act of painting (or naming) as always taking place in the absence of what it represents.

The poem is resolute. This specific poem, and by implication any poem the poet writes, may only be definable negatively as what it itself is not. The protest song is an impoverished poem. If the poet could say what it is, then it would not be the poem that he wishes to write. Whatever it is that makes it a poem — and "Protest Song" leaves open the possibility that its accumulating negations may amount to its own total cancellation as even counting as a poem — if it is actually a poem, then what makes it a poem cannot be said. What makes a poem a poem is unsayable.

So far this would seem to locate Gizzi's poem as a new apophatic poem — the new impoverished poem is the same as the old impoverished poem. Apophatic poets, as William Franke points out, tend to write in "an aphoristic, elliptical style that effectively leaves unsaid the main target and intention of their poems."[3] Aphorism is certainly a preferred mode in Gizzi's poems, but this elusive rhetorical form, in which doxa, wisdom, and logic are all implicated in a verbal singularity, is refused its prophetic credentials in Gizzi's hands. Gizzi's irony also leads him to follow through his thinking about the risks that skepticism will trounce the sensory substrate of the aesthetic. One of the most striking aphoristic lines in his poetry is the opening of "Nocturne": "To know is an extreme condition / like doubt, and will not rest" (*OUT*, 43). Stanley Cavell says something similar in *The Claim of Reason*: "consider how little of anything, or any situation, we really see."[4] "Nocturne" might seem to be a call to open the gates of perception, but is more accurately read as a reminder of the sensory worlds beyond knowledge, worlds of experience that Gizzi represents by colors.

> Is it so difficult to admit light
> in its unconditional noise
>
> its electric blur, its red
> cherry red, red of the advertisements
>
> or yellow, cool as yellow gold
> flat as mustard yellow.
>
> And bright-bright Gatorade green
> green dusky as gray forest-shade green. (*OUT*, 43)

Anne Truitt writes in her journal *Daybook*, an account of her development as a sculptor, that she "slowly came to realize that what I was actually trying to do was take paintings off the wall, to set color free in three dimensions for its own sake. This was analogous to my feeling for the freedom of my own body and my own being, as if in some mysterious way I felt myself to *be* color."[5] Allusions to music, the bluish smoke of cigarettes, and a catch in the throat from the intense feelings stirred up at a party, all tacitly allude to the Blues, and yet remain on the side of color, of its strange way of becoming part of us.

Aphorisms require a reader's confidence that claims without supporting justification can be trusted; without this, all we hear is dull pedagogy and manipulative sentiment. Poems such as "Nocturne" not only gain a reader's trust through their scrupulous emotional honesty, but they are also convincingly entangled with contemporary discourses. The "unconditional noise" of light is not merely a bit of clever poetic synesthesia, it also ties in with the use of the concept of "noise" in digital cameras, where noise is the addition of random light that can blur an otherwise clear image; and the term also alludes more broadly to the established use of "noise" to describe the opposite of information. It's a noise that makes silence all the more welcome.

There is good reason to read Gizzi this way. Before we treat his negative poetics as solely a rallying cry for an apophatic poetics, however, we need to reflect further on its intense folds of irony. Jay Bernstein eloquently speaks for such irony in relation to painting when he says, "It must seem an insult to commitments to justice and a travesty of the feelings that support such commitments (compassion for the sufferings of others, or righteous anger at those who calculate the worth of human lives as if it were a simple matter of profit and loss) that the intelligibility and validity of those commitments and feelings could be thought to hang on or be found in just 'this' painting or 'this' urgent stroke of red."[6] Substitute for the visual art examples terms from poetry such as "this poem" or this "urgent trope," and Bernstein's anxiety could be Gizzi's. Unless the poem acknowledges the appearance of insult at the enormous gap between the scale of the world's injustices and a few words marching across a page, it fails this test. But how can the poem make such acknowledgment without calling attention to its own total inadequacy? This is the question that many of Gizzi's recent poems push into. I shall suggest that an attempt to answer this question leads the poet toward a kind of irony that is as much a psychic event as a mode of rhetoric.

If we avoid too hastily acceding to the lure of the negations in "Protest Song" and hence treating these statements as purely constructed around negations because what needs to be said is unsayable, beyond representation, we can see that this poem's apophatic strategy differs from others with which it might appear to have much in common. Indeed, Gizzi's poem might at first seem to be a close cousin to the poetry of Michael Palmer and its antecedents in Edmond Jabès or Paul Celan. The difference is that this poem is inflected by an irony so pervasive that even apophasis is partially displaced into deflating self-mockery. An irony is at work that refuses to take itself either seriously or nonseriously. Consider these lines:

> Neither anthem to rally nor flag flutter
> will bring back the dead, their ashes flying (*OUT*, 88)

If the final phrase "their ashes flying" had been left out, we could just about treat this as an apophatic gesture, a recognition that we would love our poetry to let the dead speak again, to allow the national spirit to wave to itself. But that final phrase crosses a line into the black humor of post-cremation rites (perfectly caught in that moment in *The Big Lebowski* when the two slackers try to cast their friend's ashes to the wind, only to have them come flying back in their faces with a resounding gritty symbolism). And irony is there again and again in this and other Gizzi poems. Just when the darkness of apophasis appears to offer the best means to articulate the unsayable truth of poetry, Gizzi's irony cracks it open with momentary illumination.

Although I want to claim that the most recent collections take irony further, irony was already evident as a rhetorical strategy in earlier volumes too, notably *Some Values of Landscape and Weather*. This book created quite a stir in the UK when it was published a few years ago. Here was an American poet who could produce brilliant poem-like poems without apology, express subtle emotional phrasings with lovely accuracy, write with complete sonic assurance as himself, and yet balance all this with a deconstructionist attention to the "blurred sentence" (*SVLW*, 25) of language. Here was a poet whose favorite word was that sigil of imagination "if," that bridge to the subjunctive, the speculative, and the experimental. "If" is a moment that scientists, philosophers, and poets have in common, even as they cross its span to epistemologically different territories.

The Outernationale, the volume of poems that followed, carries forward the exploration of "if" in quick-witted meditative poems that entertain ideas only to interrupt their reflections with reflexive double takes, memories, and other forms of self-questioning, "to think a way / between moonlight / and the dictionary" (*OUT*, 36). This concern to "think a way" between poetic inspiration and the demands of language gives rise to a growing sense of unshakeable irony about the very act of writing poems. In "Saturday and Its Festooned Potential," for instance, Gizzi appears to venture a credo—"To be oneself becoming a poem" (*OUT*, 60)—in which the ambiguity—to be oneself rather than conform to aesthetic norms and still be able to live a life in which poems are a central part of that shaping of oneself—is an aspiration to be set alongside the demands of literary genealogy and contemporary divisions between poetry groupings. This is a poetry easily misrepresented by the critic because it is often jauntily out on those thoughtways mooning over the lexicon or carrying the language back to the moonlit world rather than looking up the moon in a book, a poetry appearing to avoid high seriousness out of a skepticism toward its pitfalls:

> The whole wide whorl
> of economics charted
> on a dart board
> in bed sheets, -th
> -onomy, -illion, -ation. (*OUT*, 99)

The claims of economics on our attention are lightly mocked by the pun, and then further undermined by the implicit comparison to a popular game of skill and chance, before contrasting the study of money with the world of love and passion. What could have been a conventional poetic dialectic of society and love is, however, then neatly turned back onto the surface of language, where the suffixes and consonantal endings that collude with the powerful abstractions of economics are lined up revealing their empty whorls. We can also glimpse here the validity of what one of Kierkegaard's alter egos, Johannes Climacus, insists: "From the fact that irony is present, it does not follow that earnestness is excluded."[7]

Kierkegaardian irony is a mode of being in which reasoning meets contradictions whichever way it turns, yet remains committed to reasoning even as the syllogisms bend. I think it helps us to understand the power of Gizzi's later poetry if we think of him as being at times acutely aware of an experience related to the philosopher's irony, but now thought of as a condition that the philosopher and psychoanalysis Jonathan Lear calls "radical irony."[8] Ordinary irony—of which there is certainly a fair amount in Gizzi's poetry—may manifest itself as the saying of one thing and meaning its opposite, or a knowingness about appearances; but radical irony goes much deeper than rhetorical inversions. Lear draws on discussions of Socratic irony and Kierkegaardian irony, linked to case histories of present-day personal crises, to suggest that radical irony is an experience of simultaneously believing in one's commitments and finding them abruptly meaningless. I believe in the power of poetry and at the same time, I don't know if poetry has any significance or value. What is the point of rhythm, imagery, form, or even of the career activities of poetry? On the evidence of *Hours of the Book*, this is a moment that Gizzi may have encountered before, though in that book it is not met with radical irony. This moment is not writer's block, there is no problem in writing poems; the problem is deeper than that, a problem about why this matters, and about what constitutes a poem.

Radical irony is a response to such a moment of deeply felt self-disruption that occurs when a lived role loses its inner—and possibly unconsciously grounded—rationale, yet remains important to oneself. Lear is very insistent that this is a first-person experience, that it happens to a me, not to a culture or society. This experience of self-disruption in the living of a role, as a teacher or poet, is not disillusion, nor is it the exposure of a false ideology.

In my view, Gizzi's later poetry manifests such radical irony most intensely when he attempts to draw back from lyric expression to justify the writing of a contemporary lyric. Take the poem "Wintry Mix," for example. It meditates implicitly on poetic method while explicitly talking about the struggle to get up on a winter's morning and go out "into the draft" of an unwelcoming dawn chill, wryly acknowledging the dilemma of being a child both of modernism and of those earlier, formerly modern movements reaching back to classicism: "Can't imagine opening / the door today in a toga" (*OUT*, 57). The present moment is both the icy winter dawn in which a robe designed for a Mediterranean climate would be insufficient, and the inappropriateness of writing poetry in Classical style. Classicism just doesn't seem sufficient any more for the "crack-o'-the-world light" (*OUT*, 56) of the cold history of the West. But what poetic clothes might be most appropriate? Indeed, would any poetic style be adequate for that light? What is the poetic equivalent of a down jacket? That this is not just a lament at lacking "This man's art and that man's scope" (as may have been the case in "Poem for John Wieners") for writing poetry is suggested by the brushstrokes of irony in the patrician toga and the plebeian contraction "o."

What I am suggesting is a kind of radical irony becomes most salient in the second "The Outernationale," where we encounter an extended struggle with a failing apophasis. This struggle manifests itself in what Lear calls "radical experience": "Why can't I just admit / I'm dead, have been dead / since I met me, -metry, -ality" (*OUT*, 94). This stuttering of "me–metry, -ality" hints that one symptom of the poet's failing encounter with the lyrical, would-be metrical "I" and its claims on "reality" is an inability to speak those predicates buttressed by qualifying suffixes. I am reminded of several of Doris Lessing's protagonists who stutter when they find themselves no longer believing the words that they habitually say.[9] In "The Outernationale," the poet narrator loses a formerly sturdy sense of poetry's significance, its meanings, and its purposes while remaining committed to writing it, and indeed, in the process of failing to find former purposes, producing what reads as a significant poem. The ironies redouble.

Lear analyzes such ironic moments as breakdowns in practical intelligibility, uncanny moments when the individual — and as I say, it is characteristic of ironic experience that it is always first person — is likely to reflect like this: "I have lost a sense of how my understanding of my past gives me any basis for what to do next."[10] Or as Gizzi bleakly expresses it, "Why can't I just admit / I'm dead, have been dead / since I met me, -metry, -ality." Lear is careful to distinguish his interpretation of Kierkegaardian irony from Richard Rorty's irony and Thomas Nagel's absurdism. Put briefly, Rorty's irony lacks the possibility of belief because all discourses are ultimately social constructions, and Nagel's is all about the smallness of the subjectivity in the vastness of the universe. Lear believes that by contrast, the kind of ironic experience that he finds eloquently defined by Socrates and Kierkegaard, and observes in contemporary life, "manifests passion for a certain direction."[11] Only by continuing to write poetry can the poet fully inhabit this radical irony that calls his poetic vocation into question.

At this point, I ought to make it clear that I am not arguing that Gizzi's poems are poetic treatments of theories of irony from the philosophical tradition, but rather that thinking about radical irony can help attune us to a feature of his poetry that I believe accounts for its possibly surprising success in appealing to readers from both the avant-garde and the personal lyric tradition of recent poetry. Nor am I offering a biographical interpretation. I am not saying that the poems are a history of the poet's own personal crisis, although it would obviously seem likely that the poet had some kind of close knowledge of such radical ironic experience. I am suggesting that Gizzi's poems offer such experience to the reader, that the poems are attempting to give the reader an aesthetic enactment of such ironic disorientation. Hence, it is the admirable persistence in believing that poetry must be possible accompanied by a sense of its impossibility that creates a disorientation.

How can the poet write about hope without losing its force to declarations of what it is to hope for? For a poet sparing of repetition, "doubt" is a word that recurs frequently in *The Outernationale*. How can he "rescue doubt into loving" (*OUT*, 33), skeptical doubt, not so much of the Cartesian epistemological kind as doubt about the conditions of possibility for poetry? These are questions that keep nervously flipping the odds back and forth in sentence after sentence in the second poem entitled "The Outernationale." It begins with one of Gizzi's signature gestures, his carefully calibrated interpolation of popular culture into a philosophical poetic meditation, as it makes a nod to the proverb "a bird in the hand is worth two in the bush," asking what will happen now the "bird's in the hand" (*OUT*, 92)? Or what will happen now a penny has been saved "in the dark belly of mr. piggy" (92)? Figuratively, the question is this: Can you say that now you have achieved your material wants, you are fulfilled? Literally, the first question has a more violent answer. That bird is about to be a captive, or most likely, a dead bird to be eaten by the likes of the owner of the hand that holds it. The real mr. piggy's belly will become strips of bacon, and the pottery pig will most likely be broken open to retrieve the coins. The poem strews such associative asides around the reader's path as it ruminates on what will happen next. Maybe a new day will dawn figuratively, and maybe the natural world will give us its wisdom? Or most likely not.

By the end of the first section, the poem has already deftly alluded to Whitman and William Carlos Williams, and then casually dismissed such allusions:

> So many strangers
> alive in a larynx.
> So much depends on *x*
> so much more
> on the book in your hand. (*OUT*, 93)

A book in the hand may be worth two in the bush, but in the era of Bush, this book, published in 2007, seems frail indeed. [Ed. note: see essays in this collection by Williams and Jennison on Gizzi's Bush-era politics.] Later the poem will look at a field through the window and dismiss that figure of poetic possibility for Charles Olson and Robert Duncan, the open field. Here in this first section, the poem already hints that its hopes, if they deserve such a positive name, fall elsewhere, on the possibilities of "nothing," a word used even more in this volume than "doubt": "Start from nothing and be / long to it"; "Start from nothing / and let the sound reach you" (*OUT*, 92). That ever-expanding American dream, to start from nothing, to start with the rich potential of nothing and become successful, is displaced by a growing interest in remaining in the state of nothing, the apophatic matrix, and listening hard to that nothing, to that unsayable Other to being. But this is hard and leads to the darkest corners of radical irony. In the following section, the poem asks in the lines I have already quoted why he as poet cannot admit that he is dead, and the lyric expressive self a dead bird (duck). This would be a bog of self-pity if not for irony's resistance to the seriousness needed to wallow.

As the poem breaks up into shorter sections, it appears that the bird is no longer in the hand, as the poet asks the skylark if it has "anything / to say to me?" to which the answer might well be "not unless you are Shelley," just as the sun told Frank O'Hara that his imitation of Mandelstam left much to be desired. Shelley's voice in "Ozymandias" can just be heard in the sand accumulating around the empty suffixes:

> Who will live
> inside the song?
> Is it only sand?
> The voice of sand
> -mandias, -icious, -rex. (*OUT*, 95)

King of kings, the rex now wrecks. From contemplating the dust of empires, the poem returns to the noise of the present-day empire laughing and boasting on the television, shuts it off, and tries to find solace in the outdoors, as if a beautiful sky might undo the influence of "bad history." But finds both "spring and death," and so starts over again.

Maybe, the poem muses, the answer is to look for hope in the forgotten histories, those histories that a series of modern poets have peered back into and found lost, silenced voices of the defeated and the marginalized. The poem reminds itself that the modern poet doesn't find "vast and trunkless legs of stone" but instead ruined factories — we might have wandered for a moment into the world of Mark Nowak's *Shut Up Shut Down*. "These old windows / bend the world" (OUT, 97) and in doing so, achieve more than the sunsets and lakeside views.

> If only I knew then
> what I know to be
> outside my head
> rain-washed and open. (OUT, 97)

Here, if it is to be found anywhere in the industrial archeology of American exceptionalism, ought to be possible the wakening of understanding that the poet is searching for. After this section the poem turns to a critique of its own former self, as lost in time as "Ozymandias," now noticing how that former self imagined itself indestructible, and in doing so imposed on itself a cruelty that "comes / from lack of everything / or so I imagined" (OUT, 98). Feeling a need for birds in the hand, for shiny pennies, or for sublime experiences, that earlier self was defined by lack, a lack that it imagined. But maybe lack was not its problem, maybe the nothing had what it needed? This self could not "save anyone / from anything" (98).

Let's step back from this poem for a moment and remind ourselves that Gizzi is acutely conscious of poetic history, past and present. He was editor, along with Connell McGrath, of one of the most significant poetry magazines of the past two decades, *o-blék*. Its distinctive style, a shape and heft similar to a smallish paperback, and a commitment to the presentation of nothing but substantial bodies of work by each poet, either a long poem or a sequence of related poems, precluded essays on poetics or the publication of other paratexts. The choice of poets was thoughtfully ecumenical: Language poets alongside earlier and more recent generations of poets, some Europeans — and always an emphasis on poetic virtues of linguistic density, metaphor, communicative and affective intensity. This training as an editor may be another reason Gizzi can even imagine wearing that toga; he often appears reluctantly intertextual, recognizing that it is not anachronistic Classicism that is the danger, but the weeds of Modernism, tropes that insistently return, still part of the ecology. His poem "Saturday and Its Festooned Potential," for instance, is a witty re-invention of motifs from Wallace Stevens's poems "Sunday Morning" and "A High-Toned Old Christian Woman."

After losing itself briefly in the "whorl" of economics, the poem then breaks off and then returns, now attending to what Olson called "the breath": "The time to breathe / is now, there will be no time / to think but perhaps / you have no doubt" (*OUT*, 99). A moment's relief, a time to breathe again, and to attend to an embodied poetics, but with a warning that thinking or reasoning may be compromised by doing so. This is not to be a moment of breakthrough similar to Descartes's realization of the *cogito ergo sum*. Crucially, there is no sense of some gradually lifting recovery, as if we were recapitulating the recovery from a loss of poetic nerve and following a traditional poetic upward recovery curve of the kind that Milton charts in Lycidas. Instead, there is an intimation that even doubt, even apophatic resolution, may not be trustworthy: "I would like / to expose doubt itself . . . to empty / once and for all expectation" (*OUT*, 99–100). This is not going to be the poetry of great expectations, of supreme fictions and maximal survey. It is at this crucial point that the poem, as one does, gets into its car and goes for a drive round the 'hood, where new poverty is indistinguishable from its predecessor, a poverty that many still believe to be the just deserts of the poor, though as the irony suggests, they are more likely the very opposite of just. Gizzi is always in dialogue with the poetic tradition, and in this instance I hear an appropriate echo of Robert Hass's poem "Meditation at Lagunas"— a poetic critique of glib American borrowings from European theories of the sign as the erasure of its referent — which begins, "All the new thinking is about loss. In this it resembles all the old thinking."[12] Loss and poverty are simply loss and poverty. Or are they? As Oppen also knew, we cannot simply treat poverty as a starting point either, as a firm ground for our politics of indignation, and our construction of good aesthetic or moral values, because we suspect, as Gizzi does, that "absolute powerlessness / corrupts absolutely" (*OUT*, 100). We are inside the loss, and in the radical irony of this realization may be the possibility of hope.

The final section of "The Outernationale" offers no consolation, only the sense of that passion directed toward continuing to write poetry, or what is now identified as the unknown, the unsayable, the "wanting that keeps us / looking hard into the dark," which in a reality dream we "hope to unpack / and move into / that one day / we might find ourselves lit up" (*OUT*, 102). The tensions between ironic style and ironic experience are wound very tight here. How often we critics of poetry offer to "unpack" a cluster of allusions, etymologies, and generic conventions in order to reveal a meaning, forgetting that the root of this metaphor implies travel away from home to somewhere new. Moving into the dark sounds terrifying. It takes radical hope to imagine that although we have moved into darkness, this new place will prove as illuminable as all those other earlier territories did, knowing the sharp vicissitudes of that history of enlightenment. It takes radical irony to find a way through the loss of meaning and confidence in the continuing relevance of the poetic tradition and out again to a firm conviction that all this disorientation will prove temporary.

Throughout this final section, the poem insists on the persistence of "nothing": "But nothing / changes everything / and we know this. / We earn this the hard way" (*OUT*, 101). How easy to imagine that all we have to do is learn it, when it is more likely that it will be hard earned before it is learned. It is also easy to miss the importance of the fact that it is asserted that "we know this." For here is the radical hope in the midst of ironic rupture, that there are things we know, even if they may seem as unhelpful as the knowledge that nothing, not even the most powerful poem or political movement, could change *everything*. But then, as Prynne ruefully concedes in "The Western Gate," "the truth is sadder but who / would ask me [the poet] to hope only for that?"[13]

Silence. The unsayable. Radical irony. Peter Gizzi's poetry more than usually compels the would-be interpreter to hesitate, not in face of a dense web of scholarly allusion or a pressing illegibility, or even a sense that subjective intentionality has withdrawn from aleatory passages of poetry. In "Hypostasis & New Year" from *Threshold Songs*, a poem whose title is a characteristic collision of high and low culture, Gizzi begins by asking, "For why am I afraid to sing / the fundamental shape of awe" (*TS*, 6). As readers, we need to meet such caution and poetic tact more than halfway. In this essay I have suggested we can do this by recognizing the poetry is engaged at times with the dilemma of how to continue to write poetry in the midst of an experience of radical irony in which writing poetry loses its meaning, when one can only feel that poetry like "daylight is historic / if you think on it / if you really feel its cold rays, / old poetry, spreading evenly / over as far as you can see" (*TS*, 75). Yet at the same time, poetry continues to offer the only hope of light, the only rays of sustaining insight, and so remains the only hope of a return to meaning. Gizzi's poems discern hope in "what is barely legible / barely in our dailiness" (*OUT*, 90), traces of feeling and thought found in the everyday. His poems remind us just how much rereading poems need before they yield what can be barely legible or only minimally audible, as they begin almost silently, understated, and seemingly unconnected; radical rereading slowly renders conscious the sonic, visual, historical, and intertextual layers so that the once quiet poem may (there is no guarantee) gradually become "bright-bright"; or, as Gizzi's poem "Human Memory is Organic" has it, "To see with a purpose has its bloom / and falls to seed and returns // to be a story like any other" (*OUT*, 27). Gizzi's poetry investigates areas of language, knowledge, and experience that have helped create the torn halves of recent poetry, promising much and leaving his readers with questions. What does it mean for poetry, as the final poem in *The Outernationale* expresses it, to "be / appendages to evolution" or "mysteries / in the face of violence" (107)? Is this sufficient, is this radical irony what we should hope for?

NOTES

1. George Oppen, *New Collected Poems*, 2nd ed., ed. Michael Davidson (New York: New Directions, 2008), 127.
2. Peter Gizzi, *Hours of the Book* (Gran Canaria, Spain: Zasterle Press, 1994), n.p.
3. William Franke, *A Philosophy of the Unsayable* (Notre Dame, IN: Notre Dame Press, 2014), 84.
4. Stanley Cavell, *The Claim of Reason* (Oxford: Oxford University Press, 1999), 143.
5. Anne Truitt, *Daybook* (New York: Penguin, 1984), 81.
6. J. M. Bernstein, *Against Voluptuous Bodies: Adorno's Late Modernism and the Meaning of Painting* (Stanford: Stanford University Press, 2006), 46.
7. Søren Kierkegaard, *Concluding Unscientific Postscript* (Cambridge: Cambridge University Press), 277. Quoted in Lear, *A Case for Irony*, 19.
8. Jonathan Lear, *A Case for Irony* (Cambridge, MA: Harvard University Press, 2011).
9. See, for instance, the opening passages of *Briefing for a Descent into Hell*, by Doris Lessing (New York: Vintage, 2009).
10. Lear, *A Case for Irony*, 18.
11. Ibid., 19.
12. Robert Hass, *Praise* (Manchester: Carcanet, 1981), 4.
13. J. H. Prynne, *Poems* (Newcastle upon Tyne: Bloodaxe, 1999), 48.

14 | PHILIP COLEMAN

"turning words to return a world"

On Peter Gizzi's "Pierced"

The title of Peter Gizzi's poem "Pierced," from *Artificial Heart* (1998), is anticipated by poems that appear earlier in that collection, most notably "Another Day on the Pilgrimage": "An absorbed earth is altered, fallow / and gusts of stinging filth pierce us / as we move from moment to task" (*SP*, 45).[1] Images of the self correlate to "a syringe" and "a pyramid," while the concluding strophe likens the "I" to the piercing action of a quill pen in the associative confluence of "feather" and "quick":

> as the old latch is gone from the back door —
> whoosh and bang all evening
> makes one's nerves sharpen to the point
> of a syringe. I like how autography is geologic
> or geographical. All my people have larger bodies.
> Will you compare me to a pyramid or a clover
> in the trash? When I am inscribed to tell
> of the beauty of innuendo
> I am like unto a feather — quick. (*SP*, 44)

In this poem's recurrent "I am," Gizzi is less interested in affirming subjectivity in a Whitmanian sense than he is in exploring the complex relationship between thinking subject and object-world, an idea summarized by the quotation from William James that stands as an epigraph to *In Defense of Nothing:*

Selected Poems, 1987–2011 (2014): "The world contains consciousness as well as atoms — and the one must be written down as just as essential as the other" (*SP*, n.p.). Objects in the world and our cognitive and emotional apprehension of them are of equal interest to Gizzi; his work represents a radical negotiation of what it means to think and act within this circuit of being and perception. As he puts it in the poem "Periplum," "to know / implies a different reading / Somewhere // faith enters / and must be pinned and sighted" (*SP*, 4).

In the context of what it means "to know," for Gizzi there is a tension between pinning something down — almost a kind of ontological lepidoptery — and what it means to be "pierced," the process whereby knowledge of the self, the world, and poetry itself are subjected to that sharp point of exploration, even to the point of dissipation. In "An Open Letter of Poetics to Steve Farmer," Gizzi explains that his long poem "Pierced" is, among other things, "a meditation on the 'long road' (the *lungo drom*)," referring to Isabel Fonseca's book *Bury Me Standing: The Gypsies and Their Journey* (1995).[2] Gizzi points out that Fonseca "describes the *lungo drom* as a nostalgia for utopia or (as she translates it) 'a return to nowhere.' Home is established only in the act of singing, the moment of a song."[3] Drawing on this idea, Gizzi sees the "return to nowhere" as what he calls "an evolutionary movement, the way Zeno's arrow has multiple sites on its arc."[4] "Pierced" may then be considered as a text that maps some of the sites targeted in the (revolutionary) movement of Gizzi's work: his poetic revolution and return to certain axes of concern — what it means to see, to think, to love, to exist — but also what it means to reconsider and revise our understandings of concepts and tropes that are germane to the whole history of poetic culture. In "Pierced," indeed, it is to the idea of poetry itself, conceived within this broad arena of concern, that Gizzi directs the arrows of his thought.

The word "pierced"— an adjective suggesting that something has been "punctured" or "perforated" as well as "penetrated by a hole or holes"[5] — may call to mind the piercing of skin, an action that can have many associations, often at the same time (personal and historical, violent and aesthetic). In Alexander Pope's translation of Homer's *Iliad*, the word appears several times to describe the slaying of various warriors by the arrows, spears, and swords of others,[6] while in Shakespeare the notion of piercing often extends beyond bodily wounds to injuries of the figurative heart and mind — as in *Othello*, when the Venetian senator Brabanzio tells the Duke of Venice that he "never yet did hear / That the bruised heart was piercèd through the ear."[7] In this example

Brabanzio is using the idea of piercing metaphorically to question the efficacy of words on a "bruised heart," but this also relates to one of Gizzi's concerns in "Pierced," which has to do with the power of poetry to do anything at all beyond the domain of its own being. It is important, then, that "Pierced" begins with a meditation not so much on the external manifestations or affects of poetry, but with a consideration of what lies at the very "heart of poetry." Indeed, before the reader reaches the fifth line of the poem, s/he realizes that beyond "the heart of poetry" there is a further, deeper space being mined by the poet here, because "at the heart is a great stillness in a tiny pocket." Taking "poetry," in other words, as his initial object of inquiry, Gizzi proceeds through the opening lines of "Pierced" to cut beneath the text's folds ("a rag folded lengthwise / placed over eyes") to move toward poetry's "heart," and then deeper still, past "a great stillness in a tiny pocket" that is posited beyond "a gap between tooth & tongue / chance, love & logic / the scalpel & scripture / tent show, RENT-A-BENCH / & Chicken Little." (*SP*, 60–69) Beyond the world within which the poet and his readers reside — the world of speech, analysis, surgery, prayer, fast food, and entertainment — there is another space beyond the surface of the poetic text, within the very "heart of poetry," that almost defeats the poet's powers of articulation.

Insofar as "Pierced" is a poem about poetry, it is then also a poem that expresses a certain kind of belief in the agency of the poetic text as well as in the poet as a mediator of its sacred message, but before these claims come into view, Gizzi takes the reader on a journey not unlike the "*lungo drom*" of Gypsy culture as described by Fonseca. "Pierced" is not an epic poem in terms of length, but the scale of the journey inward it proposes to the reader — piercing beyond worldly surfaces to the very "heart of poetry"— is equivalent to the journeys of self-discovery posited by longer (narrative) poems, from Homer's *Odyssey* to *The Dream Songs* of John Berryman. Indeed, between these approximate literary historical poles — from antiquity to high modernism — which both play with ideas of individuation and loss, self-projection and world making, Gizzi's "Pierced" suggests that "there is no actual site to return to" in these journeys, as he puts it in his "Open Letter" to Steve Farmer. In his "Open Letter," Gizzi explains that he wants "the field of [his] work to also include other works, displacing context to create narrative, emotional, psychological, and formal turbulence."[8] Reading through "Pierced," the reader hears clear echoes of many "other works" that are displaced out of their original contexts and cast into new mind- and soundscapes of Gizzi's invention. The phrase "toy majestic," for example, seems to echo phrases from Berryman's work — the title *His Toy, His Dream, His Rest* (1968), which contains Berryman's Dream Songs 78–385, together with the image of the "majestic Shade" from "Dream Song 312"[9] — while further on in the poem, a single line ("come as you are") is both an invocation of the spirit of Kurt Cobain and Nirvana's song of that title, included on *Nevermind* (1992),[10] and an invitation to the reader to follow the speaker-poet on this journey toward poetry's center.

The final line of "Pierced" ("two cars race to the horizon") makes "narrative" sense when one reads the poem in this way — as a challenge to the reader to join the poet on a kind of metaphysical journey — but Gizzi's reference to the "*lungo drom*" makes it clear that this is no straightforward road trip. Gizzi's reference to the Nirvana song title "Come as You Are" is significant here. The song begins less with an invitation than with a series of injunctions and qualifications ("Come as you are / as you were / as I want you to be") that increase in ambiguity by the end of the first verse ("as a friend / as an old enemy / take your time / hurry up / the choice is yours / don't be late"), but the chorus hangs on a repeated phrase ("*memoria*"), which alludes to the activity of remembering in the classical rhetorical canon.[11] "*Memoria*" is at the heart of Nirvana's song to the extent that "Come as You Are" is a text that invites an imaginary addressee to remember and revisit a scene that s/he may have visited before, but the speaker needs to reassure the reader that the journey is not to be feared: "No, I don't have a gun," Cobain repeats as the song concludes, but the threat of violence is already there, and it is bound up with the memories that are stored in the song's heart's own fatigued articulation. As Gizzi puts it, repeating the opening line of "Pierced" ("The heart of poetry is fatigue") just after the central point of the poem itself in line 92 ("the leafy plot is tenuous"),

> The heart of poetry is fatigue
> what the teachers left unsaid
> a whimpering man inside the child
> failed cathedral, overflowing shelter
> a woman in the shape of a man
> man in the shape of an animal
> animal shape of a children's book
> crust of bread

a skinny leg inside a blown-out shoe
at the side of an ocean
at the mouth of the delta
at the foot of a glacier
dung hill, mini mart
burial mound and parking lot
all sucked into a vacuum
the cartoon black spot
of an eye, a tiny pool of ink
through which the overload
overlord of images pour
into bodies uncensored
phantom of what we really are (*SP*, 65)

To "come as you are," then, in Gizzi's understanding as well as in Cobain's, is always already to come with many things "unsaid"— from the "whimpering man inside the child" to the "man in the shape of an animal"— a process of ever-unfolding "*memoria*" through which the "phantom of what we really are" can only be apprehended in an "overload / overlord of images."

"Pierced" performs such an overloading of images that, at times, it appears to be "overlorded" by the figure of the Poet as understood by Ralph Waldo Emerson:

> Readers of poetry see the factory-village, and the railway, and fancy that the poetry of the landscape is broken up by these; for these works of art are not yet consecrated in their reading; but the poet sees them fall within the great Order not less than the beehive, or the spider's geometrical web.[12]

In "Pierced," Gizzi provides minute glimpses of a broken landscape that includes "a decaying spider in a chain link fence" and "a rotten cushion at the bottom of a stream" (*SP*, 61), but these images are brought together as part of his poetic vision of a contemporary world in which dichotomies such as nature/culture and human/animal being are collapsed within the space of song. As Emerson writes in the same essay ("The Poet"), "the melodies of the poet ascend, and leap, and pierce into the deeps of infinite time."[13] Like many of Gizzi's poems, "Pierced" is meticulously crafted, and the poem's shape — its "geometrical" structure — is bound up with its meaning. At 184 lines, the poem's midpoint (its structural "heart") is at line 92 ("the leafy plot is tenuous"). However, before the reader reaches this point—a point that is of much greater and deeper significance than the speaker suggests—s/he must overcome certain objections to the poem's endeavor from within the poem's own theater. "The heart of poetry is a hollow man," the speaker says, alluding to T. S. Eliot, then to Fernando Pessoa ("a heteronym"), but also to Ovid ("a dog-eared copy of the *Metamorphoses*"); but these references to canonical works from the history of Western literature are troubled and threatened by "a forensic test, & casino chip / a long distance call" that tends toward the claim that "The populist's vision dims / dented at the moment of ascendency" and the exasperated (tellingly unpunctuated) question/assertion: "*is that all there is*" (*SP*, 63)?

What is there, then, beyond the "dog-eared" books of poems in translation, the random quotations overloaded in our individual and collective memories? The line "*is that all there is*" may refer to the song of the same title, popularized in the 1960s by US American singer Peggy Lee,[14] but which may be traced back to a story by Thomas Mann whose title has been translated as "Disillusionment" (*Enttäuschung*).[15] At this point in "Pierced," certainly, Gizzi's poem seems to speak to a particular kind of disillusionment regarding the fate and function of poetry, so as the poem turns toward its center, the poet appears to lay bare the process of learning again how to speak and sing in and of the world:

> m-m-moon, s-s-tring, br-r-anch
> open the throat to recite
>
> e-egg, t-twine, s-s-tick
> open the throat to sing
>
> to sigh, then sign the reply
> turning words to return the world
>
> here you are: t-t-tree, bowl of fruit
> here it is: cellow & lute
> sun shaft in garden, on dirt (*SP*, 64)

Earlier in the poem, Gizzi asks "whose home, / what letter, / what book? // whose tomb?" (*SP*, 62). In these lines those questions are answered, tentatively if not tenuously, by a self for whom "the mind of a page is the form of a body" (64). Home, letter, book, and tomb form a unified whole in this worldview, but the sense of oneness — of perceiving things not in their "broken up" state but "within the great Order," as Emerson put it — depends on song and the functioning voice of the lyric poet for its articulation. Gizzi understands "song" in a broad sense that can include the hymns of Homer as well as the popular music of the contemporary era (from Peggy Lee to Nirvana), but ultimately and at all times, he is operating as an artist whose medium (writing) is that "tiny pool of ink" through which he seeks to go beyond "the graphic surface of objects' stink." Between the discoveries of "here you are" and "here it is"— realizations of self and world in their temporal and spatial relations — the poet "open[s] the throat to sing // to sigh, then sign the reply / turning words to return the world."

Gizzi posits various things at poetry's "heart" in "Pierced," from "fatigue" (twice) to "an angry child," "a ripped sock," "an empty lot," "a hollow man," "an arc between grass / blade and gown." Deeper still, "at the heart is a great stillness in a tiny pocket" he writes in the fifth line of the poem (*SP*, 60), suggesting the kind of recursive "driving and driving / thought and austerity / nearer to lyricism" that Susan Howe writes of in *Pierce-Arrow*, published within a year of Gizzi's *Artificial Heart*.[16] What is it that Gizzi and Howe, in their different ways, were driving at as the millennium approached? Both poets express an interest, especially in these works, in the idea of looking beneath the surfaces of things and in revealing the textual character of objects, albeit by deploying radically different methods. This may be explained, in part, by referring to Howe's role as one of Gizzi's teachers in SUNY Buffalo earlier in the same decade.[17] Despite differences in craft and formal approach, they both operate within what Howe calls "the confines of poetry," and in their work they both posit a belief in poetry as the embodiment of a "secret language."[18] The poet seeks to probe beneath surfaces to get to this heart of language — to "penetrate / the mystery" to use terms deployed by Howe in one section of *Pierce-Arrow* — but for Gizzi, the positing of poetry's heart's presence is a prolegomenon to all future metaphysics and poetics. Poetry's heart exists, but it is the relationship between its beating presence and the fallen world around him that presents the poet with his most pressing artistic and existential/social dilemma. For Gizzi, then, poetry's heart persists in a world that is "faded"—"The pulse of these times is weak / an anonymous trick, tock / dirty knees and bruised biceps / a smudge below the lip / clavicle swollen from fists" (*SP*, 63) — and "Pierced" serves to affirm its persistence, painstakingly, through a slow and at times self-lacerating interrogation of its deep intentions and procedures. In the same way that Howe's *Pierce-Arrow* is simultaneously haunted by and buoyed up by C. S. Peirce's brilliant failure, Gizzi's "Pierced" (homophonically punning on Howe's subject) invites readers to consider what it means to doubt and delight in poetry's power in the same breath.

In her engagements with C. S. Peirce, Susan Howe breathes life into the logician's work that allows it to be read as a form of radical poetry, a kind of writing that strives to be "nearer to lyricism" than logic. By the same token, Peter Gizzi's work's oblique meditations on and responses to William James reclaim the visionary heart of that American philosopher's thought. In an essay on James in which she responds to the same passage that Gizzi chose as an epigraph for *In Defense of Nothing*, Marilynne Robinson writes,

> Through the whole of his work, James elaborates, without repetition, a philosophic method that never becomes a system or an ideology. This is a conscious and highly meaningful act of restraint, one that paradoxically opens and enlarges the conceptual universe of philosophy. In his *Principles of Psychology* he says, "The only real truth about the world, apart from particular purposes, is the *total* truth." This standard, though impossible in itself, permits and requires crucial inclusions that have not been characteristic of dominant schools of modern thought. He says, "The world contains consciousness as well as atoms — and the one must be written down as just as essential as the other, in the absence of any declared purpose regarding them on the creator's part, or in the absence of any creator. . . . Atoms alone, or consciousness alone, are precisely equal mutilations of the truth." James insists that reality, philosophically understood, must include humankind and all it entails, notably thought itself, on equal terms with all other phenomena. The great ages in history, he says, "have said to the human being, 'the inmost nature of the reality is congenial to *powers* which you possess.'" This may sound to us like an optimism the culture has outlived. But he may only be describing an exceptionalism we dread to acknowledge.[19]

The terms Robinson uses to describe James here may also be applied to Gizzi, and especially to the project of understanding what lies at "the heart of poetry" that is at the center of "Pierced." Gizzi's poetry never "becomes a system or an ideology" precisely because it is always seeking to understand what lies beneath systems of signification and belief — why and how we think and believe what we think and believe, how we are provoked or inspired into expressing our thoughts and beliefs. In this, then, Gizzi's work also seeks to convey a sense of the same "*total* truth" that James set as an "impossible standard" for himself, but it reflects a kind of "optimism" (or "sincerity"[20]) that is dialectically opposed to the darkness and waste of our early twenty-first-century reality. Gizzi insists that poetry's heart continues to beat: "past storefronts / through grasslands, the polluted river [. . .] between tabloid and rib / this keeps on writing" (*SP*, 68).

"The heart of poetry is // an arc between grass blade and gown / hovering beneath an eclipse," Gizzi writes as "Pierced" turns toward its closing lines, conjuring an image of the self in cosmic isolation, poised between moments of terrestrial and celestial significance. Between these spheres of influence we all search for meaning—"The sky participates in our diaries / H for silence and breath, before death"—and it is often in books that this is approached if not found: "a good book / fake book / pillow book / & notebook" (*SP*, 68–69). Gizzi does not end by insisting that truth can be found in any kind of writing, however, nor does "Pierced" neatly uphold poetry's significance as a mode of enquiry into the meanings of self and world. On the contrary, if "Pierced" appears in other parts of the poem to assert poetry's depth and provenance, the poem's conclusion seems to reduce self, world, and poem to a list of "items" by which meaning might be gleaned before the poet achieves a coherent vision of them:

> here is my instrument
> last will and testament
>
> Item: 1 locket, broken, its vowels stolen
>
> Item: to give up loneliness, give up happiness
> (poor *maudit*)
>
> Item: 1 cock, 1 comb, another evening
> a predictable event
>
> two cars race to the horizon (*SP*, 69)

The erotic suggestiveness of these images, together with the hint of betrayal in "1 cock, 1 comb" (= coxcomb?), brings "Pierced" to an ending that is as disturbing, in its way, as Nirvana's "Come as You Are," another text that is threatened from its opening line by a hint of insincerity, the idea that the speaker's true intention will never be fully disclosed to the reader ("No, I don't have a gun").

For Gizzi, however, this refusal of full disclosure at poetry's heart — which may, finally, be the major theme of "Pierced"— is central to his sense of what he has termed the pursuit of "an environment" in his work. As he explained to Steve Farmer,

> I guess what I'm after is closer to an environment, an experience of structure that collects in me. As you said about my work, "the diastolic nature" of it, "filling up and emptying out again." This condition of openness also figures a constant grappling with absence and lack. In a sense all my work is about this reckoning and displacement, enacted through an experience of lyric possession. A form of animism, but in it I would replace essentialism or soul with aesthetics or a core that is empty, a kind of holding open to allow poetic tendencies of cadence, form, tone, coloring to move through a flexible core — a force that is both a construction of self and an emptying of self — not autobiographical but autographical — flexible to accommodate figures, things, voices, documentation; to combine, build and dissolve being, boundaries — to somehow let the poem become itself.[21]

The "environment" of a poem like "Pierced" encloses and accommodates a disparate array of "figures, things, voices, documentation"— from Ovid to Emerson and on to Kurt Cobain — but it is also a poem in which Gizzi creates the "condition of openness" that allows for suggestion and association to inspire and provoke the reader toward open-ended hermeneutic conditions of their own making. Letting "the poem become itself" through a process of slow, close reading and rereading, "Pierced" also allows the reader to assume her role in a ritual of "lyric possession" that is essential to the articulation of the radically democratic vistas of Gizzi's poetic vision.

NOTES

1. In the poem "Will Call," the poet describes silence as "what we make // of eyes, trees and growing vine. It pierces" (*SP*, 48).

2. Peter Gizzi, "An Open Letter of Poetics to Steve Farmer," n.p., www.petergizzi.org/assets/an-open-letter-of-poetics-to-steve-farmer-%281999%29-revised.pdf, accessed Dec. 31, 2014.

3. Ibid.

4. Ibid.

5. The *Oxford English Dictionary* gives four main definitions of the word "pierced" but defines it principally as relating to something that "has been pierced; punctured, perforated; penetrated by a hole or holes."

6. In the first Book of Pope's translation of the *Iliad*, for example, the poet describes how the Trojan warriors "pierced the mountain boar," while in Book IV, the Trojan warrior Simoisius is killed by being "pierced by Ajax." There are dozens of such examples throughout Pope's text.

7. William Shakespeare, *Othello*, 1.iii, 218–19, in *The Oxford Shakespeare: The Complete Works*, ed. Stanley Wells and Gary Taylor (Oxford: Clarendon Press, 1998), 825.

8. Gizzi, "Open Letter."

9. John Berryman, "Dream Song 312," in *His Toy, His Dream, His Rest* (New York: Farrar, Straus and Giroux, 1968).

10. Nirvana, "Come as You Are," *Nevermind* (Geffen Records, 2011).

11. The five canons of classical rhetoric are *inventio* (invention), *dispositio* (arrangement), *elocutio* (style), *memoria* (memory), and *pronuntiatio* (delivery). It might be suggested that Cobain's articulation of "memory" as "*memoria*" is merely a consequence of musical rhythm or singing style, but at no point in the song does he sing "memory" in its standard form of pronunciation. In any case, what matters here is what Gizzi seems to be doing with Cobain's song and the intertextual relationship between that text and "Pierced," where "Come as You Are" resonates with new kinds of significance beyond its original contexts. It should also be mentioned, however, that both "Come as You Are" and "Pierced" are texts of the US American 1990s. It is tempting, indeed, to pursue the allusion to Nirvana's work in Gizzi's poem even further and suggest a connection between the infant and fish-hook imagery on the cover of *Nevermind* and "Pierced."

12. Ralph Waldo Emerson, "The Poet," in *Essays and Lectures*, ed. Joel Porte (New York: Library of America, 1983), 455.

13. Ibid., 452.

14. Peggy Lee, "Is That All There Is?," *The Capitol Years* (EMI Records, 1988).

15. Thomas Mann, "Disillusionment," in *Stories of a Lifetime*, vol. 1 (London: Secker and Warburg, 1961).

16. Susan Howe, *Pierce-Arrow* (New York: New Directions, 1998), 78.

17. In her review of *Artificial Heart* for the *Boston Book Review* (Aug. 1998), Marjorie Perloff argues that the book is "verbally, structurally, syntactically [. . .] written under the sign of the language poets with whom Gizzi studied at Buffalo and Brown," marjorie perloff.com/reviews/gizzi-artificial/#ixzz3NTBREIPt, accessed Dec. 31, 2014.

18. Howe, *Pierce-Arrow*, 101.

19. Marilynne Robinson, "Risk the Game: On William James," in *The Nation*, Dec. 13, 2010, www.thenation.com/article/156641/risk-game-william-james#, accessed Dec. 31, 2014.

20. Several critics and reviewers have commented on the ways in which "sincerity"

works in Gizzi's poetry. See, for example, Dan Chiasson's "The Higher Frequencies," in the *New Yorker*, Feb. 6, 2012. A longer essay on Gizzi and sincerity might read this impulse in Gizzi's poetry in relation to the so-called New Sincerity movement, especially in early twenty-first-century US American fiction.

21. Peter Gizzi, "Open Letter."

PART III | AFFECT AND ALLUSION

15 | LEE UPTON

Recognition, Affect, Resistance

The Poetry of Peter Gizzi

Peter Gizzi's poetry is prescient about the manner in which privacy has been depleted in contemporary culture as surveillance proliferates and rises to levels unexpected by even some of the most wary. For all his examination of ambiguity, doubt, and unfolding categories of understanding, his poetry rides on a momentum in which the real doesn't escape the imagined, nor does the imagined escape the body's intractable demands and unconscious responses. At the same time, Gizzi makes of poetry an experience that resists traceable public selves. He makes the poem a site where it is possible to intuit ungovernable and invisible aspects of human lives, as well as the slippage between affective states, emotion, and imagination. His poems function as invitations to assume sensitivity about areas of being that resonate to sound and image but that are not necessarily conceptualized. In an era of shaming, the trivializing of subjectivities, the commodification of abjection and humiliation, he would return the human subject to a recognition of resources that oppose such diminishment. As he puts it, "One of the jobs for me as a poet is to listen to the exterior world in relation to some otherwise illegible interiority. I want to connect these two and give the resulting relationship a sound."[1] Gizzi alerts us to powers that are attained and experienced and available through, among other means, poems that offer a sympathetic imagining of conceptions as they form through the affect that attends and contours sensory and cognitive recognitions.

By affect, I am referring to what Silvan Tomkins described as those bodily reactions that comprise "the primary motivational system in human beings,"[2] and what Gregory J. Seigworth and Melissa Gregg define as "visceral forces beneath, alongside, or generally other than conscious knowing, vital forces insisting beyond emotion — that can serve to drive us toward movement."[3] The extended descriptions of the workings of affect by Seigworth and Gregg are, it seems to me, uncannily similar to the workings of Peter Gizzi's poems:

> Because affect emerges out of muddy, unmediated
> relatedness and not in some dialectical reconciliation
> of cleanly oppositional elements or primary units,
> it makes easy compartmentalisms give way
> to thresholds and tensions, blends and blurs.[4]

Gizzi's poems, with their own "thresholds and tensions, blends and blurs," resist confining narratives in favor of tracing visceral feeling — as affect accompanies and even accelerates concepts: "When a thought's thingness / begins to move" ("Tradition & the Indivisible Talent," *TS*, 47). In Gizzi's poems, readers are summoned toward their own affective responses rather than simply becoming witnesses to each poem's affective content. That is, Gizzi insists on the prospect of being attuned to the full realm of affects as a common inheritance without assigning affects in his poems as the province of a specialized poetic sensibility. His direct address to readers is often put in service to an imagined projection of interiority that doesn't quite fit what might have been called in earlier eras the soul or notions of selfhood so much as an awareness that is partly neurological and partly antithetical to any prescribed definition. Such a projection splits the seams between conceptions as Gizzi refuses to allocate presence and absence, interior and exterior, to separate spheres.

Medusa thought she was looking at a shield; she was staring into a mirror. Once a beauty, she had become a terror and a paragon of surveillance. At the moment when she sees her image reflected, she turns into a stone artifact and a weapon for whoever will wield her. It's hard not to identify with her. Our reflected images threaten to make Medusas of us all, hardening subjectivities and throwing us back upon representations of surfaces that disguise experiences of affective depth.

Gizzi opens "A History of the Lyric" in *Some Values of Landscape and Weather* with the line "*Objects in mirror are closer than they appear*" (3). Reflections in the mirror ball of contemporary culture shape consciousness and necessarily influence how poems are made and read, Gizzi has argued — and who could fail to be persuaded? As he stated in an interview, "we are constantly witnessing ourselves on TV, in movies, in mirrored windows of storefronts, in magazines and newspapers. . . . We recognize and regulate and reposition ourselves, endlessly flipping from one source to another. There's no reason to exclude this in favor of some kind of static experience of the world. Why should I posit some kind of thought that's etched in stone?"[5] Reflected images may re-limit conceptions of identity, the human as a set of practices that must be supervised, contained, and predicted. In some ways, Gizzi's poems collect affect even as they enact cultural velocity. Megan Watkins, applying Baruch Spinoza's perspective to recent discussions of affect, emphasizes affect's capacity for "leav[ing] a residue, a lasting impression that produces particular kinds of bodily capacities." She draws attention to affect as it may "accumulate, to form dispositions and thus shape subjectivities."[6] By highlighting visceral experiences that resist articulation and propel bodily reactions, Gizzi's poetry functions in the same way Watkins notes that affect functions; the affect in his work gains momentum and "accumulates."

While Gizzi's images defy paralysis by registering motion and the desiring mind, he invests the reader with a heightened awareness of the process through which repeated affective experiences attain conscious recognition: "The action or an act of identifying a person or thing from a previous encounter or knowledge; the mental process of identifying something that has been known before."[7] To recognize is to recall the past, including earlier bodily responses, even while the present impinges. Just as metaphor is built on recognition and its eruptions, given that what is familiar is allied initially to the dissimilar, so too any moment of recognition is characterized by an interruption, as memory, including the memory of bodily reactions, breaks into the present. Both present and past at least momentarily inhabit consciousness. Of course, the process of recognition can be willed; we can make ourselves recall similar experiences and note their characteristics. Yet recognition is frequently unwilled. Without our prodding, recognition may force itself upon us, troubling the present moment by imparting the sensation that we occupy two or more times aligned with two or more occasions and places. Recognition — depending on the context in which it occurs — may stimulate strong affective reactions. Upon recognizing a person who has caused us pain, our bodies may react before we can control our expressions or identify our emotions. Seeing someone we love may stimulate the reverse effect. Expectancy, related to recognition, works in a similar way. Expecting a good dinner may stimulate a host of affective reactions. So too does an expectation of a negative salary review.

Poetry in particular is an attention-seeking device. At even the most elementary level, a reader navigates by means of recognition, matching letters to sounds and concepts. Given the genre's frequent investment in repetitions of sound, image, and sense, recognition in poetry is an intensive force. We're tugged by the experience of recognizing heightened patterns in poetry, meeting and re-meeting similar linguistic and spatial elements. Whereas fiction isn't usually differentiated from other prose through the visual impression it creates, the great majority of poems — including Gizzi's — use visual space and marked lineation to announce their presence as poems. As a result, we may recognize many poems as poems even before we read them.

The ambitious poet may delay the onset of the matching game between the known and the unknown in language, interrupting sequencing so that at least a sliver of the uncategorized is glimpsed, despite any reader's attempt to placate a yearning for resemblances. However ambitious he is, Gizzi presents less jarring juxtapositions than we have come to expect in the work of poets frequently considered to be experimentalists, and the rhythmic and syntactic qualities of his work create an experience that is nearly fluid, even when meanings in his poems fluctuate to the point of doubling back on logic. What otherwise might initiate the experience of delay in this poetry is at points overridden by the quietly insinuating voice he assumes and the silky tassels of his syntax. While the subjectivity that animates his poems is tentative, under threat, and at times defensive, one of his most common tropes — his preference for repeatedly tracing the workings of light — appears connected to the way that thought moves in his poems, as if conceptualizing must continually evade itself, while the lyric poem is tested repeatedly as the purveyor and generator of affective states.

Defending his continued interest in lyric strategies, Gizzi in an interview posed the rhetorical question, "Why should I apologize for, or give up on, one of the most flexible and dynamic forms of poetry?"[8] Like Wallace Stevens, who famously wrote of poetry's resistance to intelligence, Gizzi's poetry creates its own forms of resistance; it resists its limits as lyric, evading ideological complaints that would present the lyric as self-reinforcing, naïve, egoistic, and insufficiently astute in terms of fashioning new poetics that proliferate modes of reading. Gizzi has chosen to reinvest in aesthetic strategies aligned with the lyric's debt to the sonic and imagistic components of repetition and to the interactive affects that a lyric poem can stimulate. If affect is "contagious"—a term frequently invoked in discussions of affect—the lyric poem may be an especially contagious literary form for its rhythmic insistence on musicality and its ability to stimulate bodily responses.

Gizzi's poetry is recognizable in part because of choices he returns to: aphoristic-like statements that prove unstable; definition by negation; a "bleed-through" of his predecessors' language; a reestablishment of lyric obsessions with mortality, nature, and Keatsian "unheard melodies"; and the prominent use of questions, hinge words, phrases, and prefixes to suspend the drive toward settled meaning. We recognize this poetry as well by the way in which panic is muffled, whether Gizzi works with Dickinson's razor or Whitman's wide-toothed comb. The poems don't hesitate to project at least some protective calm for readers; "Lullaby," after all, titles two poems in *Threshold Songs*. In turn, these poems are animated by the act of recognition—recognition of their own strategies, of aesthetic inheritance, and of the way that time may be experienced not only as accelerated in contemporary culture with its proliferation of information and misinformation, but as a presence of sorts, occasionally less as a concept than as a companion capable of inciting and inscribing affective responses. And while conceptions of a self voicing and enacting affects and emotions may be held in suspicion by some of his contemporaries, Gizzi finds a base for understanding in the body, which, as yet, hasn't been erased from discussion.

In most ways, the body operates beyond conscious awareness and in a manner that defies a good deal of manipulation, as any listing of side effects accompanying medical interventions indicates. Ultimately, the body is not amenable to our will. If it were, some of us would live forever. For Gizzi, bodies are presented as permeable, and the categories by which we know them are similarly uninsulated: "Are we not bread-like, soft tissue, heat-seeking, and fragile?" ("A Penny for the Old Guy," *TS*, 51). As "Lullaby" from *Threshold Songs* illustrates in short form, Gizzi advances toward a recognition of what he calls "interiority"— a perception of the invisible but felt sphere of being — through the recognition of physical experience:

> the morning light is in us
>
> a stinging charge in the mouth
>
> this is something everyone feels at least once (4–5)

Gizzi's lines might initially suggest an overwhelming colonization of perceptions: *your nervous system is mine*. Here, mouth and mind are evoked while the external — the light — is internalized. The matter of biology, that is, the body and its affects and organs of perception, is the stuff of poetry through which Gizzi expresses the possibility for an enhanced recognition of interiority. To recognize an interior space becomes an insistent drive, he emphasizes. In *Threshold Songs*, this act of finding an interior reality is characterized as "the whole / vortex of home / buckling inside" (3) as Gizzi conflates depth and surface, one enfolding the other.

In practical terms, we do step into the same river twice; a repeated experience may blunt perception. We recognize a person or object or experience and consider ourselves habituated. Perceived similarity dampens sensitivity and constitutes stale predictability. While Gizzi creates in some cases poignance for the familiar, as in the concluding catalogue of "It Was Raining in Delft"— "Things that have been already said many times: / leaf, zipper, sparrow, lintel, scarf, window shade" (*SVLW*, 81) — in other poems, such as in "The Outernationale," he cites a pastoral impulse gone to seed and explores recognition of the seemingly overly familiar:

> There is that field
> in the window once again
> and to write of this field
> again is certainly a failure
> of any inward rigor
> or life. (*OUT*, 93)

Such lines register dissatisfaction with a lyric formula (the convention of the writer at the window recounting what's seen) yet Gizzi complicates the bald statement. The same field is never quite the same field, his syntax suggests, for the field is described in terms of agency as if the field roams into sight. In the same poem, he writes, "Have you a single / new idea? Yes, / I carry the oldest ones" (95). Gizzi ponders rather than forecloses on the recognized, avoiding a passive replication of experience and riddling the marker lines between past and present, the experienced and the reexperienced. His poems posit the question of how to make recognition active, a source of shared authority — a question that arises in another poem from *The Outernationale*, "A Paper Wind," with its sensitivity to time and place as his speaker notes that to experience similar situations is both "common" and "bizarre." The moon "appeared on cue," and "sank into memory," and women pick up their shawls in a scenario that draws upon familiar tropes. The poem then turns toward contemplation:

> Call it a nation, or a language.
> Call it ourselves standing
>
> in the dark in the wind
> with a friend, it was night
>
> and the book was closing,
> the city was almost asleep.
>
> We gestured toward home,
> we were home. (76–77)

"To gesture toward" is to announce future plans, while the next clause in the sentence announces that "home" is already reached. We can argue for sentimentalist versions of home, except that to be at home in this poem means simultaneously to gesture toward; a poem is made of gestures, which are by definition necessarily incomplete, and necessarily altered by the way metaphor resides in language. A poem is a home of sorts and a site where poet and reader are transformed. In an interview in *BOMB*, Gizzi remarked that he seeks "to find this 'no-place,' where I have the freedom to simply follow the poem and go where it takes me."[9] If he follows the poem and at the same time satisfies "the delicatest ear of the mind," in Stevens's phrasing, Gizzi is listening closely, tracking the language, and rearranging our sense of the poem's origin. Is the poem itself the reader? Is the reader the poem? Writing gives sensuous material form to the invisible and, at the same time, as Elspeth Probyn argues in her discussion of affect, "Writing takes its toll on the body that writes and the bodies that read or listen."[10] Does the amount of concentration a poem requires and stimulates as a form of applied recognition transform the reader into the poem and, likewise, transform the poet into the poem? Gizzi renders this metamorphosis most directly in "Saturday and Its Festooned Potential":

> to be another and oneself
> to be complete inside the poem
>
> To be oneself becoming a poem (*OUT*, 60)

While attuned to representations of time's passing, that ancient trope of the lyric poet, Gizzi enacts the way recognition is experienced in both affective and cognitive terms, as the past intersects with the present and creates a volatile afterimage. We recognize that we are recognizing—and experience a heightened perception of both time and space: *I am seeing this here; I have seen this before; I may see this again in this place in the future.* Reversing this chronology, he summarizes the experience in "Stung" from *The Outernationale*: "To want to go there / and to have been there / and to be there now" (14). The present moment is viscerally colored by the memory of previous encounters. The effect is much like what Gizzi describes in his discussion of Rainer Werner Fassbinder's *The Marriage of Maria Braun*: the director will "cut the scene just before it reaches any resolution, and you come to the next scene, but all of the unresolved feeling of the scene before bleeds into it. It's there as a kind of ghost-image."[11] The clinging afterimages of initial encounters are accommodated in Gizzi's poems as meanings hover rather than alight. Such backlighting from previous experiences is frequently rendered as a halo or nimbus of sorts. In turn, his often-cited images of and references to "ghosting" involve the recognition of forms and perceptions of delineating thresholds. He underscores this preoccupation by titling his fifth collection *Threshold Songs* and through his descriptions of trespassing boundaries in interviews: "Poetry is always about crossing lines, streets, police-barriers, lineages, time lines, taboos, lines in the sand—when it isn't, it's nothing," he has argued.[12] By crossing lines, he may find himself in the intersection rather than on the other side of a conception, while liminal elements in his poems modulate according to affective responses. As Seigworth and Gregg maintain about affect, in words that echo Gizzi's focus on threshold states, "Affect rises in the midst of *in-between-ness*: in the capacities to act and be acted upon. Affect is an impingement or extrusion of a momentary or sometimes more sustained state of relation *as well as* the passage (and the duration of passage) of forces or intensities."[13] In his stated emphasis on crossing lines, Gizzi troubles distinctions and revives elements of the journey to the underworld that obsessed his earliest predecessors, even while he locates the underworld in his own psyche, the body, and in the practice of poetry. As he states, "The ultimate line that poetry has continually crossed is between the living and the dead, or the visible and invisible worlds."[14]

His preference for illuminating the trail of past perceptions acting upon present perceptions is reflected in his rendering of the dead as cotemporaneous with the living. Tellingly, he revisits T. S. Eliot's influential essay "Tradition and the Individual Talent" as "Tradition & the Indivisible Talent"— a revision that evokes Gizzi's preference for evading the hard lines of conceptual categories. Famously, Eliot acknowledges in his essay, "Some one said: 'The dead writers are remote from us because we *know* so much more than they did. Precisely, and they are that which we know.'"[15] Gizzi extends upon this formulation; we are populated by the dead, and their voices are active within us in a manner that physicalizes them as part of the body: "So many strangers / alive in a larynx" (*OUT*, 93). That is, poets of the past don't exactly enter Gizzi's poems as callbacks or half-scrubbed presences within palimpsests. They "bleed in," a term that suggests a saturating and dyeing of the language's fabric with bodily substance: "Melville has bled / into the local runoff" ("From Here Laughter Sounds Like Crying," *OUT*, 106). The nineteenth-century American poets and first-generation modernists Gizzi favors are not obtrusive or explicitly located often by name in his poems, and their language hardly interrupts the rhythms of Gizzi's poetry. The metaphor of "bleeding in" physicalizes the matter of influence and suggests less Bloomian anxiety or misreading than a sense of indebtedness and even a celebration of contemporary poetry's biological roots in its precursors' language.

"Stung" opens with a re-visioning of Whitman's tropes before extending bodily boundaries, thinning the membrane between the physical self and presumably outer reality. The ending with its allusion to *Hamlet* suggests how the seams between inside and outside are enfolded:

> To be and not to understand.
> To understand nothing
> and be content

to watch light against
leaf-shadowed ground.
To accept the ground.
To go to it as a question.
To open up the day inside the day,
a bubble holding air
bending the vista to it.
To be inside this thing,
outside in the grass place,
out in the day
inside another thing. (*OUT*, 15–16)

Syntax reorders perception, embracing the inward and the outward simultaneously, illuminating what Gizzi has called in an interview "the vast spaces inside consciousness."[16] Once again, Seigworth and Gregg describe affect in terms that strike me as applicable to the way Gizzi's poems perform: "With affect, a body is as much outside itself as in itself—webbed in its relation—until ultimately such firm distinctions cease to matter."[17] Gizzi's poems would seek to blow open distinctions between outside and inside, darkness and light, and time as it is perceived and time as it defies perception.

Two of Gizzi's poems in particular illustrate a heightened recognition of interiority. In "That's Life" from *The Outernationale*, Gizzi fills internal space with patterns discerned through imaginative will: the constellations, those most distant of outer realities that become inner realities in the space of the poem:

Remember the day
you first took in the night sky?
I mean really let it enter
and unfold along the interior
when the architecture of the body
resembles a cauldron for a dying star,
twinkle twinkle inside, and inside that
a simple hole. (41)

The same set of images reappears in the collection's title poem (the second poem in the book to use that title) delineating a permeable consciousness within a planetarium of sorts. Images of constellations in "The Outernationale" again enhance awareness of remote realities that can also be figured as internalized immensities:

> Throw back your head
> to the milky tears.
> All types and shapes
> of silent light.
> Here the crab, the bear,
> the dipper, the wheel
> and the little tightnesses
> that keep us wanting.
> The wanting that keeps us
> looking hard into the dark.
> The dark we hope to unpack
> and move into
> that one day
> we might find ourselves lit up. (102)

Both poems afford Gizzi an opportunity, as he has described it, "to give a sound to the invisible world animating [his] nerves"[18] and to dispel final distinctions between outer and inner conceptions through an invitation to "Throw back your head," to be taken into and taken up by forces that cannot be contained. "[L]et it be thought breaking in your view," he asks in "Fragment" from *Threshold Songs* (18). Thought "breaking," as a wave breaks, suggests that thought is in perpetual motion, splitting open the received and allowing the possibility for discovering dimensions of being. In that sense, Gizzi's practice aligns with the perspective on "poetic thinking," which Durs Grübein argues "will make certain places visible for the very first time — individual branches of the otherwise intractable psychic cave system that runs through the bodies of all humans and can be discovered only by a resourceful imagination audaciously pushing forward into still unsecured galleries."[19]

Early on in this essay I invoked Medusa, but I'll end with a reference to one of the most airy creatures of imaginative literature. For all the tough fiber of his musings on meaning, if poets were lined up under Ariel or Caliban, Gizzi would most often be under Ariel's wing for the breathing spaces that open in his poems, for the poems' ascensions, even for their pursuit and embodiment of an ethereal beauty, their adjectival plush, their capacity to enchant and baffle. In *The Tempest* Ariel's voice provokes and disarms. In his poetry Gizzi projects a voice thrown back to us like an echo, for an echo transforms the tone, rhythm, and duration in which words were first spoken. No doubt he agrees with Gertrude Stein, "There is no repetition." An echo delivers a resemblance, not an identity. We listen for the difference as much as for the similarity. As Gizzi remarked in another context, "I am forever fascinated by the space or threshold between seeing and feeling, knowing and not-knowing, and how the fact, and the affirmation, of not-knowing, call it doubt and discovery, can be generative for the creation of meaning in poetry."[20] Gizzi is not alone in this; many poets have argued that the unknown or "not-knowing" is generative. Yet the unknown is limitless territory. Which unknown is calling? What element of mystery is the poet responding to, given that the mysterious unknown is vast, the known miniscule? Yet the unknown is closer than we may at first realize; the unknown is as near as our own bodies. The words and phrases Gizzi uses may begin as familiar, until lines shift and words turn, newly charged, new to their own strangeness, alive to the body's responses and to both the richly bewildering past and the confounding present.

NOTES

1. "Literature Q&A with Peter Gizzi," interview with Levi Rubeck, *BOMB*, *Bomblog* 23, Nov. 2011, n.p. bombmagazine.org/article/6301/q-a-with-peter-gizzi.
2. Silvan Tomkins, "What Are Affects?" in *Shame and Its Sisters: A Silvan Tomkins Reader*, ed. Eve Kosofsky Sedgwick and Adam Frank (Durham: Duke University Press, 1995), 34.
3. Gregory J. Seigworth and Melissa Gregg, "An Inventory of Shimmers," in *The Affect Theory Reader*, ed. Melissa Gregg and Gregory J. Seigworth (Durham: Duke University Press, 2010), 1.
4. Ibid., 4.
5. "In the Moment of Looking," interview with Peter Gizzi by Aaron Kunin, *Rain Taxi*, n.p. www.petergizzi.org/assets/interview-with-aaron-kunin-for-rain-taxi(2003).pdf.
6. Megan Watkins, "Desiring Recognition, Accumulating Affect," in Gregg and Seigworth, eds., *The Affect Theory Reader*, 269–85 (269).
7. *Oxford English Dictionary*.

8. "Poetry at the Threshold: Peter Gizzi on Lyric Selfhood and the Perils of Singing," interview by Ben Lerner, *Poetry*, Mar. 15, 2012, poetry.org, n.p. www.poetryfoundation.org/features/articles/detail/69780.

9. Rubeck, "Literature Q&A with Peter Gizzi."

10. Elspeth Probyn, "Writing Shame," in Gregg and Seigworth, eds., *The Affect Theory Reader*, 76.

11. Kunin, "In the Moment of Looking."

12. Rubeck, "Literature Q&A with Peter Gizzi."

13. Seigworth and Gregg, "An Inventory of Shimmers," 1.

14. Rubeck, "Literature Q&A with Peter Gizzi."

15. T. S. Eliot, *The Sacred Wood* (London: Faber and Faber, 1997), 39.

16. Lerner, "Poetry at the Threshold."

17. Seigworth and Gregg, "An Inventory of Shimmers," 3.

18. Lerner, "Poetry at the Threshold."

19. Durs Grübein, *The Bars of Atlantis: Selected Essays*, ed. Michael Eskin, trans. John Crutchfield, Michael Hofmann, and Andrew Shields (New York: Farrar, Straus and Giroux, 2010), 90–91.

20. Lerner, "Poetry at the Threshold."

16 | DANIEL KATZ

Peter Gizzi's Emotion Machine

"and what memorials what or what is the role of art if any / within your particular emotion machine" (4), Peter Gizzi asks in "Lullaby," the second poem of *Threshold Songs*, and the first of several to imply a musical form in their titles. Gizzi's poems are often — and rightly — praised for their intensity, for their dedication to the lyric charge that Gizzi himself stresses by his very frequent emphasis on song, as topos and model. Often for Gizzi, "song" is at once the buzzing, humming interference of both the without and the within, along with the moment of attentive clarity that pierces it: "There is a spike / in the air / a distant thrum / you call singing" (*TS*, 1). This distance, as is often the case in Gizzi, is among other things the ambience of the body's relationship to itself. The poem continues: "and how many nights / this giganto, torn / tuned, I wonder if / you hear me / I mean I talk / to myself through you / hectoring air / you're out there / tonight and so am I" (1). "you're out there / tonight and so am I" implies a solidarity between the "I" and the "you," locating them on the same plane, but it also indicates the distance of the "I" from itself, and points to an I that only speaks as it hears itself, that is, an I that uncannily "receives" the voice with which it sings. Gizzi's lineage here is one he is happy to point to. The epigraph to *Threshold Songs* is the first line of Samuel Beckett's *Company*: "A voice comes to one in the dark. Imagine."[1] And the importance of Jack Spicer's trope of poetry as dictation is unmistakable in relation to these questions. In his own work on Spicer, Gizzi stresses Spicer's opposition to certain midcentury credos of spontaneity, subjectivity, and authenticity precisely by way of the example of Beckett: "dictation also works as a joust with culturally sanctioned myths of poetic authorship which were definitive in Spicer's time, from confessional poetry to the Beat aesthetic. The very process of dictation is one of vigilance, which is both spiritual practice and materialist tedium, placing Spicer closer to the sensibility of Samuel Beckett than to the automatic writing of the dadaists and surrealists, the first-thought-best-thought of the Beats, or any other form-driven mottoes of the New American Poetry."[2] This "vigilance" is an apt term for the stance of Gizzi's own poetry, which frequently presents itself as a form of intense attentiveness, not least to its own processes of attending, which makes it a poetry of inattentiveness too. For these reasons, one must markedly qualify the many readings of Gizzi as a self-conscious but ultimately unreconstructed poet of lyric immediacy, upholding the values of transcendence in a bleak, postmodern poetic landscape dominated by irony, détournement, and pastiche. Gizzi, like Spicer and Beckett before him, is at his most compelling as a poet of failure. "Try again. Fail again. Fail better" writes Beckett in *Worstward Ho*.[3] In "Pinocchio's Gnosis," a sequence dazzled with color and light, Gizzi writes, "Let it be said I made an attempt to give relief to the dark. It didn't work. Won't work. Don't really want it to work. It's hard to say" (*TS*, 34).

The valences of failure are manifold for Gizzi, but must certainly be related to the "emotion machine" or, to cite the title of an early book, the "artificial heart." That is to say, if Gizzi is definitely a poet who seeks intensity, intensity itself is opened to questioning by his work, for both the poet and the receiver. The moments of clarity and brightness in Gizzi are often also ones of blankness and bewilderment (to use another of his favorite words), in which the values of light and day are suspended. In *The Holy Grail*, Jack Spicer writes, "I have forgotten why the grail was important / Why somebody wants to reach it like a window you throw open. Thrown open / What would it mean?"[4] Similar questions hang over much of the magisterially shining openness of Gizzi's work. "A Panic That Can Still Come Upon Me" is an excellent example of this. Throughout we find instances of this familiar brilliance, of which these are only a few: "If I break into pieces of glitter on asphalt / bits of sun" (*OUT*, 1); "if sunshine hits marble and the sea lights up" (1); "if in the auroras' reflecting the sea" (3); "If the sun sharp and hot and still / but deep and clarifying, walking its boulevards" (7); and in what might be an echo of Spicer, "If behind the grail and new elm / the pink light saying welcome earthling" (6). This poem is one of the most striking examples of a device that has become prevalent in Gizzi's later work, that is, the stringing together of dependent clauses, often beginning with "If." Almost always, these conditional clauses remain grammatically uncompleted by the logical consequence their structure demands. Gizzi has commented on this in interviews with Aaron Kunin and Daniel Kane, explaining to the latter, "Doubt is always generative for me, and here I found that I could revise each statement by interrupting it with a further complication. So instead of completing any single, definitive statement, I chose to keep the movement open and tumbling forward by using a series of conditional phrases."[5] This "doubt," then, quite literally suspends the value of the proffered moments, leaving us grammatically hanging in wait of a resolution that does not come. If Gizzi is very much a poet of subjective registration, recording, and imprinting, in ways that recall the paratactic modes of important predecessors such as Whitman and Schuyler, his use of the dependent clause distances him from such precedents in significant ways. While parataxis eschews syntactic subordination in order to leave each recorded element in a position of equivalence, appearing to suspend judgment in an opening toward what simply "is," it also can shamelessly indulge the fiction of a stance to be imagined as nonsubjective, or beyond the subject, as if the "thereness" of what is recorded were speaking for itself. This is precisely the fiction that Gizzi's work refuses by its recusal of the illusion offered by seemingly neutral grammatical structures and moods. Gizzi's dependent clauses are a form of parataxis, yet precisely, a *modalized* parataxis, which erases the paratactic fiction of the subjectless utterance. At his best, Gizzi mobilizes this grammatical incompletion to open new spaces of instability with regard to the positioning of the lyric subject, to foreground language as an inherently charged vector of investment and desire. In this respect, for Gizzi language is no different than the senses, whose "impressions" it might otherwise be seen simply to record.

That is to say, at the core of all these questions is Gizzi's sense of the somatic, itself the object of so much of his "vigilance." His poems are notable for how they register the transitory as it disappears, becomes gone, but even more so, for their ability to capture the fragility of the moments that the human subject or process not only navigates, but quite literally *is*, as a creature of time, with time its only medium: "tick in *t,* imp of *i,* / the *m* in mountain, *e*'s empire" (*SVLW*, 78). Time in Gizzi is markedly sensible as well as intelligible, very much a process of the body. That said, one of the principal accomplishments of this poetry is its ability to register the embodiment of the perceiving subject without fetishizing a biological/physical/sensory "ground." Gizzi himself puts it this way: "that the sensory data recorded in my poetry is, at the same time, a fiction of consciousness and the physical reality of my nervous system."[6] Or again, "So for me selfhood is also a biological phenomenon, enacted by the body I have to work with; it's my instrument. In one of my poems in this book I say 'the biology that composes I is shared with I.'"[7] The poem Gizzi refers to here is "History Is Made at Night," a ten-part nocturne that begins with the body as site of time's passing:

> Out of the old place and out of time
> the present inches into view
> into prospective blue
> and what the colors apprehend
> in the eye, in the head, here
> revved and pounding night is
> alive to such thinking. (*TS*, 66)

"Eye" and "head" here parallel the "nervous system" and "consciousness," whose relationship Gizzi is interested in probing throughout. This is made yet clearer in the first line of the second section: "The eras come as chemistry. Felt" (67). The stress on chemistry, however, leads to neither of the outcomes one might expect: biological materialism or a phenomenological position based on the primacy of sensory experience. On the contrary, once the emotions no less than the senses are seen as a product of biology, the former become as materially grounded as the latter, and just as the mind can no longer be conceived as the subject of the body, nor can the body as the sensory or sensation be grounded as the source of the mind. Gizzi's poetry constantly rides between these unfixable sites of selfhood and sensation: "A child I became a question / sitting on the grass. / To be told how lucky I am. / An open field. / This corporeal expanse / was a body too / in silver magnetism" ("Stung," *OUT*, 13), or as the poem ends:

> To open up the day inside the day,
> a bubble holding air
> bending the vista to it.

To be inside this thing,
outside in the grass place,
out in the day
inside another thing. (16)

Or again, as he writes elsewhere, "Some say the current in the wall is the ground / some say the nervous system does not stop with the body / some say the body does not stop" ("Plain Song," *SVLW*, 90). In this way, Gizzi's poetry powerfully answers to the real fictitiousness of nerves and consciousness, senses and resonances, but even more, as the lines just quoted indicate, understands senses as always already extrasensory. Lawrence Rickels has written of the "endopsychic sensurround" to discuss the imbrication of media broadcast technology with early Freudian theories of projection, in which "endopsychic perception" is cast out into the world by the subject in the form of religious systems or "the construction of a *supernatural reality*."[8] What Rickels points to here is not so much an externalizing of psychic interiority, but the necessity to rethink the psyche as something other than a conventionally conceived interior space. Without mythologizing, Gizzi's poetry pressures the way the "fictions" of both consciousness and the senses find their locations within and without the various topographies of self, body, mind. Gizzi's somatic psyche floats like a drunken boat through the banal everyday, which — another point of Gizzi's achievement — is arcana. This is not defamiliarization, but rather what is unsoundable within the patently known. This is why "Objects in mirror are closer than they appear": "they are right next to you / in the lanes, hugging a shoulder. . . .

they are closer than comfort
closer than night breaking

over the mountain face

empurpled, its silhouette
ragged, silver

unquantifiable in pixie dusk ("A History of the Lyric," *SVLW*, 5)

At the same time, body chemistry plays a far less theoretical role, as Gizzi's life as a poet coincides historically with the greatest and most widespread chemical intervention in the human "emotion machine" in history — the normalization of SSRI antidepressants, starting with the mass marketing of Prozac in 1987. Given Gizzi's position, the question of the relationship between Prozac and poetry has to be posed, as the implications of the new chemical regimen are, quite simply, that what is most intimate and personal to our own sense of meaning and fulfillment may be more powerfully inflected by molecular adjustments than by song. In a manner resonant for Gizzi, Spicer took Orpheus as the model of the poet: "Orpheus was a singer. The proudest boast made about Orpheus was not that his poems were beautiful in and of themselves.... The proudest boast was that he, the singer with the songs, moved impossible audiences—trees, wild animals, the king of hell himself."[9] And recalling Gizzi's title "Lullaby," one could see the genre invoked there as archetypally "Orphic" in that it is by definition perlocutionary, its goal nothing other than to create an effect, that is, to "move" an audience, if only to sleep. Of course, sedatives do this much more effectively, which is one reason the question of the role of art within the emotion machine remains open. But the possibility of better living through chemistry only points to the fundamental estrangement of what the "I shares with I." As Gizzi puts it in an interview with Ben Lerner, he aspires "to be the ethnographer of my own nervous system."[10]

And all of this means that for Gizzi, the machine is not a closed system. The body and the mind both remain ever present but also virtual, available only as "fiction" because the underlying chemical-biological real quite literally has no meaning. How does the fiction of poetry relate to these other fictions? Writing on James Schuyler, Gizzi notes, "Objects are never as real in life as they appear in Schuyler's poems."[11] This is more than hyperbolic praise; it's also recognition of the way in which Schuyler, despite much of his reception, is *not* a poet simply devoted to recuperating, preserving, or recording the "real world." Schuyler's hyper-reality is not mimetic, or not simply so. In a similar vein, I'd like to suggest that objects are even less real in Gizzi's poetry than they are in life. Witness the last half, more or less, of "Bardo":

The trees the air warms into
a bright something

a bluish nothing into

clicks and pops
bursts and percussive runs.

I come with my asymmetries,
my untutored imagination.

Heathenish,

my homespun vision
sponsored by the winter sky.

Then someone said nether,
someone whirr.

And if I say the words
will you know them?

Is there world?
Are they still calling it that? (*TS*, 77)

This passage moves from the visual, to the aural, to the linguistic, dissolving outlines of forms of mediation as the elements segue into one another. This is typical of Gizzi in that while one comes away from the passage with a feeling of the world's immanence, it is the immanence of how things lose their outlines and names: "a bright something," and a "nothing" that is not blue but "bluish." The words mentioned are "said" but it's not clear by whom, or why, or how they refer to what the poet's words have been evoking, although "whirr" could seem to echo the poem's first lines: "I've spent my life / in a lone mechanical whine" (76). Does this isolation derive from how the mechanical world impinges on and invades a subject who can't find an ideal solitude, or is it the whine of the emotion machine itself? The poem's ability to slide between these alternatives is again reminiscent of the positionings of subjectivity in Beckett, for example, in his short text "Neither": "To and fro in shadow from inner to outershadow / from impenetrable self to impenetrable unself by way of neither / . . . . till at last halt for good, absent for good from self and other / then no sound / then gently light unfading on that unheeded neither / unspeakable home."[12] It is in this context that the name "world" is provisional, and, by extension, so are all the words that we can know the world or ourselves by. This winter poem, like so many others of Gizzi, if reminiscent of a great New England tradition, doesn't freeze into place as those of Dickinson and Stevens often do, but rather seems to melt into a different sort of nothing than that of the Snow Man. It's not clear in "Bardo" that even a Stevensian nothing is there, beyond a bluish instant.

This question of situatedness is at once metaphysical, historical, and empirically concrete in Gizzi, as is brilliantly enacted in his long poem, "Etudes, Evidence, or A Working Definition of the Sun Gear," a poem which, as its final note indicates, is very much about being "à Marseille" (*SVLW*, 78). Throughout, Gizzi at once locates morning breaking in the old port town as well as the cosmological time that allows the "now" of the poem through the medium of the poet's body, as in these lines:

> In the stone port
> the cubed volume of public air floats the plaza,
> the waves near shore startling things,
> a body's slow aperture takes its time
> allowing a ray from three or four thousand years
> to want the present, record the terrain,
> the language and customs of leaves
> in early winter, burnt orange fresco in pieces,
> a blushing cheek on a triangle chip (75–76)

This startling moment of presence, when the body meets the interplanetary sunbeam, is contrasted with the increasing virtuality of the early twenty-first century, which interrupts every ambience based on the proximity of sensory data, or the mind's proximity to itself. So if the poem asks, "How much sun can a body carry" (76), it quickly moves to the mundane, in every sense of the word:

> "Work is no longer a place," said Jorma Ollila,
> CEO of Nokia Oy, "You can do anything
> from anywhere or will be able to soon,"
> walking the streets of Paris.com
> to see Notre Dame.com in the evening light,
> writing a love poem.org to Montparnasse.com
> filled with brassy boulevard talk (76)

The humor here derives not only from the poem's wry insistence that Paris .com isn't Paris, and that therefore, you in fact cannot do *any* anything from just *any* anywhere. It also comes from opening the "place" of the poem to CEO banalities on spatial boundaries and locations. Of course, the Utopia (in the strict sense) promised by the cited phrase is a nightmarish one, threatening to extend the capitalist regime of wage-slavery quite simply everywhere. The poem returns to this phrase a few lines later, in order to reverse it: "Picture this: work is no longer a place / but place is constant work" (77). This is the virtuality that truly underwrites Gizzi's "vigilance," a virtuality much deeper than that which names digital media. And the work required for Gizzi seems much less to establish a grounding to counter this virtuality, than a labor relating to the forms of dis-placement that take us on their ride. As Cole Swensen has pointed out, Gizzi's poems are very much poems of motion, in which the perspective given is clearly in transit.[13] The constant "work" of place, for Gizzi, means constant departure and arrival. Gizzi's poetry is literally transgressive in this way, breaking the heightened enclosure of the poetic space with humor, bad jokes, detritus, and banality — elements that are always allowed the possibility of being nontranscendent, of not helping. Gizzi's poems are full of gestures of breaching, crossing, opening — thresholds — but these crossings, unfoldings, emergences don't always have a self-evident value: "Thrown open, what would it mean?" Yet one of the openings Gizzi consistently thematizes, again by way of Spicer, is the breach into the underworld — a move that shows Gizzi's dialogue with Pound and Williams as well as Spicer and Beckett.

"Why can't I just admit / I'm dead, have been dead / since I met me" (*OUT*, 94) he asks in "The Outernationale," sounding a note familiar to anyone who's read Beckett. For Gizzi too, the writer writes and the poet sings from the space of an unobtainable subjective intimacy and agency that can go by the name of "death." But Gizzi also often spatializes the site of the ghostly voice, sketching it as the realm of history, of ancestors, of inheritance — of all the voices that speak along with us, in our voice, as ours mixes with them: "I am on the other side now / have crossed the river, have / through much difficulty / come to you from a dormer closet / head full of dark / my voice in what you say / . . . . / every thing is poetry here" ("*The ethics of dust,*" "A History of the Lyric," *SVLW*, 6–7). Pound starts *The Cantos* with the "nekuia," with the descent of Odysseus into the underworld, where he meets his mother —"And Anticlea came, whom I beat off"[14]— as he seeks out Tiresias. Gizzi gives us "Basement Song," the maternal underworld in a minor key: "How deep the mother / deep the basement // the body, odor of laundry / the soul of a bug. // The grass inside / the song stains me. // The mother stains me" (*TS*, 37). *Threshold Songs* is then clearly about the threshold between life and death—the threshold crossed by the book's three dedicatees, the poet's mother, brother, and close friend Robert Seydel—but also about the thresholds that separate bodies and voices in whatever spaces they try to negotiate in common. It is a book of traces—stains, odors, and shadows—but also of legacies. "Apocrypha" takes the form of a last will and testament, a twenty-first-century Whitmanian bequeathal of the poet's legacies, numbered one to twenty-eight. Gizzi will not be waiting for you under your boot-soles,[15] but in your pixels: "To Times Roman I give my stammer, my sullenness, my new world violence, form and all that, forms, and all that paper, gusts. Little buttress" (54). But if a will, more than almost any document, places demands on the signature and its validity as a proper stand-in for the dead donor, this one, as the title tells us, is apocryphal, and an apocryphal will is a contradiction in terms, where the "I" erases itself before it can anticipate its departure across the threshold, into death. Perhaps that's why the previous poem mentions, "And now that the things for jack are coming to an end, I'm a nursery rug away from naptime. // Here on the other side, the water grasses waving, deep under" ("A Penny for the Old Guy," 52). This is an obvious reference to Spicer's line, "Now the things that are for Jim are coming to an end, I see nothing beyond it"[16] from *A Textbook of Poetry*, and thus, a nod to Spicer's poetics of dictation and the underworld, as Spicer's poem ends with "The real sound of the dead" and "the noises alive people wear."[17] Gizzi himself, however, explains his entire project best, in the closing lines of the final poem of *Threshold Songs*, "Modern Adventures at Sea":

When lost at sea
I found a voice,
alive and cresting,
crashing, falling
and rising. To drift,
digress, to dream
of the voice. Its
grain. To feel
its vibrations. Pitch.
Its plural noises.
To be upheld

in it, to love.
Whose book lying
on that table?
And where does
the voice
come from?
What life
was attached
to its lift,
to its feint,
its gift of sight.
To understand
oneself. With-
out oneself.
How to live.
What to do. (*TS*, 84–85)

The question of the legacy of writing is presented here not as the trace of a disappeared presence, but as the trace of a "voice" that was itself never entirely emerged from whatever "origin" allowed it to be found. This is the legacy of a network of transmissions, of Spicer's dead men — and women — talking to each other. All the more so, as the poem ends with the words, the book, maybe the voice, of another poet: "How To Live. What To Do" is the title of a Wallace Stevens poem, which offers little concrete advice on either subject. Gizzi's poem suggests that "To understand / oneself. With- / out oneself" is what one must do, to live inside, or beside, or without the emotion machine.

NOTES

1. Samuel Beckett, *Nohow On* (New York: Grove Press, 1996), 1.

2. Jack Spicer, *The House That Jack Built: The Collected Lectures of Jack Spicer*, ed. Peter Gizzi (Middletown, CT: Wesleyan University Press, 1998), 176.

3. Beckett, *Nohow On*, 87.

4. Jack Spicer, *My Vocabulary Did This to Me*, eds. Peter Gizzi and Kevin Killian (Middletown, CT: Wesleyan University Press, 2008), 357.

5. www.petergizzi.org/assets/interview-with-daniel-kane-for-teachers-and-writers-(2000).pdf.

6. "Literature Q&A with Peter Gizzi," interview with Levi Rubeck, *BOMB*, *Bomblog* 23 Nov. 2011, n.p. bombmagazine.org/article/6301/q-a-with-peter-gizzi.

7. Ibid.

8. Laurence Rickels, *The Case of California* (Minneapolis: University of Minnesota Press, 2001), 48.

9. Spicer, *The House That Jack Built*, 230.

10. "Poetry at the Threshold: Peter Gizzi on Lyric Selfhood and the Perils of Singing," interview by Ben Lerner, *Poetry*, Mar. 15, 2012, poetry.org, n.p.

11. Peter Gizzi, "Review of *Collected Poems of James Schuyler*, epc.buffalo.edu/authors/schuyler/schuyler_gizzi_collected_review.html.

12. Samuel Beckett, *The Complete Short Prose, 1929–1989* (New York: Grove Press, 1995), 258.

13. In a piece to which I'm indebted in many ways, Cole Swensen mentions the "fascination with motion" in Gizzi and goes on to specify: "In Gizzi's work, the motion is usually double: both the thing seen and the seeing thing are moving" (109). Cole Swensen, "Peter Gizzi's City: The Political Quotidian," in *American Poets in the 21st Century: The New Poetics*, ed. Claudia Rankine and Lisa Sewell (Middletown, CT: Wesleyan University Press, 2007).

14. Ezra Pound, *The Cantos* (New York: New Directions, 1986) 4.

15. In the final section of *Song of Myself*, Whitman writes, "I bequeath myself to the dirt to grow from the grass I love, / If you want me again look for me under your boot-soles" (247). Walt Whitman, *Complete Poetry and Collected Prose*, ed. Justin Kaplan (Library of America, 1982).

16. Spicer, *My Vocabulary Did This to Me*, 313.

17. Ibid.

17 | DAN BEACHY-QUICK

To Arrive in Zeno's Thought

Reverie On, Thinking In, Peter Gizzi's "A Panic That Can Still Come Upon Me"

If-When, If-Who

There exists a chasm, though nearly imperceptible, between reason and rationality—despite the depth of its abyss, regardless of the extent of its span, every day, heedless, helpless, hardly noticing, with nearly every step we take, we cross and cross it again and again. Or so I like to think. More than a motion of body, it is a movement in and of mind. Though so often the current state of poetic culture chides that reader who wants to ask of any given poem what work it does, what necessity it bears, I cannot help myself from doing so. To merely watch language perform itself on the page bears that meager interest of watching a person's face—be it stranger or lover—as she thinks: something there is happening, we might feel, but to it we have no access. Quietly, subtly, just by holding this image in our mind, another person's face caught in that outwardly blank look of inward attention, we bring ourselves to a primary ethical crisis. Do I trespass? Do I assume? Do I feel jealous, spurned, knowing she is within herself in ways I cannot join or enjoy? Do I risk asking her of what she's thinking and so dispel the vision?

Or do I see for myself with her eyes what in the dark, electric recesses behind the eyes seem almost to fill with? Do I imagine in myself what I suppose she is imagining and so possess for myself the vision that had been her own? If so, what of this experience is mine? — the face with thinking on behind it.

Stranger still, to be brutally honest, to confront myself not in my self-knowledge, but all I know of my own ignorance — should I stare at my face in the mirror, would I feel the same mystification, some banal horror, that to my own mind my access is just as obscure? Do you wonder, as sometimes I do, that the very page the poem is printed on is just such a mirror, and in watching another mind go through the work of thinking, you see demonstrated back to yourself the dark difficulty of doing the same? Do we gaze into the face of the thinking page and learn to think ourselves, or do we find that rational desire to discover the shared point of expressed connection severed by reason's ever-inward obscurity? And yet —

And yet, against this labyrinthine blank amazement of consciousness, as Peter Gizzi shows, as he knows or strives to know, "we ask that every song touch its origin / just once" (*OUT*, 2). We do this asking in words that torment the boundary between inner life and outer expression. *Origin* opens the fundamental paradox of Gizzi's vision in the long poem that opens his collection *The Outernationale*. Perplexing and illuminating the entirety of "A Panic That Can Still Come Upon Me" revolves the ongoing crisis of source, of origin, an idea that insists that every utterance mimic and repeat some first utterance, some initial calling out aloud that not only pulls from within the mind those thoughts gathering to themselves the awkward garment of words, but mines through all that inchoate echoes through perception and memory and insists the same must urge the world toward cosmos. Origin in its deep paradox lives so deep within us and our songs that it feels true to say that it exists outside of ourselves — but it is an outside found only within. The poems I love most bear this audacity: they risk becoming the thing they pursue. In seeking to touch origin just once, a poem cannot help but become — just once — an origin in and of itself. I might call this work "devoted betrayal." But maybe not. Maybe that's easy; maybe it's coy.

Peter Gizzi begins his poem: "If today and today I am calling aloud" (*OUT*, 1). The simple line opens us to complexities. "Today" posits *now*, the given world in a span of time, and so our ability to experience it, to wander in it, to have something of it, some proof stored away in nerve or mind. Its relation to time is reasonable, adding to the storehouse of individual experience so easily, if so erroneously, labeled "fact." But here "today" doubles. At once, "today and today" offers a sense of urgency, as if repetition creates insistence. It also implies sequence: that the second "today" is not the same as the first, but each day is a source of itself, a new *now* that requires the same call to be given not merely again, but again for the first time; the position of the singer is to sing always the same song for the first time. Lastly, with more difficulty, "and today" posits within time another time, a day within the day, a repetition uncanny in its placement that suggests simultaneity and containment both: the other world that is, as Paul Eluard suggests, found only within this one. Adding to the Talmudic depth of the initial "calling aloud" is the phenomenological work the line knows it must accomplish. Evoking the ancient invocatory mode, it also marks within it difference; for here the call is without end, to no god or goddess, but instead, in the very language of its own utterance, these words must create the world in which their cry can be heard. Gizzi ushers us into a poetic mode deeper within us than memory can chart; and then subtly, honestly, ethically, creates shades within that bright archaic light which reveal not only that an ongoing relation with origin lives within this day of our living, but another day lives there, too. The day in the mind. The day of the mind. Reason's viceroy that precedes the beginning of the ancient song with the philosopher's most basic word of conditional conjecture: *if.*

That word undermines the reality it posits, and hearing it, we feel that specific kind of doubt best described as conceptual realization. I can imagine it, I have an idea about it, a conceptual range in which it is true — but what is the reality of such ambiguities, such etherealities? Unlike more immediately poetic imaginings, *if* connotes the world of logic. We hear, it cannot be helped, some theoretical *then* biding its time in reason's anteroom, twiddling its conceptual thumbs, just waiting for the cue, after the comma, to make its appearance to muted, if still relieved, applause.

But not here. Gizzi holds off that reflex of the reasonable mind. He offers us no *then*, but more necessarily, more beautifully, only a *who*, only a *when*. In doing so, he opens a space of consideration in his poems very few poets are capable of creating. He lets thinking become something another can enter, a work so intimate as to verge into the erotic (if by the erotic we can understand the absolute crisis of the ethical, point of greatest reality not of ourselves, but the sought and loved other). Within the cogs of reason, he points out the asymptotic distance that cannot help but threaten the gearing of logic's *if-then* clockwork. He pushes us into that imperceptible chasm and, as a poet must, accompanies us in our fall. There we experience that which poetry alone might offer us who love it, who feel we must continue to learn how to love it, who enter into the page not for the comfort of intimacy, but the difficulty of it: that break where every *if* tends toward a *when*, where each *if* reaches toward a *who*, and reason is replaced by rationality. That *ratio* within rationality reminds us of the need for each one of us to continually renegotiate the relations that keep us connected to all that in our "unhappy discovery, too late to be helped"[1] we've come to find is real: that *if* we exist, we exist. And so does the world.

Gizzi's repeating *if*, prevalent in the poem's first section, but also its dominant prosody throughout, posits at the far end of conditional conjecture actual being. He casts us into a necessary form of doubt (the very marker of poetic faith *rather than* that which must be suspended to be poetically devout) whose beginning pushes out from hypothesis into this astonishing if unsupportable fact: that the end of poetic possibility is nothing less than ontology. When the poet calls out aloud, "today and today," the teleology reaches past the bounds of logic, and promises the *who* and the *when* of not yet encountered actuality. It is as if we have learned, so the poem has taught us, how to step into the face of the thinking other — not a trespass, but a kind of inevitability, if not an invitation entire.

Solar Sincerity

To find we "have arrived in Zeno's thought" (*OUT*, 1) steps us into eternity even as it crashes us into the day. Zeno saw, millennia ago, that time presents us with a crisis we cannot escape. Not mortality. Death is not an event of life. Of it, we can reason; but to it, we have no rational connection. Time's crisis — or our crisis in time — bears itself out in Simone Weil's thinking: Time doesn't exist; we live in time.[2] Of the arrow sprung from the taut bow, Zeno realized that even as it coursed through the singing air, it would never, could never, hit its mark. Taken in any instant of its flight, the arrow is caught in the ever-decreasing distance between its point and the object of its aim. Living in time, we see the arrow pierce its target. Being within this other time that doesn't exist, we can glimpse that infinitesimal gap nothing can cross that exists between us and all with which we're in relation. Then we glimpse the arrow in its rational life: the arrow that is still even as it flies. Time hurtles its barb toward us, and we suffer this impossible harm of being caught always in the safe forever of being about to be struck and finding, even as we realize it cannot be wholly true, that we already bear the wound.

Gizzi puts us into such paradoxical motion because he so adroitly sings its qualities. Against the personal so bound by time that he finds "our loves anointed with missiles / Apache fire, Tomahawks" (*OUT*, 2), he sings also from the impersonal vision where "sunshine hits marble and the sea lights up" (*OUT*, 1). More so than Zeno's arrow, light alone is that piercing principle by which our open eyes every instant of waking are wounded. The syllable *sun*, the syllable *sea*, sung at the first moment of conscious realization, inscribe within their own utterance that fugitive *now* that contains within it its own undying source; simultaneously, we recognize, we remember, we recall through the mind's vast storehouse those images of like experience that in our own minds provide some timely match, some sense of experience not as original, but similar, familiar, a reasonable approximation, and the near mythic spell dies. Gizzi's *if* creates in the opening, longest section of "A Panic That Can Still Come Upon Me" the profound ambivalence of sincere poetic experience: an arrow that in stillness flies, a world that is and is not, time's own agony, the eye open to the sun's light, and the I that in that light by others may be seen.

Light and time — light that is particle and wave at once, time that exists and does not — infuse the second section of Gizzi's poem with a strange measure of perception:

> There are things larger than understanding
>
> things we know cannot
> be held in the mind
>
> If the sun throbs like a drum
> every five minutes
>
> what can we do with this
>
> the 100,000 years it takes a photon
> to reach the surface of the sun
>
> eight minutes to hit our eyes

If every afternoon gravity and fire
it's like that here

undressed, unwound (*OUT*, 4–5)

The eye, organ most attuned to the instant, sensitive in its periphery to the slightest animal motions and light so dim that some stars can only be seen out the corner and disappear when looked for directly, encounters the very moment only by utilizing a medium so ancient each particle of it contains more then the whole of human history. Gizzi sees that to witness anything — be it "nothing save Saturdays at the metro" (*OUT*, 2) or "the auroras' reflecting the sea" (*OUT*, 3) — unfolds within the lived moment a span of time so large as to reach back past the mind into some mythic origin in which minutes, hours, and years exist in such overabundant supply that to measure them would be a fool's reasoned effort. If we learn to see truly, and if we can admit the unfashionable truth that still we turn to the pages of poems in order to accomplish just this good — work of seeking clarity, work of seeking cosmos and in so doing seeking order — then vision becomes not an experience that occurs *in time*, but something stranger, more essential, nearly magical, in which sight itself is filled with time, overflows with time, and any given image that fills the eye does so, for all intents and purposes, eternally.

When we open our eyes, we see by a light that makes infants of us all. I want to call such light *sincerity*, if by that word we can hear not a tone, not a style, but a focus — as of sunlight poured through the intensifying curvature of a lens (and so the open eye, just such a lens, finds a way to inscribe in the mind what it sees, as a child burns his name with a magnifying glass onto wood). Robert Duncan, in "The Truth and Life of Myth" (from which the title of Gizzi's poem derives), speaks toward the necessity of the poet to see according to such sincere light: "The roots and depths of mature thought, its creative sources, lie in childhood or even 'childish' things I have not put away but taken as enduring realities of my being."[3] The open eye, ever awakening to its own enduring infancy, must be the blossom that feeds the deep root that, in refusing reason's dark self-sufficiency, grows the ratio that connects the bright sun to inner thought.

And yet —

A Panic; or, Built in the Gap

And yet, Gizzi's poem strives for honesty, humility, where an easier route might seek "wisdom." As Duncan praises Socrates because "he knew he did not know," Gizzi too holds himself within the bounds of his knowledge so that he can all the more feel the limit beyond which knowing ceases. Over the course of the first three sections of "A Panic That Can Still Come Upon Me," a gradual drift takes place, one nearly infinitesimal, almost asymptotic, as hard to discern as the gap between reason and ration, seen first, maybe best, in the difference between the first line of the poem and its variation that opens the third section: "If today and today I am speaking to you, or" (*OUT*, 6).

Against the first section's "calling aloud," which signaled invocation and so opened within the poem's initial gestures that ushering in of mythic time in which time-as-such seems not to pass at all, here Gizzi diminishes, deflating the ancient, epic gesture down into the human scale of "speaking." The word implies social intimacy, asserts the political and personal realities that bind us together and that depend on speech as a shared construct of creating interpersonal harmony. The poem widens the scope of its relational, rational life past the mythic epistemology of the poem's initiating crisis while not repudiating it. Gizzi's particular genius may well reside in such subtle shifts — felt best in how that pendulous "or" gathers within itself contradictory possibilities without negating the first. He moves the poem away from those philosophical paradoxes inherent in finding "we are still in motion / and have arrived in Zeno's thought" (*OUT*, 1) not as a departure, but to show more thickly, more complexly, the ways in which no area opened in a poem is able in the same poem to be abandoned. Gizzi holds himself to a kind of fate. It is a fate of the poem, a fate of the poetic page, in which Form as a metaphysical reality, more than form as an act of prosody, requires that every word establish a fact from which the poem can find no honest escape. Within the difficulty of such an idea, we brush again against the type of paradox Zeno establishes as part of the impossible order of the actual world.

A poem is, in its way, similar to Zeno's arrow. The song in every moment of its singing reaches that socially intimate "you" to whom it is addressed; at the same time, it is caught eternally in that address to the nameless You whose intimacy resides not in the interpersonal, but in the impersonal. Gizzi's poem is but one stunning example of such work; a poet, as was Duncan, who realizes that the "poem that moves me when I write is an active presence in which I work."[4] If the point seems minor, it does so only because it gains its greatest meaning within the asymptotic infinitesimal interval the poem opens within itself as the boundary-gap between mythic timelessness and daily life. There "every struggle ice-cream truck tinkle" interrupts "the cosmological" (*OUT*, 7). Gizzi knows, and so he shows, that the poet dwells within the poem he writes, and is subject to the world, and every law of that world, the poem creates. He is not some god removed from the reality he makes. The very crux of the poetic act requires that we take the meaning of *poeisis* (to make) as seriously as possible, for only through it do we come to the necessary impossibility of the poet's position: one is maker and made at once, creator and also created. Stranger still, the poet exists most essentially within the work he's made: the poem. "Creative immediacy," as Duncan puts the effort of the poet's highest aspiration, inverts teleology in such a way that origins and ends intermix and cannot be told apart. Nor can one assume, as the reasonable *if-then* logic would assert, that cause precedes effect. Form subverts sequence in such a way — absurd it may be, it feels most fair to say — that the poem precedes the poet.

And yet the poet within the poem doesn't reside in security, doesn't dwell forever in that eternity housed within its stanzas. The poem attunes the poet to the dangers it manifests within itself: this world that is worlds, this singular plural, this place in which reality is invested by imagination and made more real for the fiction. Duncan writes, "In the world of saying and telling in which I first came into words, there is a primary trouble, a panic that can still come upon me where the word no longer protects, transforming the threat of an overwhelming knowledge into the power of an imagined reality, or abstracting from a shaking experience terms for rationalization, but exposes me the more."[5] Gizzi's poem is written within this panic. His *if* creates the nervous ambivalence inherent in Duncan's primary trouble. Rather than try to resolve that crisis, Gizzi allows us to experience — through the gift of the poem creating the experience it suffers — what it is to be "bound by the most ignoble cords / if squatting in time" (*OUT*, 7). The tension of those cords pulls taut by the rational connection between the world of myth and this one in which, like squatters in an abandoned house, we take our impermanent residence until the Author kicks us out. Duncan feels the terrifying strain in which knowing and imagination fray and pull apart — a place in which the grounds for keeping the ratio between unlike worlds in relation dissolves. That fear then sentences daily life to the mere drudgery of time's indifference. The same fear lets us live merely fictional lives unconnected to the actuality that must — for life to be a substance poetic — interfuse and confound thinking, feeling, imagination. But to live within the panic is to refuse to allow the ratio to break, and it is there, as Gizzi writes, where "these gaps I feel are also the gaps / I am built inside" (*OUT*, 7). He has gained the feel of not-to-feel, that Keatsian ideal that also is Keats's highest reality, in which the subject hovers before us divorced from subjectivity, sensing absence as actual, negatively capable, in which perception turns apperceptive, and to feel gaps within oneself is also to discover oneself in the gap.

I Am a Bridge I Am Standing On

It is within perception that the fourth section of "A Panic That Can Still Come Upon Me" opens:

> A branch and the scent of pine in summer
> the bridge and the water in the creek
> the stones and the sound of water
> the creek and my body
> when hair and water flowed over me (*OUT*, 9)

Each subsequent line moves through a different sense: smell, sight, sound, touch. In this turn toward a more traditional lyric mode, one that finds in its own history a means of escaping the philosophical paradoxes that torment the poem entire, Gizzi gives us what we thought could no longer be our own: the immediacy of the nervous body as the very base of our epistemological life. The world he here describes is discovered in the mind via the senses that bring it to him, and the one omitted sense of taste finds presence in the orality of the words themselves, bearing in them the sensuous nature of that which they name. The body is immersed in the material it discovers, a unity with the world reminiscent of the eye opening always to its infancy. We find ourselves, as does the poet find himself, at the midpoint between those mythic ur-parents whose authority in the deep recesses of our minds still reigns supreme: father-sun and mother-earth. Just to sense the world one is in is to be an obedient child.

But thought rebels — even if it does not want to do so. That conditional syllable, *if*, returns — significant, increasingly so, of the inner life of mind that pivots from the senses and their connection to the very stuff of the world to the resources stored in the mind's dark.

> If I am a bridge I am standing on, thinking,
> saying goodbye to myself
> when I stood by the water in life
> thinking of my life, pine boughs
> the hill next to water *(OUT,* 9)

In curious parallel to the previous section, in which "or" hovered at the end of the line, not in denial, but in accumulation of alternate possibilities, so this "thinking" energizes the poem's deep crisis at the very point at which we hope we might have put it away. That crisis is nothing less than consciousness itself. It is as if by *thinking* alone that the body is lifted out of the water and put onto the bridge. Hints at the self gazing at its own image riddle the stanza. "I stood by the water in my life / thinking of my life" vacillates between deep interiority and a continuation of the landscape given us in the section's opening stanza. In both cases — imagining myself so as to think about myself, or staring down into my own reflection in the water — we catch ourselves in this moment of trouble, one that happens so quickly as to be nearly unnoticeable, in which that old construction, *I think, therefore I am*, reveals not the unity of self, but its doubleness.

But this same force of consciousness, that removes us from the elements of which we think, becomes the structure of our contemplative life, and in so doing, expands as it must the limits of those experiences that count as actual. A poem such as Gizzi's here offers profound example. "I am a bridge I am standing on" gives paradoxical image to our thoughtful, poetic condition. Not only does the line imply that, just as the poem must become the world it discovers and so the poet must be the bridge he stands upon or crosses, it speculates (for what certainty is there?) that this thinking life is the one that, even if it lifts us out of the river, offers us that means of connecting unlike points together, and making of the unified, immersive world, something more vastly grand, the reality of the metaphoric one. That reality requires impossible bridges to be built over fathomless abysses. But to think that bridge is solid is to over-assume if not to miss the point entirely. For the bridge — if Gizzi's line is to be taken as literally as we must — is itself a nervous thing, constructed of the very perceptions whose drift into apperception removed him from the cool creek. This apperceptive life, that inward work in which the senses learn to perceive themselves, each in such inexplicable ways self-aware — sight that sees that it sees — creates that very complex of imaginative realization that is a furtherance of actuality rather than a separation from it. Only then does our initial hope become manifest: that the work of the poem participates in the reality to which it also contributes. Then the moment of the day — say, the tinkling of the ice-cream truck — indeed is part of the cosmological.

Symphonic Dailiness Is Felt Order

In the final section, when Gizzi says simply, "I'm not stupid" (*OUT*, 10), we might hear in the declarative mode a humble realization beneath the tonal play. I hear, at any rate, the declaration of a mind knowing it works, even if it can posit that only in the negative, only in the colloquial, only in the bratty. The line sounds like the answer a middle-school child gives to a question she thinks below her intelligence. At the same time, it speaks in, and of, self-realization. Hidden within it is some extension of Keats's parable about the nature of soul creation:

> I will call the *world* a School instituted for the purpose of teaching little children to read — I will call the *human heart* the *horn Book* used in that School — and I will call the *Child able to read, the Soul* made from that *school* and its *hornbook*. Do you not see how necessary a World of Pains and troubles is to school an intelligence and make it a soul?[6]

Gizzi's panic, inherited as it is from Duncan, is but another version of Keats's "world of pains and trouble." Unlike easier modes of poetic epistemology, such thinking never assumes the soul, or the mind, or the human heart are givens in the human condition. For Keats, the heart inscribed upon by the damage of the world is that book the mind comes to read, and when the words are understood, the soul begins. It might be, asked by a teacher some question, say, "What is the color of the sky?" that the soul would answer, appropriately enough, "I'm not stupid."

Hearing that line in such a way allows us to enter most fully into the achievement of Gizzi's long poem — though perhaps "achievement" is the wrong word. As Duncan describes hearing a teacher of his read Blake aloud, a poem undoes our expectations of what marks it as good: "what was important was not the accomplishment of the poem but the wonder of the world of the poem itself, breaking the husk of my modernist pride and shame, my conviction that what mattered was the literary or artistic experience."[7] So too does Gizzi's poem seek to break the husk of our pride; it does so by breaking the husk of its own. That break in pride allows the poem's thinking to become our own, and vice versa, allows ours to become its. We see behind the eyes of the other what those thoughts picture; we put on the voice, so to speak, as a child might put on a mask — save the magic of the poem is that the mask is worn behind the face, and its image ends up being our own.

Once again, that syllable *if* looms. The doubt it contains becomes a winnowing force just as it becomes the figure that damages the heart in such a way that the intelligence of the poet moves past the anonymous and beyond the personal to some soul-like entity that contains both at once, coexisting opposites. Such a poem seeks its power not to control the world it creates, but far more importantly, to open itself to those powers — mythic, cosmological, and daily, mundane — in which our basic sympathies must be continually reawakened to the magic they are most persuaded by. It is a magic of being within non-being, of time within timelessness, of actuality within image, where

> There is my body and the idea of my body
> the surf breaking and the picture of a wave (*OUT*, 11)

NOTES

1. Ralph Waldo Emerson, "Experience," in *Emerson's Essays* (New York: Harper Perennial, 1981), 292–323 (292).

2. Simone Weil, *Gravity and Grace* (London and New York: Routledge, 2002).

3. Robert Edward Duncan, *The Truth and Life of Myth: An Essay in Essential Autobiography* (Fremont, MI: Sumac Press, 1968), 13.

4. Ibid., 23.

5. Ibid., 13.

6. John Keats, *Selected Letters of John Keats* (Cambridge, MA: Harvard University Press, 2005), 291.

7. Duncan, *The Truth and Life of Myth*, 13.

18 | ANTHONY CALESHU

Divine Allusion and Refraction

Beginning, Ecstasy, and the Dead in the Poetry of Peter Gizzi

In the Beginning

"In the beginning God created the heaven and the earth," begins Genesis, moving through the creation of day and night, water and earth, beasts and fowl, man and woman, who have dominion over all on "earth" and "air."[1]

"Song of the Interior Begin," the first poem of Peter Gizzi's first book, *Periplum,* begins in "sky," lands on a "tree . . . / a twig   O branch   O earth," refers parenthetically to "(psalm)," then on to "day spills / to where is   O water" before commanding "Begin!   Begin!" It concludes with an anatomical reference to sight and an emphatic sense of sound (via four hard-rhyming sound strings):

Are eyes
shy?   O iris   O onyx
Into blouse of

Air go there ! (*PEROP*, 3)

In this poem, sung from the vantage of the "interior" self, the "I" is conspicuously absent, a mere phoneme in "eyes" and "iris." Still, in the presence of "go" and "there," we just might hear the "I" sing its own beginning, a discombobulated sampling of the familiar phrase: "There but for the grace of God go I."[2]

The idea that Gizzi's poem uses language that alludes to Genesis and transfigures the coinage of sixteenth-century evangelical preacher John Bradford is a deliberately loose one; but it's in this looseness (and loaded-ness) with language — allusion, suggestion — that this essay's argument is built: an exploration of Gizzi's refraction (divergence, substitutions, amendments) of certain tropes, rhetoric, and images of religiosity, particularly Judeo-Christianity, in order to claim and affect the poem as a devout space. I use the word "devout" in the same way that Gizzi, parenthetically and without capitalization, uses the word "psalm"— outside the religious worship of a godhead, but as a way to expose Gizzi's sacred feelings about poetry and the language that poetry claims as its own interior subject. To say this is to enter the territory of Wallace Stevens, a poetics of "miraculous influence" (tying God to the imagination via Blake and other poetic forefathers), to use the phrase Edward Clarke uses in his discussion of Stevens's late poem "Final Soliloquy of the Interior Paramour."[3] Stevens's legacy, as it applies to Gizzi, could be explored at length (and has been by others),[4] but it's enough for this essay to note that Gizzi's poetics shares what Clarke refers to as Stevens's awareness "that words . . . are transient things made by God."[5] In a later poem, Gizzi will write, "I am fighting for love / but I need a new god" (*ARCH*, 32), a statement that clearly expresses that no lower-case supreme being will do the job; what will do the job is a new language. Paradoxically, that new language has to come in tension with the "old language," as he writes in another poem (*ARCH*, 5).[6] Beyond Genesis and Bradford, "Song of the Interior Begin" returns us to Stevens's old language, not only in the "interior" of its title, but for other semiotic structures as well; "we make a dwelling in the evening *air*," writes Stevens (italics mine),[7] not to mention both poets' interest in *light*:

> Light the first light of evening
> (Stevens, "Final Soliloquy of the Interior Paramour")
>
> day spills
> (Gizzi, "Song of the Interior, Begin")

In another poem, Gizzi will literally speak the light ("If to say light to inhabit light," "Fin Amor," *SVLW*, 82), but in "Song of the Interior, Begin," light resides just below the surface, at that place of *beginning*, where the old language is readily heard as biblical stock: "And God said, 'Let there be light,' and there was light."[8] Though Gizzi pursues interior space to be a "day spill[ed]" site of religious-like invocation, he ultimately refracts God in favor of finding in language and poetry the possibility of contemplating human consciousness and existence. How to constitute the beginning — of thought, of life on Earth, of death beyond? — remains the great unknown for neuroscientists and poets alike. And it's necessarily altered by Gizzi via a language that is as playful (punning, intertextual, substitutive) as it is precision engineered: the first two lines of "Song of the Interior Begin" refer to "hydraulic / spring," putting the man-made metal coil in homographic tension with the natural world's season of beginning.

Gizzi's interest in metaphysical *beginning* is everywhere in his work: from a reference to compositional process (see "Beginning with a Phrase from Simone Weil," *SVLW*, 95), to a springboard for contemplation: "If Monday a whole world begins" ("Pinocchio's Gnosis," *TS*, 33). To *if* is to speculate ("if to build a flower, if naked at the base of a sycamore, if animated camouflaged bark" continues "Pinocchio's Gnosis"), or, to put it another way, to *if* is to not know "what happened in the beginning," as in these opening lines from another early poem employing biblical sentiment and language, "Thirty Sentences for No One":

> It begins with socks in a drawer and continues to laundry bags to the future. In the Food Mart everything is above the child's head. Always looking up. Always lifting our eyes to heaven. The horizon is your mother's repose on the divan after daily chores . . . I was born on the third chapter of the novel forever asking what happened in the beginning. In the beginning sky. In the begining earth. (*PEROP*, 110)

To be "born on the third chapter of the novel" is to return — via memory — to that point of awareness of one's world: to "socks" and a mother who cares for those socks. It's the domestic sphere this time that is conflated with the mythic Judeo-Christian one, and it moves us from where the "I" was begat (to use a biblical term), and through a life of evolving consciousness of self: "I have grown into the sweater my aunt gave me . . . I have grown into this sky I wear about my shoulders everywhere I am" (*PEROP*, 110). I'll explore Gizzi's use of the biblically derived "I am" later (from Exodus 3), but note here and now that it appears four times in this poem which explicitly complicates real-world experience by reconstituting "I am" in the context of "mind," "body," and, what seems a religiously refracted sense of God's existence within us, *spirit*.

This, by no means, comes to us as a straightforward rendering of what one thinks or is. "The hamper in the mind," continues Gizzi in "Thirty Sentences for No One," "is endless." All that dirty laundry of our childhood (literal and metaphorical) that defines our experiences either smells up the *mind* or gets washed until it's transformed into something we misremember, something we can live with as adults: "Let me work my image into soil and treebark and leaf-stem. This is not who I remember." As the poem begins to conclude, Gizzi's disrupted sense of self is further complicated with the introduction of "you" and the I's relation to that "you": "In my dream you are real. I am as one who each day stands behind the tapestry and receives the needle to pull the thread taut and pass it back through. The design is no one's" (PEROP, 110). The "I" assumes the faint figure of a godhead; the self is active in a type of creation "design"— albeit assigned almost absently, self-effacingly, to no one.

At the poem's end, Gizzi puts in tension a subjective vision of various selves and a desire to metaphysically understand distinctions between life and death (that ultimate domain of God), though just whose death is being contemplated is obscured: "Then I read 'death is not being unable to communicate but no longer being able to be understood' or something like that." The emotional pathos of "Thirty Sentences for No One" comes in its perpetual *beginning*: of life, of death, and even of sentences that are conjoined but also parataxically and peripatetically distinct as new starts of grammatical expression. The beginning documented isn't personal so much as an attempt to document what it means to begin, to become conscious of self, subject, and audience; and/or conversely, what it means to eschew self, subject, and audience in order to perpetually begin again and again (again, these are "Thirty Sentences for *No One*" [italics mine]). To treat a life in time, in concrete terms of rendered image and object, is to move us from states of "beginning" to *becoming*, even if it means declaring the "self" insufficient in the process in the penultimate lines: "I am incomplete. Indeed" (PEROP, 110). This propels the poetry into ecstatic territory.

Ecstatic Bewilderment

A paradox pertaining to "knowledge" is voiced by the Ecstatics and their descriptions of enlightenment. Here is St. John of the Cross:

> It is an act of His great Clemency
> That keeps us there uncomprehending,
> All knowledge transcending.[9]

Within the transcendent space of the poem, Gizzi shares the idea of perpetuating knowledge by not knowing. The title poem "Periplum," also from that first collection, is exemplary for Gizzi's questioning of what it means "to know":

> The person who knows where
> has made an accurate study
>
> of here
>
> As to know
> implies a different reading (*PEROP*, 6)

Thereafter, knowledge runs parallel to "faith" as the subject of diminishing returns:

> Somewhere
>
> faith enters
> and must be pinned and sighted
>
> A church tower is good for reference
> but losing ground (*PEROP*, 6)

There are few more famous sentences that put knowledge and faith into relationship than Kant's: "I have . . . found it necessary to deny *knowledge*, in order to make room for *faith*."[10] Gizzi's interest is not in contemplating religious "faith," but in contemplating faith in language, specifically poetry, and how one can both earn and proffer it. To put one's faith in such is to begin to contemplate, as he does in another poem, "How to live. / What to do" (*TS*, 85; not incidentally, lines cribbed from Stevens's poem of that title).[11] For Kant, denying knowledge is a denying of certain aspects of science; likewise, Gizzi explores the potential of science as perhaps offering a substitution for faith: "satellites orbiting the earth"— before ultimately rejecting them as "perhaps too grand" (*PEROP*, 6).[12] Gizzi concludes "Periplum" with a declaration of pressing on despite, or rather in favor of, bewilderment ("unknowing") that might well rival the Ecstatics:

> And never mind about the bewilderment.
>
> "I'm at sea" (*PEROP*, 6)

Faith in the significance of our interior consciousness can be overwhelming to the point of "bewilderment," but therein one can experience transcendence by accepting that state of being lost, that is: being "at sea." "I'm at Sea" is a disembodied language fragment, spoken by no one and spoken by everyone. Either way, being "at sea" seems more rehabilitating than debilitating, an ancient emblem of our world of (re)generation. Or, as Gizzi puts it in "Modern Adventures at Sea," being "lost at sea" can be "an adventure" where one can find a "voice":

> When lost at sea
> I found a voice,
> alive and cresting,
> crashing, falling
> and rising. To drift,
> digress, to dream
> of the voice. Its
> grain. To feel
> its vibrations. Pitch.
> Its plural noises. (*TS*, 84)

In interview, Robert Casper cites Gizzi as saying, "At best, I'm always in the process of narrating my bewilderment in the world, language, in society."[13] As Gizzi has it,

> not-knowing . . . plays itself out in the writing of poetry. . . . plays a signal role in the production of reality in a poem . . . not-knowing can come to some sort of order that allows meaning to happen, mystery.

Paradoxes, or "asymmetries" between states of knowledge and states of being, drive the tension throughout all of Gizzi's work, as we find in the more recent poem, "Bardo" (*TS*, 77). Judeo-Christianity may provide the dominant foundation for Gizzi's poetics of spiritual enquiry, but Gizzi's "Bardo" refers to that intermediate Buddhist state between lives on Earth whereby one's consciousness is disembodied after one takes a final outer-breath. "I come with my asymmetries, / my untutored imagination. // Heathenish, // my homespun vision / sponsored by the winter sky" (*TS*, 77). To be "heathenish" is not only to *not* belong to a widely organized religion, but it's also, in the old English of Germanic origin, to "inhabit open country."[14] Gizzi's poetry is of this openness — less about proclamation than wonderment: "Is there world? / Are they still calling it that?" (*TS*, 77). Partiality is declared for the imperfect, unrefined, and the misunderstood within the context of its cogent opposites: "I am not sure about meaning / but understand the wave" (*TS*, 76). It's also in this poem that we're given a direct reference to St. John of the Cross, a reference of oxymoronic wonder for the fact that the "I" no longer has the saint in his life: "No Juan de la Cruz singing / 'I do not die to die'" (*TS*, 76). Meaning, like the imagination, like one's vision, like the paradoxical religious paradigm that we live to die and die to live, is constructed through the very manipulation of reality and fiction in language.[15]

In interview with Levi Rubeck, Gizzi tells us that

> the sensory data recorded in my poetry is, at the same time, a fiction of consciousness and the physical reality of my nervous system. Sometimes I think that I'm only an ethnographer of my nervous system; it's certainly peopled. So what do I mean when I say that I want to be clear and to suggest something larger? One of the jobs for me as a poet is to listen to the exterior world in relation to some otherwise illegible interiority. I want to connect these two and give the resulting relationship a sound.[16]

"Knowing" and "not-knowing," listening to the "exterior world" and processing it through an "illegible interiority"— or what Stevens, in "Final Soliloquy of the Interior Paramour," dramatizes as "[our] feel[ing] the obscurity of an order, a whole, / A knowledge"[17] — constitutes Gizzi's "fiction of consciousness." But Gizzi's construction of consciousness isn't artificial in an ironic sense. Instead, he uses the "sound" of language to expose that being "at sea" is a legitimate response to both one's interior self and one's external world. To be "peopled" is to be plural: in voices, points of view, meanings, and subjects. Consider, for example, how the title of a poem like "Periplum" moves us through the plurality of existence in *time*: "Periplum" being an allusion to Pound's early twentieth-century use of the word (Canto LIX), derived from the ancient Greek *periplus* to refer to an account of traveling by ship, and leading to the use of the idiom to be "at sea" (first coined in the eighteenth century).[18] Likewise, consider the use of a deliberately unfixed language of those "plural noises" cited in the aforementioned "Modern Adventures at Sea," a poem whose penultimate lines present the paradoxical ideal —"To understand / oneself. With- / out oneself"— before concluding with those very declarations/ questions already cited, lines that both document and disturb one's nervous system: "How to live. / What to do" (*TS*, 85). As Stevens-inspired declarations/questions, they represent a mode of disjunction (with religion/faith) and spiritual confusion. As (re)citations, they are emblematic of the "plural noises" or voices that come to Gizzi via the "air," and that he uses to populate the devout space of the poem, a space of both ecstatic confusion and "clarity": "I am silly with clarity. / Born of air I am . . . I remake my life" ("Eye of the Poem," *TS*, 12).

Calling the Dead

In the air of Gizzi's poems, the dead, in Jack Spicer–derived parlance, can exist as "ghosts": "When I say the ghost has begun / you understand what is being said," Gizzi begins "True Discourse on Power" (*TS*, 61).[19] In the afterword to his edition of Spicer's *Collected Lectures*, Gizzi writes that "Spicer's "logos/low ghost" pun (referring to the Holy Ghost) situates God within the language; this gets extended when Spicer speaks about his own poetry as "largely using the *incarnation* of Jesus as a metaphor for poetry" (italics mine).[20] Because Gizzi refers to a Spicer poem as a "word game with Whitman, Dickinson, and the Bible," and further writes that "[t]he presence of the divine can only be accommodated, invoked, and addressed through linguistic structures, and hermeticism only furthers the process,"[21] I'm keen to continue pursuing Gizzi's own "incarnational" poetics, where the dead are given voice and body among the living.

An early poem such as "Despite Your Notices" refers to his father's death in the crashing of "flight 405" and becomes an occasion to bring the two states of being together: "I mate with these voices on the other side" (*PEROP*, 37). In "Hard as Ash," also from that first collection, Gizzi breaks deeper ground: "Do I have to die for you then to hear these lines / that I make profligate and plaintive for you" (52). Self-sacrifice is the very stuff of more than just Judeo-Christian doctrine, and returns us to the paradox that the end can be a beginning. In the case of "Hard as Ash," that beginning is represented as a "morning" (a conscious homophone of *mourning*):

> The morning you woke up and for a moment forgot
> to call them "dead," it was the morning
> of the poem. (*PEROP*, 48)

"Hard as Ash" is a meta-discursive, polyvocal poem, in which Gizzi slips in and out of the persona of a Miss Newcombe, who "combusted before a roomful of people while waltzing in a dance hall," we're told in the epigraph (*PEROP*, 48). The poem's deliberately multiple "I" serves as a way of "chumming for clarity / and a pronoun to share" (50); note the different conceptions: from the bathetic to the Beatles to the biblical: "I am sad and strange" (52), "I wanna hold your hand" (52), and "I am who sent me" (54) are just a few. With this last "I am," Miss Newcombe presents as a godhead of sorts, with direct reference to Exodus 3:14: "And God said unto Moses, I AM THAT I AM: and he said, Thus shalt thou say unto the children of Israel, I AM hath sent me unto you."

But Gizzi's quest isn't to articulate God, so much as to refract Him, to riff off and diverge in order to pursue ideas about transformation, from one state to another, between different forms, between the living and the dead, about interior consciousness, again, about *becoming*. A fuller context from the poem follows:

> [. . .] Now bring about words to heal.
> Sentences to bring about change. Grammar
> that shall inhibit evil? Now: clap hands.
> Father tell me what you think
> of me. Is it a face or a factory? Come here
> to distinguish the burden of a smile. Attached
> to lightning. As the world was revealed then returned
> to your sandwich. I am who sent me.
> Obvious and otherwise a trope was. This laundry
> line strung from year to year reaches
> to the woman I am becoming. (*PEROP*, 54)[22]

In Gizzi's construction, language is what changes us, even saves us. It's what allows us to be heard and to hear long after we've died (combusted or not). In *words*, *sentences*, and *grammar* there is a semblance of the divine, as in the Gospel of John: "In the beginning was the Word, and the Word was with God, and the Word was God" (John 1:1). "Light," in its myriad forms, is in abundance in this poem —"I have come to tell of the discrepancies of light" (*PEROP*, 27) — and light (in the form of "lightning") is "attached" to a "face" and a "Father," sending us again to John: "Then spake Jesus again unto them, saying, I am the light of the world: he that followeth me shall not walk in darkness, but shall have the light of life" (John 8:12). The "reveal[ing]" of the world is indeed a revelation, and it's one where a "trope" such as "I am" stands in to witness our turning away from such a revelation — offering, instead, the observation of the banal act of eating a sandwich. And who makes our sandwich? The same woman who does our laundry, that familiar woman from "Thirty Sentences for No One" (also look toward "Hypostasis & New Year" as discussed later in this essay), making "Miss Newcombe" love object, godhead, and, indeed, mother figure. And though an occasional phrase such as "O mommy is it true?" allows us to hear the voices of children, the poem is much wilier than to propose womanhood (or motherhood) as its subject (*PEROP*, 50). Motherhood opens the poem out so that gender fluidity and physiological transformation during reproduction can be contemplated: "When all forms have been / emptied can I begin? I doubly derive my body . . . I knew then this body was not invincible" (*PEROP*, 53). To "doubly derive" is to enthusiastically exclaim one's derivation, but also to extract a body from a body. Once that body is extracted one has to care for it, to ask questions not only of oneself but of those children being cared for: "Are you shy are you lost / are you blue? Is there nothing left for you? . . . From boneyard to schoolyard . . . waiting in a parking lot" are our mothers (*PEROP*, 54).

Almost 20 years later, in his fifth collection, Gizzi's mother has passed away and he directly takes on the elegiac form as he straddles the personal-impersonal divide between the living and the dead. The book's dedication reads, "For Robert, for Mother, for Mike / called back."[23] As Gizzi tells us in interview,

> "Called back" is not only Dickinson [her last spoken words, and also inscribed on her tombstone], but Orpheus. As we know, the ultimate mission of the poet in the Western tradition is to bring back the beloved. For a poet, it also means bringing back all our beloved unread, unsung poets of the past and reanimating them.[24]

In dramatizing the disintegration between the binaries of death and life, however, Gizzi isn't just interested in bringing the beloved back, but in assuming the posture of the dead, one gone over to the other side. Here's a short compilation of lines from some of the poems in *Threshold Songs* that project the self as living among the dead and dying:

> I am rooted but alive.
> I am flowering and dying. ("Tradition & the Indivisible Talent," *TS*, 46)

> now that you're gone
> and I'm here or now

that you're here and
I'm gone or now
that you're gone and
I'm gone . . .
I am just learning
that threshold
and changing light ("Analemma," *TS*, 16–17)

I am alive today, yes alive not being alive

being with the lost ones and the living lost
("On Prayer Rugs and a Small History of Portraiture," *TS*, 26)

And when I died
I entered a moonlit canvas
from the late 19th century
. . . .
I am no more
alive than canvas.
No more dead than alive.
("Moonlight & Lace, after Blakelock," *TS*, 44–45)

In his essay, "'One's Own Sad Stead': American Elegy as Self-Elegy," the American poet-critic Richard Jackson cites a great variety of American poets who've written self-elegies, including some of Gizzi's fore-poets Emerson, Dickinson, and Whitman.[25] Jackson defines self-elegy as follows:

> The dominance of the self in American poetry is a defining characteristic. Then indeed, why not think of the essential American elegy as "self-elegy," a kind of poem where the author projects his or her own death? . . . But the American self-elegy tends to use, as the best American poetry seems to, a first-person "I" that serves, as Ralph Waldo Emerson suggests, as a "transparent eyeball," a self that observes, discovers its shortcomings, and attempts to transform and transcend what it sees in an empirical rather than philosophical way.[26]

While useful, it's important to note that Jackson's definition isn't completely comparable with Gizzi's poetics (which is as philosophical as it is empirical). There's also the fact that Jackson is more interested in self-elegy as a way to epiphany, a way to "transcend death and mortality," where Gizzi's speakers are more prone to slip between the thresholds of life and death in less knowing ways.[27] One must also remember the purpose to which Gizzi's speakers "imaginatively enter [their] . . . own death"[28] — to reanimate the dead (Orpheus-like), but also to sing their own refracted songs. Again, it's useful to go to Gizzi in interview:

> The ultimate line that poetry has continually crossed is between the living and the dead, or the visible and invisible worlds. When I read the long-gone, the nearly-gone, the newly-gone, or the contemporary writers who are unread, unsung, under-appreciated and misread, my job is to animate their work, to bring it to life, and to bring it into my room (call it my body, my nervous system, my consciousness). And as that work has been brought to another life within my consciousness, bent and refracted in my own voice, I can call them back. The dream of a phenomenal syntax that can reanimate that which has been otherwise lost to the world . . . an animated and affective kinship you simultaneously discover and build in the construction of voice — your own voice.[29]

"Hypostasis & New Year"

And yet, questions about the impossible process and dubious validity of voicing, of *singing*, appear throughout: "For why am I afraid to sing / the fundamental shape of awe," Gizzi's speaker asks at the opening of "Hypostasis & New Year," the poem I want to dedicate the last section of this essay to discussing (*TS*, 6). In interview, Gizzi answers: "Madness? Overindulgence? Failure?"[30] All of these are risks in theory, but in practice what we get is the conflation of fear and awe so that the poem becomes a projection of divine sublimity.

"Hypostasis," by philosophical definition, refers to the substance, essence, or underlying reality of something.[31] By medical definition, it refers to a settling of solid particles (often of blood into an organ). In Christianity, it refers to any person of the trinity, or in some theological debates, the *indivisible* idea of the essential person of Jesus in which His human and divine natures are united.[32] All three of these are functional in a poem that works through a complex series of unpunctuated questions. Consider the openings that begin the early stanzas:

For why am I afraid to sing
the fundamental shape of awe (*TS*, 6)

. . . .

Of what am I afraid
of what lies in back of me of day (6)

. . . .

Then what of night
of hour's unpredicated bad luck (6)

. . . .

Of what am I to see these things between myself
        and nothing (7)

It's not until the poem's penultimate stanza that the speaker introduces another figure, a figure who ultimately grounds the speaker with, if not exactly a subject, a motivation to "sing": "Mother where from did you leave me on the sleeve / of a dying word" (*TS*, 8). In the Christian tradition, the Mother of God is second in importance only to the Father and the Son she bears. In John's gospel, Christ's dying words are both to his mother—"Woman, behold your son"—and to the disciple standing next to her—"Behold your mother" (John 19:26).[33] Gizzi's poem offers us an inversion; it's the mother who has left the speaker with a "dying word." The "word" is very much the "world" for Gizzi, and his speaker makes several references to both throughout: from "the vowels themselves free" (*TS*, 6), to his "love [of] the unknown sound in a word" (8), to a question that asks "what world and wherefore / will it shake free" (6). The *freeness* of the word/world subject is referred to in a line that follows the speaker's cry to his mother: "I compel and confess open form" (8). Where Charles Olson, in "Projective Verse," might be said to compel Creeley's idea that "FORM IS NEVER MORE THAN AN EXTENSION OF CONTENT" (Olson's capitals), Gizzi's "confess[ion]" situates the idea within religious doctrine.[34] Olson's "open form" refers to an energy transfer between poet and reader, and for sure, Gizzi is interested in this transfer: "Dear Ghost. Dear Reader," he writes imploringly in the aforementioned "Hard as Ash" (*PEROP*, 48). But in "Hypostasis & New Year," the energy transfer is between speaker and subject, son and mother, a relationship both divisible (due to the singular element of her "[leaving]") and indivisible, due to the speaker's need to stay with her in that liminal region between life and death, past and present: "Of what am I afraid / of what lies in back of me of day / these stars scattered as far as the I" (*TS*, 6).

Gizzi's signature-scattered "I" (a homophone of the expected "eye") pushes us into the territory of a divided self; but that same "I" also serves to unify mother, son, and "word," a not-so-distant holy trinity for a poem of seemingly spiritual concern for that line between life and death. The line drawn is one between the real world and the "shadow world" where "when a thing comes back / comes back unseen but felt and no longer itself," as the speaker states (*TS*, 7). This "spirit" or ghost-like condition is exacerbated in a poem that fleetingly exploits the temporality of what it means to occupy external and internal space. We move from nature's "willow spear" and "sky," to what seems a hospital room "between curtain and stain," to "street," "desert," and finally to the underworld, "hell," at the poem's conclusion (*TS*, 7–8). The speaker's self-declared fear, as he begins the poem, starts with an expression of disassociation with "song," but there's also the fear of disassociation with his progenitor subject (his mother). The "I"'s challenge, within the terms of this poem, is to reconcile himself to living with that fear of disassociation by singing songs that bridge the past and present (and future), songs that bridge the living and dead: "it is the old songs and the present wind I sing" (*TS*, 8), he tells us; and it's at this point that we hear the New Year song of the poem's title: "Auld lang syne," literally meaning the "old long since," that "song of farewell." To fear, and to live with fear, is the speaker's predicament. In its most viscerally interior moment, it forces him to assume "hypostatic scenes of breathing":

> Of what am I to see these things between myself
>   and nothing
> between the curtain and the stain
> between the hypostatic scenes of breathing
> and becoming the thing I see
> are they not the same (*TS*, 7)

"Hypostatic pneumonia" refers to pulmonary congestion due to the stagnation of blood in the dependent portions of the lungs. To see death on the other side of the curtain and to become it (to drown in one's own blood), and to not fear it, to occupy that space between worlds (to live in the "shadow world"), is the goal of this threshold song, which slips between the threnodic and the will to sing "awe" with ecstasy. The "underlying reality" of the "I"— as son, as Christ figure (resurrecting the dead mother), as one who bears witness to these "hypostatic scenes of breathing"— is one of literal empathy. The speaker assumes his mother's dying, extreme in his need to "[become] the thing I see" in order to "sing." To exist on one side of the curtain, and then to see the "stain" on the other is, again, both of this world and not of it: though we're not given them, we see blood stains from pneumonic coughing. We might also hear a reference to the "stain of original sin" as in Adam's, as in that which Mary, the Blessed Virgin Mother, according to Catholic dogma, is without.[35] It's only a few poems later in this collection that we'll read, "The mother stains me," which furthers the idea that Gizzi's poet is stained by the dead, and it's a stain to revel in, not to scrub away.[36]

The trace of religious tropes continues at the end of this poem, when the speaker tells us, "I can't remember if I made a pact with the devil when I was young / when I was high" (*TS*, 8). Though he doesn't say it, the reader knows what the speaker is thinking: that he *must've* made a pact to live while all those others around him are dying (again, in the context of this book, mother, brother, friend). To make a pact with the "devil" might eventually send this earthly (less-than-divine) speaker's soul to "hell," but even this isn't feared as the poem finds its way to redemptive whimsy in its conclusion:

> hell
> I'm just taking a walk in the sun in a poem
> and this sound
> caught in the most recent coup (*TS*, 8)

The casualness of the rhetorical "hell" is such a smooth transition for us to contemplate the warmth of the son/sun (another homophonic pun) in the underworld. The conception of such a space that unites the dead is not, of course, only of Judeo-Christian tradition but exists in the realm of classical mythology or even other canonical and heretical religious traditions, from Buddhism (recall "Bardo," discussed earlier) to Gnosticism, as Gizzi refers to in interview:

> I am interested in what I would like to call the borderless nature of selfhood and tradition. I don't know where it begins and I end or where I end and it begins . . . Every time someone dies it's not an isolated incident; it brings back all the other deaths that I've experienced. It's layered just like one's voice is layered. Here it gets interesting because my bibliography, all the books I've read, is a huge part of my autobiography. So when I say the borderless nature

> of selfhood and tradition, what I'm saying is that it's not only the people I've lost who are called back through the book, but so are all these other poets that I've read throughout my life. They're here in the language, in the layering of the voice.[37]

Gizzi's poets include David, the "sweet psalmist of Israel" (Psalm 108:1); Moses; the Gospels' Matthew, Mark, Luke, and John; Asaph; Ethan; St. John of the Cross; and God, Himself, speaker of the "word" that gets written down in the Old and New Testaments.[38] At the end of "Hypostasis & New Year," Gizzi puts sun and song together in a poem that aspires to live with the fear of singing "awe," that hopes to engage that threshold between living and dying, between knowing and not knowing what's to come. "I love the unknown sound in a word," the speaker says earlier in the poem, and that unknown sound is the sound this poem, like so many of Gizzi's poems, works to capture. It does not pretend to know how that sound works to convey emotion, consciousness, or spirituality. Instead, it aims for the poetic equivalent of transubstantiation — the desire to lift language to that divine state where it is not merely sign or symbol, but an intrinsic demonstration of transformative change: language in the state of *becoming* a poem.

"I contend that the greatest poetry can make us apprehend that God, the centre of religious celebration, whatever we call that nothingness or darkness, incomprehensible and vast in its own being, is a force within man," writes Edward Clarke in *The Vagabond Spirit of Poetry*.[39] Gizzi's poetry is not one of religious art, but it aims to be of religious "awe." His poetry refracts religious principles and texts to explore Clarke's interior force within, a force that is demonstrable of our capacity to change ourselves via language. The aim for a "mutable" poetics — in "Hard as Ash," Gizzi calls for a "mutability of forms" (*PEROP*, 50) — is an ambition for sound to meld into words, into poetry, before (re)turning us to the beginning of sound, of syntax breaking, and subsequently mending, syllables of poetic instrumentation. The last word of "Hypostasis & New Year"— the homophonic and onomatopoetic "coup"— gives us the sound of a dove: the form by which the Holy Ghost descended. It's also emblematic of the tensions that Gizzi's poems thrive on: existing at the threshold between something beautiful (even peaceful) — a "song" of bird-like cooing — and a language that is likewise sudden and violent in its disruptions, its coup-like overthrowing of our sensibility and experience. By the end of this metaphysical metapoem, the desire to replicate that "unknown sound" has sparked a song of becoming, a song of ecstasy, a song that calls back the dead. With threnodic timber, Gizzi projects a loved one's death onto his speaker's own "self," complicating the exchange between resurrecting the dead and going down into the underworld to resurface, if not with the deceased, with new songs to sing.

NOTES

1. Genesis, *King James Bible.*

2. The idiom stems from "There but for the grace of God, goes John Bradford," attributed to sixteenth-century English evangelical preacher John Bradford. See Bradford's entry in *Oxford Dictionary of National Biography.*

3. Edward Clarke, *The Vagabond Spirit of Poetry* (Winchester, UK: IFF Books), 185. Among other things, Clarke's wonderfully wide-ranging book explores poetry in terms of spirituality. "From the perspective of our world we discern poetic influence as if it flows from the past when in reality it discloses on earth the future in eternity. Ultimately, or anagogically speaking, poetic influence denotes miraculous influence. . . . In distinctive ways, great poets speak from the same source" (186–87).

4. See essays by Altieri, Perloff, and Middleton in this volume. Middleton notes Gizzi's "Saturday and its Festooned Potential," for its "tink tink," as explicitly dialoguing with two of Stevens's most famous poems, "Sunday Morning" and "A High Toned Old Christian Woman."

5. Clarke, *The Vagabond Spirit of Poetry*, 198.

6. The most noticeable example of Gizzi's interest in "the old language" comes in his long poem, "Field Recordings" (*ARCH*, 5–21). See also Gizzi's discussion about his interest in "the old language" in "An Interview with Peter Gizzi," ed. Anthony Caleshu, Periplum Video, www.plymouth.ac.uk/periplum, accessed May 11, 2016.

7. Wallace Stevens, "Final Soliloquy of the Interior Paramour," *The Collected Poems of Wallace Stevens* (London: Faber and Faber, 1959), 524.

8. Genesis 1:3, *King James Bible.*

9. hpb.narod.ru/tph/TPH_SJCR.HTM, accessed Sept. 15, 2014.

10. Immanuel Kant, preface to Critique of Pure Reason, trans. and ed. Paul Guyer and Allen W. Wood (Cambridge: Cambridge University Press, 1998).

11. Wallace Stevens, "How to Live. What to do," in *The Palm at the End of the Mind: Selected Poems and a Play* (New York: Knopf, 1971), 235.

12. Aside: Willis Barnstone's translation of St. John of the Cross directly refers to science in its refrain: "I remained not knowing / Beyond all science knowing." hpb.narod.ru/tph/TPH_SJCR.HTM, accessed Sept. 15, 2014.

13. Robert N. Casper, "Interview with Peter Gizzi," *Jubilat* 14, poems.com/special_features/prose/essay_gizzi.php.

14. www.oxforddictionaries.com/definition/english/heathenOld, accessed Jan. 7, 2015. "English hǣthen, of Germanic origin; related to Dutch heiden and German Heide; generally regarded as a specifically Christian use of a Germanic adjective meaning 'inhabiting open country,' from the base of heath."

15. "Death and the imagination equals life itself," writes Gizzi in "A Telescope Protects Its View" (*OUT*, 24).

16. Levi Rubeck, "Q&A with Peter Gizzi," *BOMB*, bombmagazine.org/article/6301, accessed Sept. 15, 2014.

17. Stevens, "Final Soliloquy of the Interior Paramour," 524.

18. Ezra Pound, *The Cantos, 1–95* (New York: New Directions, 1956).

19. Peter Gizzi, ed., *The House That Jack Built: The Collected Lectures of Jack Spicer* (Middletown, CT: Wesleyan University Press, 1998), 189, 197. In addition to Spicer's self-declared practice of "dictation" or "transmission" from "ghosts," Spicer refers to "spooks" and "Martians."

20. Gizzi, ed., *The House That Jack Built*. Spicer is referring specifically to his long poem, "A Textbook of Poetry" (21). Gizzi's reference to the "logos/low ghost" pun that functions in that poem appears on page 185.

21. Gizzi, ed., *The House That Jack Built*, 184, 178.

22. Note: Gizzi's instruction to "clap hands" shares its context of language, song, mortality, and God, with Yeats's "Sailing to Byzantium": "Soul clap its hands and sing, and louder sing / For every tatter in its mortal dress" (cited with thanks to Edward Clarke).

23. The same phrase, as Gizzi alludes to in interview, appears on Dickinson's tombstone.

24. Caleshu, "In Conversation with Peter Gizzi," *PN Review* 209, 39.3 (Jan.–Feb. 2013): 50.

25. Jackson's citations of twentieth-century poets (Bishop, Plath, Merwin, Levine, James Wright) are not in the Poundian/Stevens/Spicer lineage in which I read Gizzi, but his sense of self-elegy is useful nonetheless. Aside: it would be interesting to consider Gizzi's elegies in the context of Spicer's "Imaginary Elegies": "It is as if we conjure the dead and they speak only / Through our own damned trumpets, through our damned medium" (from "Imaginary Elegies," *My Vocabulary Did This to Me: The Collected Poetry of Jack Spicer*, ed. Peter Gizzi and Kevin Killian [Middletown, CT: Wesleyan University Press, 2008]), 27.

26. Richard Jackson, "'One's Own Sad Stead': American Elegy as Self-Elegy," in *Radiant Lyre: Essays on Lyric Poetry*, ed. David Baker and Ann Townsend (Minneapolis: Graywolf Press, 1997), 21.

27. Ibid., 29.

28. Ibid. See also Spicer's "Orpheus" poems.

29. Rubeck, "Q&A with Peter Gizzi."

30. Lerner, "Poetry at the Threshold," www.poetryfoundation.org/features/articles/detail/69780, accessed Jan. 25, 2017.

31. Aside: Pound uses the word "hypostasis" in the libretto to Canto LXXXI: "there came new subtlety of eyes into my tent, / whether of the spirit or hypostasis."

32. www.thefreedictionary.com/hypostasis, accessed Sept. 15, 2014. See also Joseph T. Lienhard, "Ousia and Hypostasis: The Cappadocian Settlement and the Theology of 'One Hypostasis,'" in *The Trinity: An Interdisciplinary Symposium on the Trinity*, ed. Stephen T. Davis, Daniel Kendall, and Gerald O'Collins (Oxford: Oxford University Press, 2002).

33. In other gospels, Luke's Christ cries, "Father into your hands I commit my spirit," and in Matthew and Mark, the self-elegy looms largest: "My God, My God, why have you forsaken me" (Matthew 27:46; Mark 15:34).

34. Charles Olson, "Projective Verse" (1950), in *Collected Prose*, ed. Donald Allen and Benjamin Friedlander (Berkeley: University of California Press, 1997), 240.

35. *Catechism of the Catholic Church*, Vatican Archives, www.vatican.va/archive/ccc_css/archive/catechism/p1s2c1p7.htm, accessed May 6, 2016.

36. See "Basement Song" (*TS*, 37): "The grass inside / the song stains me. // The mother stains me." Also, in "Despite Your Notices," mid-poem, we're told "[that day] came and went without the anxiety of anticipation and its finality of passage and unannounced significance stains us good."

37. Caleshu, "In Conversation with Peter Gizzi," 50.

38. Though this essay doesn't speak of Gizzi's poetry as one of enthusiasm, its relationship to knowledge and the poetic voicing of God would be a relevant study. Though I have to relegate it to a footnote (as also done in my introduction to this volume), there is great value in reading Gizzi alongside David Herd's *Enthusiast! Essays on Modern American Literature* (Manchester: Manchester University Press, 2007), 5: "In enthusiasm the poet will be 'out of his senses and reason is no longer in him' . . . 'God himself is the speaker, and . . . through (the poet) he is addressing us' (Herd's citations are from *The Dialogues of Plato*). The opposition is clear: the mental state known as enthusiasm, the state of poetic composition, is counterposed to reason, and requires that the poet be in some sense 'out of his senses,' from which it follows for Plato . . . that the poet, or the enthusiast generally, doesn't know anything . . . Except, of course, that the poet does know something. He or she does in some sense know the god, the inspiring divinity" (5).

39. Clarke, *The Vagabond Spirit of Poetry*, 18.

19 | AARON KUNIN

Love at Both Ends of the Western World

Gizzi conceives the poetic sequence "Fin Amor" as a western in reverse (*SVLW*, 82–96). I will begin by sketching the plot that he reverses. In classical Hollywood film, the western genre follows one of two plots: either the beginning of the West, or the end of the West. In the beginning plot, civilization comes to the wilderness; cowboys travel west, bringing with them the codes and tokens of civility. When they succeed, the place becomes civilized (end of West), and they must depart, traveling further west. Although their careers prepare territories for civilization, the cowboys do not belong in civilization, and in fact prefer wilderness to civilization.

The Man Who Shot Liberty Valance tells a story about the end of the West. In the film's "legend that becomes fact," a lawyer played by James Stewart replaces the historical figure of the cowboy played by John Wayne, who has done the dirty work of civilizing the territory. John Wayne is "the man who shot Liberty Valance," but this act is nearly suicidal, for Liberty Valance represents the wildness of the West, the liberty that the cowboy seeks and in which he feels at home.

The beginning plot is far less common. Sticking with westerns directed by John Ford, consider the example of *My Darling Clementine*. At the center of the film, in a sequence seemingly extraneous to the main plot, Wyatt Earp leads a dance on the future site of a church. This set piece is actually the entire plot of the film. The cowboy is a civilizing force who lives not in civilization, but on its threshold. Thus the dance occurs where the church will be erected after Earp departs.[1]

Gizzi's immediate source, which he cites in "Revival" (*SVLW*, 47–52), another poem from *Some Values of Landscape and Weather*, is Jim Jarmusch's *Dead Man*, not a classical Hollywood film but a 1995 indie film. Jarmusch inverts the paradigm. His cowboys lack civilization. They bear the names of great poets — the killer is named William Blake, and his first victim is named Dickinson. But the language of poetry is unknown to them. They may be a civilizing force only in the sense that they are unconscious carriers of the treasures of nineteenth-century poetry. The singular figure of conscious poetic wisdom is Nobody, the American Indian who directs William Blake in a series of scenes restaging lines from poems. The cowboys go west not to bring civilization to the wilderness, but to receive an education in poetry for the first time — and not until after their deaths, as Nobody tells Blake at their first meeting. To notice the poetry that was always in the air around them.

"'Here are my flowers,' / what do they smell like? 'Paper'" ("Revival," *SVLW*, 51). For Gizzi, the allusion to *Dead Man* is a way of acknowledging a relationship to literary and art history. The flowers smell like paper because, in the story of the film, a woman makes them. They are also made of paper in the sense that they belong to the mise-en-scène of a performance captured on film. They did not grow in the earth or in a greenhouse; they are props, made by human hands. (It would be interesting if Jarmusch had photographed real flowers to represent the paper flowers in this scene, but this would not change the force of the allusion. Whether they were blossoms cut from living plants, or paper folded to look like blossoms, the flowers are artificial because they are props in a film.) Behind both the film and the poetic sequence is the entire history of literature. The flowers smell like paper because they have appeared in other poems before this one; they carry the smell of the medium in which they have resided for so long.

I

Gizzi reverses the paradigm by traveling in the opposite direction, writing a new history of the American West and of Western civilization. He brings poetry east, to the cradle of civilization, the Mediterranean. He brings courtly love to the place where the Troubadours invented courtly love. In the process, he transforms it into something more demotic, no longer "refined love," but "if love."

> If love if then if now if the flowers of if the conditional if of arrows the condition of if ("Chateau If," *SVLW*, 82)

Perhaps there is no great mystery about "if." Gizzi uses it throughout the book as a formula to generate statements, and, in this poem, to generate all of the statements. It creates a mood—grammatically conditional, emotionally doubtful—but its more important task is to provide the speaker with things to say.

Ten years ago, when I interviewed Gizzi about the poems in *Some Values of Landscape and Weather*, I started by asking him to talk about the word "if," on the principle that something repeated many times must be important. Today, if I were to interview him once more on the same subject, I might begin by asking about the second word in "Chateau If." "Love," unlike "if," is not repeated ostentatiously. It never generates a statement. The concept of love nonetheless has a special prominence, if only because of the title of the sequence, "Fin Amor" (*SVLW*, 82), a phrase in Old Provençal, which means, literally translated, "fine love," or, conventionally, in the modern critical tradition, "courtly love."

So the first thing you might notice about love in this sequence is how utterly poetic it is. "Fin amor" is archaic, a conventional phrase in a dead language. By the time it reaches Gizzi, it has been thoroughly poetized by the generations of Provençal poets who used it in their poems, and the generations of readers who studied them. Refined indeed.

The second thing you might notice is almost the opposite. The relationship between the title "Fin Amor" and the first line of "Chateau If," the first poem in the sequence, reveals both a tradition of poetic wisdom and an attitude of indifference to maintaining it in its traditional form. In the title, love has an Old Provençal name, "Amor," which "Chateau If" swiftly translates into modern English, "love," and into classical Greek, "eros," which appears here in the guise of its modern English homophone, "arrows." There are other possible plays on these tenuous relationships between sound and meaning. "If" arguably echoes "fin" by inverting it, turning the sound "fi" into "if," and specificity into vagueness; and "arrows," even without echoing classical diction, may suggest the iconic accessories of the classical god of love, his archery.

For the Troubadours, the phrase "fin amor" functioned like Gizzi's formulaic use of "if." Gizzi doesn't perform such operations on love. One line in "It Was Raining in Delft" refers to a certain kind of poem, "a they-love poem," in other words, a genre of poetry that uses love as a formula to provide the speaker with things to say, as in the poems of the Troubadours. The poems in "Fin Amor" have formulas for if-statements, but not for love-statements. When they discuss love, they avoid saying who loves or what is loved.

I suggest two possible interpretations of the phrase "If love." (1) A broken statement. For one thing, there is neither a subject to express love nor an object to be loved. For another, this if-statement is missing its then-clause. Love may be the condition, but what is the consequence?

Even the if-clause may be incomplete. Perhaps the condition is a modification of love, an extraordinary refinement of love, to which the line gestures without naming fully. The prospect of incompletion appears with greater force in the continuation of this line: "if to say it is you if love is if your form is if your waist that pictures the fluted stem if lavender" (*SVLW*, 82). "If love is" could be a longer way of saying "if love": if love exists, if there is such a thing as love. Or "if love is" could be a statement broken before the completion of its predicate. "If love is"—what? And, if so, then what? In effect, love has been abstracted from the world of persons, things, actions—all of which appear, but in separate if-statements. "Fin amor," a "fine romance," as Dorothy Fields put it, "with no kisses."

(2) This statement is not in the conditional mood at all. Rather than acting as a conjunction, "if" is an object: "if love," that is to say, love of "if." A feeling of affection for the coordinating conjunction. A wish to inhabit the state of possibility and doubt. To build a castle out of it. Something like what Marvell meant by "vegetable love"—love of vegetables, or between vegetables, or in a part of the soul that is barely aware of itself, imperceptibly growing.

2

Are they really statements? This one is a statement: "If I were to say hummingbird it might behave as an adjective here." A complete sentence. First a condition, then a consequence. The speaker is not just saying the word "hummingbird," but imagining a situation in which he did so, then imagining what would happen as a result. Thus the conditional statement stands in for an utterance that it also includes. The phrase "if then," although a sentence fragment, could be considered a statement on the same model, a condensation into two words of the movement from condition to consequence.

However, on this account, most of the if-statements in "Chateau If" would appear incomplete. "If in this field" (*SVLW*, 82): a grammatical fragment, giving merely a condition, with no consequence. "If not if the heart's a flutter if nerves map a city if a city on fire" (82): merely a list of conditions, none of which develops a consequence. (The list progresses outward horizontally, from motion within a body to motion within a city to the city's violent disorder, but not vertically; there is no way to blame the fire on the heart's rapid beat.) "If the conditional": not even a condition, merely apposition. Accepting these phrases as statements means accepting any utterance, any part of an utterance, any word at all, as a statement.

"Plain Song" makes the same demand. Many of the lines in "Plain Song" make statements according to the most rigorous definition: "some say leaves are green 'cause it looks good against the blue / some say the grasses blow because it is earth's instrument" (*SVLW*, 89). Each line predicates a quality on an object, suggests a reason for the condition, and, finally, albeit vaguely, identifies the source of the statement, attributing it to a group of voices called "some." Although the title "Plain Song" suggests singing in unison, as in a medieval chant, the community of the poem is not a monoculture. Larger movements in the poem trace divergent accounts and disagreements between the groups of voices, and the formation of factions within the groups. In the following passage, two groups of voices produce divergent accounts of the same object: "some say the way of the beekeeper is not their way / some say the way of the beekeeper is the only way" (*SVLW*, 91).

But the poem ends by treating a series of individual words as discrete statements: "Some say molecular some open others porous some blue / some say love some light some say the dark some heaven" (*SVLW*). These lines seem to be more interested in the task of partitioning speech into groups of voices than in the continuity and completion of their utterances. At the same time, as in "Chateau If," the small scale of the utterances makes it difficult to keep track of the partitioning. Each line could be a series spoken by one group, or a catalogue of utterances spoken by several different groups.

"Just a Little Green Untitled" frames similarly truncated statements in an interrogative mood. "Do you ever say / runner, or buttons?" "Do you ever / say helix or fairy dust, just a little green?" (*SVLW*, 87). The words are ordinary in the sense that they are not obviously literary — they do not allude to a literary tradition, as the words "fin amor" do — but not so ordinary as to occur frequently in conversation. My answer to these questions would be a little uncertain. Yes, I might say. Probably. In some situation, in response to something I heard or read, I probably have used all of those words, although not in that combination or order.

The limits of the questions are vague. What is being said, "runner, or buttons"? Or simply, "runner"? What kind of answer to these questions would satisfy the speaker's understanding of what it means to say something? Is the speaker asking whether in some circumstance I have ever used any of these words? Or, in order to give a positive answer, is it necessary for me to have treated the word "runner" or the word "buttons" as a complete statement, to have met some circumstance by uttering, "Buttons," and nothing more? The limits of the speaker are also unclear (which is not true in the other examples). In a sense, the first person is now speaking on behalf of someone else, the second person, tentatively. The speaker is not putting words in someone else's mouth, but entertaining the fantasy that this word or series of words might have been in someone's mouth.

Despite its thoroughgoing vagueness, "Just a Little Green Untitled" includes the one place in the sequence where love settles on an object: "Color of my true love's hair" (*SVLW*, 88). This line also happens to be the one place where color is objectified. Everywhere else, colors are abstracted from objects. Not an object, just "something" in blue. (Which could mean an object, unidentified, that isn't blue, but dressed in blue, or in a blue light, or against a blue background.) Something green that lacks a name, "untitled." The object in this case sounds like a punk rocker, although the line probably alludes to the unhappy nonconformist played by Dean Stockwell in *The Boy with Green Hair.*

3

What happens to the codes and conventions of Troubadour poetry when, in Gizzi's western in reverse, they return to their place of origin? They become industrialized. The five sections of *Some Values of Landscape and Weather* represent differing values, the second to last of which is "Industry," and the last of which is "Song." The poems in the final section are not necessarily more songlike in form or more concerned with song than the other poems in the collection. The sequence "Masters of the Cante Jondo" (in the section representing "Nerves," *SVLW*, 57–66) may be closer to words written for music, although it has no particular tune; the sequence "A History of the Lyric" (in the section representing "Forensics" (*SVLW*, 3–16) may be more densely allusive to songs. Other poems in the collection refer to particular songs ("Stars of Track and Field" [19]) and recordings ("Kathleen Ferrier singing Kindertotenlieder" [47]).

Meanwhile, the poems representing the value of "Song" might not seem particularly musical. They are written in sentences, and broken like paragraphs, and their vocabularies are plain, flat, prosaic. How do they represent the value of song? What is this value?

> Instances when one came to sing,
> the motor of the voice box, to see it,
> to see the mouth open to take air.
> The notes weeping, even willow,
>
> insistent willow.
>
> Noise surfaces at a circumference —
> that sudden rush of air, a small tick
> smaller *tsk tsk*, a timely emphasis
> on prayer, voice, a body. (*SVLW*, 88)

A view into a mouth. Someone, called "one," is singing. Someone — maybe the same one, looking into a mirror, maybe someone else — is in the audience. Rather than listening, the audience is looking. Maybe this is the value of song: to demonstrate where voice comes from, whether the voice is singing or speaking.

The thread of continuity between the "Industry" section and the "Song" section is the "motor of the voice box." Because it manufactures something, the voice box, a part of the body, is a machine, and an industry unto itself. (In the title of his previous book, Gizzi gave the same meaning to a bodily organ: "Artificial Heart" either refers to a machine that replaces the heart, or imagines the organic human heart as a kind of machine.) In the "Industry" section, Gizzi mechanizes song: "song / is an engine" ("Etudes, Evidence, or A Working Definition of the Sun Gear," *SVLW*, 75). In "Fin Amor," he is still doing the same work, concretizing voice into the parts of the body that produce the voice, which are engine parts. At the same time, the poem abstracts body parts from particular bodies, reducing the mouth to a diagram, "a circumference."

The imagined engines reappear in the poems as verbal formulas, if-statements and some-say-statements. These machines for producing sayings are formal manifestations of the engine figure.

NOTES

1. The classic analysis of both paradigms is Richard Slotkin, *Regeneration Through Violence: The Mythology of the American Frontier, 1600–1860* (Middletown, CT: Wesleyan University Press, 1973); Slotkin looks at Hollywood westerns in *Gunfighter Nation: The Myth of the Frontier in Twentieth-Century America* (New York: Atheneum, 1992).

20 | GRAHAM FOUST

"Trembling my standard returned"

Two Versions of "Hard as Ash"

> "Print reminds." The voice serves, but never gives a complete vision. Yet if the text is lost, the poem is lost. If the voices falter, the poem has no occasion. The poem is like a person. It has a mind-body problem.
> — Allen Grossman[1]

Navigate to writing.upenn.edu/pennsound/x/Gizzi.php. Scroll down to "Reading at the New Coast Festival, Buffalo, April 2, 1993," and listen to the recording of "Hard as Ash." What do you hear?

I hear that "Hard as Ash" is both the last poem of Gizzi's reading and the last poem in his book *Periplum*. I hear of Gizzi's own "need to hear" the poem and an impromptu epigraph from Bertolt Brecht: "To he who does not know that the world is on fire, I have nothing to say."[2] I hear the poem's actual epigraph — a brief narrative concerning one "Miss Newcombe," a twenty-two-year-old English woman who supposedly met her demise in 1938 by way of spontaneous human combustion — followed by the poem's title. I hear Gizzi come down hard on his title's first word, his pause between "hard" and "as." And over the course of the next minute or so (roughly one-tenth of Gizzi's performance) I hear something like this:

> *Some* trees cannot grow without fire. Private catastrophes at the speed of Phaethon. What *was* X? Without faith an integer of light broke into cities

> of geometry. Define Y. In the desert it is all calculus. In an overcoat in winter without socks I wandered into night. One by one all the bars fell into place. The day of the talking stones is no longer. The dreams of metamorphosis. The morning you woke up and for a moment forgot to call them — dead — it was the morning of the poem. The subject *is* the content into which I step, lovingly. This lapidary effect of all suns sets where houses invest the notions of home, or hearth, and heat gives, even as the earth rolls over into night and is contained or content to remain itself, while still breaking into flower or streets with cadences of wind. *Your* musics insist to inform me by remaining plastic. With you, I will revise the entire possibility of twilight. The day is woven into images we adhere to, only memory of light against a screen-door ajar. Then children's faces appear, a thematic see-saw, silhouetted now — romantic and real.

But when I open Peter Gizzi's *Periplum* to page 53 and read "Hard as Ash" as printed, I see something rather different from what I heard. I see a text broken into lines, a poem punctuated and "voiced" somewhat differently than the one I heard during Gizzi's reading. Moreover, I discover a radical mishearing on my part — it's "sons," not "suns"— that also seems an honest mistake, given that our own sun sets every day.

In her essay "Lucent and Inescapable Rhythms: Metrical 'Choice' and Historical Formation," Marjorie Perloff writes,

> [M]etrical choice becomes an important indicator of the historical and cultural formation in which it takes place. The question for us, as readers of contemporary poetry, is then not, "Is it a good thing for, say, Lyn Hejinian to have written *My Life* in prose?" but rather, "What does it mean that she chose to do so?"[3]

I concur, and I'd like to take Perloff's assertion a bit further by bringing her idea to bear on Gizzi's poem and his performance of it, for now that you've listened to and looked at "Hard as Ash," it should be obvious that on April 2, 1993, in Buffalo, New York, Peter Gizzi read — and now on any given day on the Internet *reads* — the entirety of "Hard as Ash" with almost no vocalization of the printed poem's line breaks. What, if anything, does this choice mean?

Of course, it may mean very little, for although there are poets who voice their written line breaks with a notable intensity (for example, Robert Creeley) or whose quantification of the duration of the silence after a line break may still hold some sway within the general context of the creative writing workshop (for example, Denise Levertov and her "half-a-comma" rule), it does seem that poetry's right-margin effects, which have largely been freed from their dependence on rhyme or syllable count, are now mostly visual, which is to say that they are meant more to be seen than heard. At the very least, the presence of a more or less nonarbitrary right margin indicates to the reader that he or she is to read the text at hand as poetry — that is, as a text that involves the writer rather than a typesetter making choices about its look on the page. And yet Gizzi's audible insistence on the prose convention of the sentence during his reading seems undeniable and very different from the performances of, say, Louis Zukofsky, who, while often inattentive to his line breaks as they are written, certainly makes use of pauses and musical phrasings that feel governed by something other than punctuation.[4] Perhaps it's best to say, then, that I'm not so much interested in Gizzi's inattention to his line breaks as I'm interested in his vocalized attention to the sentence, which is a unit of writing and not speech.

In his book *Line Break: Poetry as Social Practice*, James Scully makes an interesting claim with regard to technology having a hand in "prescribed" verse giving way to free verse, noting that prescribed verse forms "have a mnemonic function that [free verse] does not typically have." He continues:

> Free verse needs *and assumes* a memory that may be consigned to memory banks such as books and notebooks, not to mention their electronic extensions. With increasing dependence on such repositories, and with less individual need to remember, free verse becomes possible and even, perhaps, inevitable.[5]

This notion seems right to me, and I might take it even further by asserting that this decline in the "individual need to remember" texts is eventually accompanied by an increase in the *collective* need to perform them, though this collective metrical space is very different from, say, the group chanting encouraged by accentual meter, in which, as Antony Easthope notes, "rhythmic repetitions take complete priority over natural intonation, subsuming it."[6] Rather, as our ability to access multiple and varied linguistic structures increases, thus causing the "need to remember" to wane, the individuality of the poetic subject fades as well, a phenomenon outlined by Perloff as follows:

> [A]t a time when the spoken and written word are more pervasive than ever, when our visual fields are bombarded by billboards and manuals, and our aural fields by overheard snatches of conversation and catchy TV jingles, the individual voice can no longer be In Charge. Rather, the text gives the impression that the story is telling itself, that it is available for communal use — a kind of score that we endow with meaning by "speaking it" ourselves.[7]

Perloff's example of a text that features a withered "individual voice" is Samuel Beckett's short prose piece *Still*, and what I find most interesting about her treatment of it is that she cannot help but find *lines* (or something very much like them) therein; moreover, her findings are tied directly to the rhythm of Beckett's words as they are *spoken*. (Prose is solid, poetry breaks, and yet it seems that the latter can be found inside the former, just as the hardest objects are full of spinning electrons.)

"When [*Still*] is read aloud," Perloff writes, "(and I have heard it read by the actor Alec McGoweran)," the rhythmic unit of the prose is heard as something resembling lineated poetry: "a short phrase of irregular length and primitive syntax . . . a phrase heavily accented, discontinuous, and repetitive — a kind of shorthand by means of which the human consciousness tries to articulate what it perceives and remembers."[8]

If *Still* is a block of text that becomes audibly lineated when read aloud, we might say that Gizzi's oral erasure of his scripted lineation makes "Hard as Ash" a series of post-Beckettian sentences that ultimately pave the way for their own repair (as in both their *being fixed* and their *going elsewhere*) into something both more and less traditional.

"Your musics insist to inform me by / remaining plastic," writes Gizzi, his sentence yoking together notions of firmness, data, and malleability; his line break after "by" briefly morphing the verb "to inform" into something like the verb "to pass" (as in "pass me by"); and his pluralization of "music" suggesting that a poem might have multiple ways of being sounded. These lines provide us with an example of a free-verse line break in which enjambment results in polysemy, for had these lines been written as prose, it's unlikely that the reader would have isolated "inform me by" and so yoked the concept of "information" with the concept of "passing," a notion that can be fed back through the line in which "sons" on the page passes for "suns" in the air (or, later in the poem, the line break that nearly causes the iambic "content" to pass for its trochaic twin, which appears a few lines earlier).

But if the right-margin elements of "Hard as Ash" can at times be said to be of some interest, it seems to me that Gizzi's lines don't contribute to his poem's motion and meaning as often or as intensely as his sentences do, and I would argue that his "prosed" vocalization suggests that a more recent poetic technology is in fact this poem's prime mover. In his essay "The New Sentence," Ron Silliman writes that "sensitivity to syllogistic movement" is characteristic of the poems that make use of that device, observing that each sentence in such poems "plays with the preceding and following sentence" and noting that enjambment's "torquing" has been relocated to "the interiors of prose," thus *proscribing* the free-verse line break while also *having been prescribed* by it.[9] As we proceed though "Hard as Ash," we can see that it does largely consist of sentences that attract and refract one another (and often themselves), and it is perhaps this fact that accounts for Gizzi's close attention to that unit during his performance.

Heard or read, Gizzi's poem's very title prepares the reader for some New-Sentence torque, for if one thinks of cigarettes or cremation, the words "hard as ash" seem oxymoronic, which may in turn move the reader to assume that the word "ash" refers to a type of wood. An ash tree is of course harder than the ashes of a cigarette or a cremated body, but the wood from ash trees is soft compared to many other trees, so the phrase is still a little off, perhaps meaning something akin to "not as hard as oak." Another possible twist becomes visible in light of the fact that the Latin root of the word "hard," *durus*, has much in common with the Latin root of the word "endure," *durare*, which perhaps bends the title toward the notion that ash is irreducible, as in "ashes to ashes." That said, once one has heard or read the epigraph about Miss Newcombe, one is likely to reassume that "ash" refers to human remains and not to trees, although the memory of the effort required to make this kind of sense is a kind of prophetic remainder, a reminder of how the poem will continue to move. As Allen Grossman writes, "surmised possibilities remain as semantic dissonance."[10]

The poem itself begins by keeping the title's and epigraph's references to trees and fire in play, while also introducing additional narrative elements that fold around or telescope into one another. Harking back to *Periplum*'s opening poem, "Song of the Interior Begin," in which Gizzi writes, "So the tree for even / a twig" (*PER*, 9), the first sentence is likely a reference to trees such as Ponderosa pines, which rely on forest fires to germinate their seeds so that new trees will grow, thus allowing us to remember that what we often think of as an accident or a crime is in some cases a natural and necessary phenomenon. "ONLY YOU CAN PREVENT FOREST FIRES," says the famous cartoon bear, voicing the sign that appears on the screen (we like to read what we hear and to hear what we read). Were there no "you"—which is to say no *us*—lightning would strike, fires would erupt, and forests would burn and grow in turn, but this uncontrolled process would hardly be of concern to nature itself. Of course, as it continues to encroach upon nature, culture at times becomes obligated to play the role of nature; that is, to *make* lightning strike—or, to put it more accurately, to make it *as if lightning had struck*—so that nature can take its mediated course in a way that accords with culture's needs and wants. Born from the tension between natural and artificial language, poetry seems capable of a similar process, and we need listen no further than Gizzi's controlled burning of his written line breaks into something like New Sentences to see evidence of this. Moreover, it strikes me that the process described in this first sentence, which also happens to contain the name of a poem and a book by one of his influences (John Ashbery's "Some Trees" and *Some Trees*), is a terrific metaphor for poetic lineage, which might be said to require younger writers to rise from—and perhaps even start—the fires that burn their predecessors away.

The poem's second sentence, the fragment "Private catastrophes at the speed of Phaethon," makes reference to an ancient story of the mishandling of fire. In Ovid's version of the myth, the son of the sun god Phoebus scorches Earth after losing control of his father's chariot and is in turn killed by one of Jupiter's lightning bolts. Phaethon's demise is the result of a query and a desire. In order to prove his godly status to his son, Phoebus agrees to grant him whatever he wishes. Phaethon's wish to drive his father's chariot proves fatal to himself, grievous to his father, and disastrous to the African continent. Yoking the speed of the "[p]rivate catastrophes" of interior life to that of Phaethon's fall to earth, Gizzi relocates the epic's public contents to the more intimate world of the lyric.

It's worth noting that the first two lines of "Hard as Ash" are also its first two sentences, a move that allows the poetic convention of capitalizing the first letters of lines to coincide with the prose convention of capitalizing the first letters of sentences. This initial synchronicity is squelched by the lowercase beginning of its fourth line.[11] Fittingly, the fourth sentence's breaking of the poem's formal unity occurs between two sentences that make reference to the components of the Cartesian coordinate system, the X-Y axis on which one might plot a line. (This sentence also mentions "faith," which ghosts the first syllable of "Phaethon" and could be said to be math's antithesis.) At this point, mathematical references begin to saturate the poem's opening — *integer, geometry, calculus* — perhaps reminding us to make note of how the poem's sentences are adding to and subtracting from one another. "In an overcoat" echoes "In the desert," and the sentence "One by one all the bars fell into place" suggests a slot machine, which, given that machine's association with the city of Las Vegas, may in turn return us to the "desert" and the "cities of geometry." Does the speaker's possibly being in Las Vegas account for his not wearing socks in winter? And does a possible reference to Las Vegas ("the meadows") point to Robert Duncan's "made place" of "first permission"? The line about "talking stones" not only suggests the demise of the fixity of print culture, but also echoes Talking Heads, whose first live album, *The Name of This Band Is Talking Heads*, contains stage banter that Gizzi samples later in the poem when he writes, "The name of this song is new feeling, because / that's what it's about" (*PER*, 56).

If the aforementioned sentences encourage connective and intertextual reading and listening, others, like the following clunky-but-lovely Ashberian moment, draw our attention to the fissures within and between sentences:

> The day is woven into images we adhere to
> only memory of light against
> a screen door ajar. Then children's
> faces appear. (*PER*, 54)

Of course, our ability to make connections hasn't been completely shut down here — "memory of light" echoes the "twilight" from the previous sentence (and prefigures twilight's reappearance in the poem's penultimate line) while the "screen-door" is re-conjured by the mention of children's faces in the next one, the words "ajar" and "appear" echoing one another in what seems like a scene from a summer evening — but the most notable moment here is the torqued first sentence, which isn't so much disrupted by the line breaks after "to" or "against" as it is by its odd construction, for even without the line break, there seems to be something missing between "to" and "only." To my ear, this sudden breach of grammar seems a more visceral transmission of the not-all-there experience of looking out a screen door into the sun — not to mention the not-all-there experience of recollection — than any enjambment might achieve.

Elsewhere in the poem, the transition from one sentence to another affects the reader's movement in a somewhat different way:

> This is only a poem to say I love you.
> I love you too. I've been so happy.
> Happy! (*PER*, 54)

In this echo of Frank O'Hara's "A Warm Day for December" (and perhaps of Keats's "Ode on a Grecian Urn"), we hear Gizzi's speaker professing his or her love to two people and/or a call of love followed by the response of some other speaker, though the poem hasn't thus far managed enough narrative normativity to allow us to jump to an immediate conclusion. Later on, the poem makes a similar move —"You should've seen it. / I did."— thus shifting our earlier uncertainty with regard to who is speaking or being spoken to into what feels like a more frictional circumstance (*PER*, 55).

Contrary to Perloff's earlier commentary, we often think of the speakers of lyric poems as being alone with their thoughts. But if the "I" in "Hard as Ash" is unaccompanied, his or hers is an aloneness gone somewhat double, as the poem codes its utterer as both male and female. Early on, we see the speaker worrying that "someone will die / and I'll have to wear a tie, again," while afterward s/he speaks of "a voice I misplaced when I was a girl" and of "a laundry / line strung from year to year [that] reaches / to the woman I am becoming" (*PER*, 54–55, 60). Noting that the subjectivity of the writer is neither absent nor the center of attention in poems that make use of Silliman's "New Sentence," Bob Perelman asserts that the "multiple shifts" of such writing help to "encourag[e] attention to the act of writing and to the writer's particular position within larger social frames," and surely Gizzi's doubly gendered speaker is one of many operations that prevent the objects and events in "Hard as Ash" from being given what Perelman calls "novelistic treatment."[12] Yet if, as Perelman claims, a poet like Silliman allows us to place a narrative detail such as the damage done to a child in "a larger economic context" by way of a compositional process akin to the "finite but focused" moments of attention one pays to individuals and perceptions in "crowded urban settings," it seems Gizzi has managed to turn this approach outside in, allowing the reader to recognize the crowd of identities and visions that might constellate and constitute the lyric "I."[13]

While "Hard as Ash" often refuses to "construct narrative wholes [thus forcing the reader to] renarrativize," it also always presents us with something other than a loose linguistic schematic of late-capitalist relations.[14] For even as one "renarrativizes" the poem's contents, one is always renarrativizing *along with* the speaker, whose constant use of the first-person singular pronoun encourages us to see him and/or her as someone whose task it is to narrate his or her own recreations. Just as a listener can "see" "Hard as Ash" as the speech of a single person as it's being read aloud, the reader can "hear" "Hard as Ash" as the speech of a person — that is, as a representation "not of an action or the chronicle of an action, but of an utterance."[15] While Gizzi's poem does more than simply deploy the "fictitious totalization" (Perelman's term) that characterizes countless other literary narratives, it also manages to present us with an at-once shattered and intact *speaker* — a fictive "I," or what Grossman calls "a fiction of a self seen from within"— who, like the reader him- or herself, comprises a large and complex set of continuities and discontinuities.[16] But if it's true that the speaker of Gizzi's single quantitatively unrecognizable stanza is composed of Whitmanian multitudes, it's also true that he or she cannot seem to contain them (in both senses of the word *contain*) or, indeed, be contained him- or herself.

Gizzi's introductory claim that he "need[s] to hear" "Hard as Ash" at the New Coast festival echoes the very poem he's about to read, in which he writes,

> So what is an anthem, and growing up there
> is a lesson in it. I doubly derive my body.
> Running ahead of myself, beyond memory's reach,
> the source sprang incarnadine. Teeming
> with information. Trembling my standard returned.
> I knew then this body was not invincible.
> Who shall know this posture, this morning's slide rule.
> I needs. I wants. (*PER*, 59)

Unlike "Your musics insist to inform me by," which uses the line break to overdetermine the sentence, the first two lines here are another example of a moment when a line break doesn't cause but may simply heighten our attention to a moment of ambiguity that's already built into the sentence, for even in prose the reader could not determine whether the sentence concerns "growing up" in the "anthem" of "so what" or if there exists "a lesson" in "so what" that's learned by simply "growing up." "I needs" and "I wants" echo both Rimbaud's famous dictum that "Je est un autre" and Robert Creeley's "The Language" ("As soon as / I speak, I / speaks"), suggesting that if the first-person singular noun is in fact an entity that necessarily differs from its users, then any given "I" will have its own set of requirements and desires. I read the poem's I's assertion that it "doubly derives [its] body" as a description of a nexus of awarenesses — the speaking poet's awareness of his donation of his body to the poem, and the poem's own strange awareness of its line-and-sentence tension regarding the various methods by which it might be disseminated. Indeed, one of this poem's artifices is that of the poem's "own" voice, as when Gizzi writes, "Saying leave me alone, I am only a poem, / what do you want from me?" (*PER*, 56).

Elsewhere in "Hard as Ash," another reference to the very text we're reading and/or listening to occurs:

> Do I have to die for you then to hear these lines
> that I make profligate and plaintive. (*PER*, 58)

Again, it's Gizzi's sentence that's strangely ambiguous — is the speaker asking if s/he has to die in order for the *reader/listener* to hear her/him, or is the speaker asking if s/he has to die in order to hear *her/his own voice*? In order to see "these lines" as part of a line, we need to be out of earshot of Gizzi's recording — or at least within eyeshot of his book — and so perhaps the sentence conjures a sort of figurative death in which to "die" would mean to lack the breath of performance, leaving the reader alone with just the poem on the page, a twist on a scene from a Neil Young's song "On the Beach," in which the singer goes to a radio interview only to find himself "alone at the microphone."

Roughly halfway through his poem, Gizzi mashes up these lines from that very song —

> All my pictures are falling
> from the wall where I placed them yesterday.

— with two other lines from the same song —

> Though my problems are meaningless
> that don't make them go away.[17]

— in order to write these lines of his own:

> This thought bit me the other day. As all
> my pictures have fallen but that don't make 'em
> go away. (*PER*, 57)

Having substituted "falling" pictures for "meaningless" problems, Gizzi prefigures his future performance, a moment when the poem's mind-body problem becomes visible in the tension between its printed lines (which "go away" during Gizzi's performance) and its sentences, which seem to dominate the poem's organization, even when broken on the page. If the poetic line, to quote Grossman again, "is a picture of the sentence," then the line breaks in the printed version of "Hard as Ash" suggest that Gizzi still has a use for such pictures.[18] Moreover, his pictures are falling toward the past and into his final line ("from Eden toward history," as Grossman says, though Gizzi's is an Eden in flames), and this finally thrusts the poem into an older artifice than we might have anticipated.[19]

The last line of "Hard as Ash" ends not only the poem but the book, *Periplum*, with a noun-phrase sentence fragment that references "I Gave My Wedding Dress Away," a song recorded by country singer Kitty Wells in 1963. Wells's vocals are both sung and spoken, and they tell the story of a woman who not only loses her fiancé to her younger sister, but ends up giving her her wedding dress as well:

> My baby sister wanted him and so she took my place
> It's worth a broken heart to see the smile upon her face
> I've cared for her since mother went away
> So I gave my wedding dress away[20]

In the last line of "Hard as Ash," the poem's speaker rewrites (or respeaks) the sentiment so that the poem ends with a line of perfect iambic pentameter:

> The dáy I gáve my wédding dréss awáy. (*PER*, 61)

While the song's narrative describes the renunciation of social, symbolic, and even descriptive traditions (it's usually the bride and not the dress that's "given away"), the iambic music of the poem's last image has of course been prescribed for centuries. Antony Easthope tells of how the iambic meter was invented twice — once in the Middle Ages and again in Early Modern times — and Pound, of course, famously advocates for poetry's break with it: "(To break the pentameter, that was the first heave)," he writes in Canto 81.[21] And yet not even Pound wanted a total upheaval, because "to heave" is also to rise and fall rhythmically. Likewise, Gizzi returns us to tradition just as quickly as he subverts it in a book titled after Pound's use of the word "periplum" in Canto 59. Ultimately, in the air and on the page, two versions of "Hard as Ash" meet apart. Gizzi is able to have poetry *both* ways — as both writing and performance, as both invention and precedent, as both social music and interior song.

NOTES

1. Allen Grossman, *The Sighted Singer: Two Works on Poetry for Readers and Writers* (Baltimore: Johns Hopkins University Press, 1991), 281.

2. I've not been able to track down the source of this quotation, though it appears in several places on the Internet. It may well be a popular misquotation of these lines from Michael Hamburger's translation of Brecht's "The Buddha's Parable of the Burning House":

> I went out again. These people here, I thought
> Need to burn to death before they stop asking questions. Truly, friends
> Unless a man feels the ground so hot underfoot that he'd gladly
> Exchange it for any other, sooner than stay, to him I have nothing to say. (291)

3. Marjorie Perloff, "Lucent and Inescapable Rhythms: Metrical 'Choice' and Historical Formation," in *The Line in Postmodern Poetry*, ed. Robert Frank and Henry Sayre (Urbana: University of Illinois Press, 1988), 16.

4. Numerous recordings of Zukofsky reading his poems can be found on his PennSound web page at writing.upenn.edu/pennsound/x/Zukofsky.php.

5. James Scully, *Line Break: Poetry as Social Practice* (Willimantic, CT: Curbstone Books, 2005), 142.

6. Anthony Easthope, *Poetry as Discourse* (London: Metheuen, 1983), 73.

7. Perloff, "Lucent and Inescapable Rhythms," 37.

8. Perloff, "Lucent and Inescapable Rhythms," 34.

9. Ron Silliman, *The New Sentence* (New York: Roof Books, 1989), 89–90.

10. Grossman, *The Sighted Singer*, 281.

11. This self-referential enjambment is echoed later in line 18, which ends with the words "still breaking" (53).

12. Bob Perelman, "Parataxis and Narrative: The New Sentence in Theory and Practice," *American Literature* 65.2 (1993): 316–17.

13. Perelman, "Parataxis and Narrative," 317.

14. Perelman, "Parataxis and Narrative," 318.

15. Barbara Herrnstein Smith, *Poetic Closure: A Study of How Poems End* (Chicago: University of Chicago Press, 1968), 122.

16. Ezra Pound makes a similar point when he writes, "One says 'I am' this, that or the other, and with the words scarcely uttered one ceases to be the thing" Pound, *A Memoir of Gaudier-Brzeska* (1916; New York: New Directions 1970), 85.

17. Neil Young, "On the Beach," in *On the Beach*, Reprise Records, 1974, LP.

18. Grossman, *Sighted Singer*, 315.

19. Grossman, *Sighted Singer*, 262.

20. Kitty Wells, "I Gave My Wedding Dress Away," in *The Kitty Wells Story*, Decca Records, 1963, LP.

21. Easthope, *Poetry as Discourse*, 54: "The first time was in the fourteenth century when it took the form of Chaucer's Middle English pentameter. Between then and the early sixteenth century massive phonological changes took place in the development of Modern English from Middle English, so that poets could no longer discern Chaucer's metre and the pentameter was reintroduced."

21 | BEN LERNER

From Seeing to Saying

On Peter Gizzi's "It Was Raining in Delft"

The poem takes place in the long shadow of its title: *It was raining*— the past progressive, a grammatical aspect that creates the expectation of a concurrent action ("It was raining while I was writing") or of action interrupted, the simple past breaking in ("It was raining when you called"). The title establishes an atmosphere of indeterminacy and suspense: What else was happening or about to happen in that particular period of rain?

A verbless first line, and then we encounter the simple past: *I saw* (which, the poem makes me see, is "was" backwards). It was raining in Delft when "I saw rooftops. The sun after a shower." But then — how can it have been raining when the speaker saw the sun *after* a shower? Maybe because, while it was raining outside the museum, he was looking at the sunlit roofscape of Vermeer's *The View of Delft*, where it has always just stopped raining, storm clouds in the foreground breaking up. Or, if you look closely at the canvas, can you still see, despite the sun, droplets striking the surface of the River Schie? Was it raining in Delft when Gizzi wrote the poem sometime around the end of the twentieth century? Was it raining in Delft when Vermeer painted his canvas in the early 1660s, or was — and is — it raining in the painting perpetually? I sound — the poem makes me sound — like I'm turning over Moore's paradox, which so exercised Wittgenstein:

1. It is not absurd to assert the past-tense counterpart, for example, "It was raining in Delft, but I did not believe that it was raining."
2. It is not absurd to assert the second- or third-person counterparts to such sentences, for example, "It is raining in Delft, but *you* do not believe that it is raining," or "It is raining in Delft, but Peter Gizzi doesn't believe that it is raining." But:
3. It is absurd to assert the present-tense "It is raining in Delft and I don't believe that it is raining."

It's not absurd, however, to assert number 3 if there are two Delfts and one rain and if the speaker is partly projecting himself into the painting he stands before; the tension between the tenses of art and life is one of the organizing dramas of the poem.

Gizzi's details abet the crucial temporal and spatial and diegetic ambiguity the title helps establish. In part, this is the effect of selecting architectural language (cornerstones, marble pilings, and so on) — language that describes forms that persist across centuries (in or out of paintings) — and in part, it's the effect of vocabulary that at once sounds contemporary and antiquated: "There are . . . Yellow wrappers in the square / Just what you'd suspect: a market with flowers and matrons, handbags" (*SVLW*, 81). "Yellow wrappers" could be outer garments from whatever era (one of the women in the foreground of the painting wears yellow; she carries a basket or handbag) or detritus from today's candy or pack of cigarettes. I also hear the "yellow wrappers" of a rare book, another echo of artifice and age (beauty ages everything), and I think of the *petit pan de mur jaune* in Vermeer's canvas that Proust so loved. One expects handbags, "real" or knockoffs, in any contemporary market, but juxtaposed with "matrons," it's difficult to locate this particular one in time. Much of what the speaker sees could be encountered in the (actual or depicted) Delft of 1660 or the contemporary Hague or any other global city. The ambiguity of these particulars makes me think of the percepts Whitman selects in "Crossing Brooklyn Ferry"— seabirds, waves, masts, and so on — particulars *general* enough to be perceived across the years by anyone, objects in the past progressive. However, unlike Whitman, who was projecting himself confidently into the future, Gizzi's details keep threatening to pull him back into the stasis of the past.

From his location or dislocation in a zone that is at once the past, a lived present, and a painting (which can stand as a metonym for artifice more generally), the speaker is calling. Again, "call" takes on an uncanny power here because it evokes both canonical literary diction (think how often you encounter "call" in, say, Shakespeare's sonnets) and contemporary speech ("I will call in an hour"). The poem addresses "Liz," but without the apostrophaic fiction of response; indeed, Liz is unconscious: "I will call in an hour where you are sleeping. I've been walking / for 7 hrs on yr name day" (*SVLW*, 81). Marking time by a "name day" is anachronistic, distinctly "old world," but killing time for seven hours sounds like the complaint of a jetlagged American. Or maybe he's calling from the frozen time of art: I see that the tiny clock on the Schiedam Gage in *The View of Delft* shows it is forever just past seven; perhaps the speaker is trapped in a painting where it will never strike eight, never be time to dial. If the speaker is locked in the past or a painting, he can't make a sound; indeed, "will call" starts to feel less like it denotes speech conveyed across the Atlantic than it does a ghostly visit. He will call not *when* Liz is up, but *where* she is sleeping — he will pay a call, but his presence is so like an absence that it seems unlikely to wake her. Regardless, the speaker isn't speaking, he's writing — "hrs" and "yr" serve to refocus our attention on the writtenness of the address, that this is a mere image of speech. Without the vowels, the words are unpronounceable (and "yrs" looks like a shorthand for "years"); writing is as inaudible as paint; the call is as mute as the colonnades it echoes but cannot echo off. Despite the casual register of "I will call you in an hour," the poem powerfully emphasizes that the speaker and Liz are not coeval.

"Dead, I am calling you now" (*SVLW*, 81). The first instance in the poem of the present continuous cancels itself; the now of the I and the you can't correspond; if he can call, she can't pick up; this poetic temporality is no more an actual "now" than the past continuous of the title. (The felt impossibility of addressing the present is only made more acute by how we could also read "dead" in the line as the recipient of the call and not as an adjective apposite to the "I.") What the first eight lines of the poem so expertly establish are varieties of belatedness, a kind of poetic desynchronosis (which I recently learned is the technical term for jetlag). But Gizzi knows that even his concern with belatedness is belated, that it's a well-worn trope of the lyric, that it is, in a sense, "just what you'd expect" in the marketplace of poetic speech. Part of what's novel in Gizzi's handling of these problems is that he makes no claim to novelty: "I am far and I am an animal and I am just another I-am poem, a we-see poem, a they-love poem" (81). The challenge the poem faces is to find some way to resist the belatedness it acknowledges or to establish within it the possibility of correspondence across time.

None of the grammatical positions is live, the first and second and third person are tropes, not viable vantages for seeing and speaking, but the repetition of "I am" also makes us hear "iamb"; the copula without the possibility of complement is transformed sonically into the name of the foundational metrical foot. And for me, the volta in this almost-sonnet is a turn from seeing to speech, from the ekphrastic to the literal "noise" of the poem — from things that have been seen to things that have and can be said. The last line of the poem is a litany, an incantatory recital that unites reader and writer in a present tense of recitation as a way out of the desynchronosis of poetic address.

> There is so much stone here. And grass. So beautiful each
>   translucent electric blade.
> And the noise. Cheers folding into traffic. These things.
>   Things that have been already said many times:
> leaf, zipper, sparrow, lintel, scarf, window shade. (*SVLW*, 81)

"Cheers folding into traffic" might represent the sounds of the past centuries becoming the sounds of the modern present, another way the poem collapses temporal distance, one of Gizzi's signature dissolves. This is a list of things, but because the emphasis is on articulation, "thing" refers to the materiality of language as much or more than to its referents. And it's in our attention to the signifier that relations between the terms in the list emerge: The "f"s at the end of the monosyllabic "leaf" and "scarf"; the double consonants in "zipper" and "sparrow," which rhymes with "window"; that "zipper," "sparrow," "lintel," and "window" are all trochees; the strong rhyme of "blade" and "shade," which offers the poem an affect of formal closure without necessarily promising thematic resolution — and so on. There are many ways to interpret the selection of these particular well-worn words, but I think what's crucial is the fact of saying: that the poem both narrates recitation and can be recited, "folding" the time of composition into the present tense of whatever reader's — Liz's, mine, yrs — enunciation. And at this point, "Dead, I am calling you now" no longer sounds — or doesn't only sound — like Gizzi lamenting his inability to reach Liz from within the poem/painting; instead, the sentence now also sounds the possibility of posthumous address through the technology of the poem as a durable score for the breath. I do not claim this erases the poem's melancholy; Liz and the speaker cannot interact in time. But "now" can now mean both Gizzi's time of composition and whenever a reader picks up the call and says the things that have been said many times before. In the renewable present tense of reading, the temporality of art and life can be made, however briefly, to correspond.

AFTERWORD | COLE SWENSEN

"Sonic Sense"

Working on a collection to be titled *Archeophonics*

an arc in the phoneme
 eco-mnemonics

or he says[1] perhaps instead "Strangeness Becomes You"
makes you
 and makes you fill up with windows.

 Sitting in Emily Dickinson's bedroom
looking out the window, writing about windows.
 Watching "a dove with a broken
window."[2]

Archeophonics is the science of extracting ancient sounds from porous surfaces — walls, woods, books. It's based on the conviction of universal attention; there is nothing that is not listening, and remembering it —

"it" being both what it heard and the act of remembering.
 Remembering, not recording —
the former includes an occupation;
 it enters and makes a home in you.
Perhaps,
he says,
a metaphor for poetry in general or perhaps simply a description

of a window etched on the inside by all the sliding voices. It
becomes strange in you.

The lyric is at a critical moment in American poetry, at an American moment that distrusts anything that rhymes in any and all senses of the word, suspicious of anything that claims to add up (because that, in a sense, is what the dynamic net of the lyric implicitly claims — an elaborate field-weave of sounds and rhythms that arrives at an integrated, inviolable whole).

Suspicious because, clearly, *it* (the big global one) doesn't add up at all.

So perhaps the lyric's challenge at the moment is to use sound in ways that not only acknowledge this inherent incongruence, but that make use of it to create yet more complicated, intricate sound patterns, patterns that incorporate trouble and dissonance, that play with ragged collisions, that model the resounding contradiction that is the warp of contemporary social, political, and cultural (dis)order.

Contradiction: to speak against — which works for both content and form — one counters a claim, one asserts a difference, or one uses language *à rebours* — against the grain, heading upstream — it's a strain, and inherent in resistance, in insistence.

This implies that there's a correspondence between the field-weave of a poem and that of a society, the former replicating the latter through analogous proportions and dynamics. Someone asked Gizzi yesterday what he was working on — "A series of short lyric poems."[3]

                    passing
through a series of rooms
                    in which he listens to the walls
                    where the lyric is rooted
in relation to the interior — right on the edge of it,
                    a permeable membrane
between the mind
               and what is largely outside

all those rooms
               that build within
                         which then within them

in repetition

"Some say a baby

Some say birds

Some say a body

does not stop"[4]

Anaphora:

always on the verge of starting out

an endless

and let's begin again, a room
with three walls
in the sunlight when

a constellation of common nouns takes on a density of anchoring gravity: mirror, lens, the many in the grain.

The lyric as a common town.

And so we begin again.

Gizzi's lyric attempts precisely this grapple with the incongruous, and in part by engaging another element considered by some to be also inherent to the lyric, the hyper-problematic *I*—well known for implicating everyone and therefore fitting no one. It's always a lie. Thereby leaving us all namelessly engraved in the cool shade of anonymity.

"If I break"[5]
If I forget
If I am

a shattering of affect across a reflective surface.

The repetition of the anaphora and the repetition of the I are inherently connected, in that the I, every time it's enunciated, also begins again; it cross-sections any life's continuum; it's a snapshot making a permanent instant within and out of a continuous flow, and in that way, it's a slippery bit of sleight-of-hand, yet despite that, the instant instantly becomes a distinct and anchored point from which the speaker begins a new life. And then someone across the room, or in another city or country, a split-second later, says I, and the life of that someone begins again—as does the word I itself.

Gizzi's I is particularly dynamic because it strikes a precarious balance between the personal I and the public I — the personal, that is, the confessional, in which the I is not tied to the writer, but is tied to the interior, to interiority itself, and thus to the potential for an inner life, with the concomitant potential to expand the internal world, to carry the reader into that internal world, and thus also to expand the reader's internal territory — as contrasted with the public I, the externalized I, which walks out into the world as witness, as an entirely exteriorized surface upon which the world reflects, sees itself, and is thus held accountable. This I is the capacity of an individual to walk out into the world with responsibility — that is, with the ability, and therefore the obligation, to respond.

Gizzi constructs an I that has it both ways; it heads toward an infinite inner world and an infinite outer one simultaneously, annihilating the boundary between the two, sacrificing it to the smooth running of a continuum that connects the individual to the entirety, seamlessly.

That boundary, that wall between self and world, is an ancient one.

It's the one that's always been listening
and its dissolution releases
to the world of archeophonics
the memory of all languages
made, as all languages are, of wind.

"I remember, in the coo of shade
my body . . ."[6]

as an artifact of voice
as a shadow walking the length of the beach, La Boule, July, 2013

or along the Cam one afternoon when water is the only sound.
I see him always walking on.
A gentle time seeping from his hands
lightly at his sides
all the cities he has lived:
New York, Providence, Santa Cruz,
Cambridge, Amherst, all
haunted. All noted for harboring poets.

And all their poems, like all their languages of wind, the soft wind that lofts from the mouth that brings the air from the city inside

("I have eaten the air / of that city"[7])   aslant.

Archeophonics opens with language itself centered as subject, named as such through the question of the name

coming back again, tracing the ways
syntax connects us
to the sky. And the question of "the old language,"[8] too, returns, aging time. The man walking beside the moving water feels it sliding through him, the ocean perpendicular, the river parallel, and the old language, a diagonal field; it, too, aslant.

Slanting through, in fact, which troubles the surface, a rhythmic disturbance that breaks up the reflection, shatters and then scatters it. We call this the poetic. It underlies the semantic and is still there when the latter has been worn away.

Gizzi, in all his work, works on and with the trouble on the surface of language:

"I was more ing
these days to
every surface. So
what's in this morning
that will solace?"[9]

Two grammatically clear sentences; the syntax holds. But the adjective *ing* is not only itself devoid of semantic content, but it prevents all the other words in the sentence from accruing such meaning as well. We're then offered a sonic parallel, a sentence that does "mean" in a "normal" way, but only barely. Such slippery semantics provoke a certain level of anxiety, too low to be consciously noticed, particularly by readers familiar with poetry and able to summon up a dose of negative capability, yet, as humans, we know that our lives literally depend on our ability to glean semantic meaning from language, so the lack of it cannot but create concern. And just when that concern is at its peak — in this case, at the end of the second sentence — when, again, complete clarity is not delivered, something else is. Sound kicks in. A rapidly clicking equation, one that aligns *surface* with *solace* and *more ing* with *morning* and holds them all in place through rhythm, replaces the anxiety around the lack of semantic meaning with the pleasure of the presence of sonic meaning, and creates a slight emotional shock that makes us realize that sound has meaning in itself.

If the anxiety and the lack weren't there, we wouldn't be able to recognize the meaning that resides in sound. And like all modes of non-semantic meaning, and what distinguishes them from the semantic, the meaning in sound and sound relationships can never mean anything *else*, anything but itself, and so we find ourselves delivered to the present of the poem — a solace, indeed.

No matter what else his work is grappling with — history, sorrow, embodiment, sky — it is always also grappling with the multiplicity of modes of meaning and the ways that they conflict or conflate. And though the grapple is vigorous, almost physical, Gizzi's principal approach is always through subtlety. Often things seem semantically clear, only to be destabilized, but only slightly, and only by a slight detail, maybe just a line break:

"The wobble of light on wood-grain late
 in the day."[10]

The alliteration and consonance of light and late are so strong and so strongly supported by the line's rhythm that they make the line into a sealed unit, and in the process, change the meaning of "late" because it's suddenly rendered wholly ambiguous — suddenly, it might be a noun, or any number of other opening things.

And the *slight* is very much the key because it catches us with our guard down; we let a lot of difference in when we don't notice that we're doing so. And things grow. Beyond measure. Precisely as we're measuring them — rhythm — and its counting — rhyme — and its counting back. Back up and add. The whole map of intricate sound relationships can be graphically tracked and would give us a cartography entirely other to the proclamation of progress implicit in semantics. We are not going forward, but ever outward in odd arrays.

Gizzi's work on different modes of meaning is all supported by a conscious choice of a particularly elemental vocabulary — light, sun, sail — single-syllable words that go directly to the heart of our cultural mind. Mind, time, spine.

In English, all the important things are said in single syllables, are hard seeds, tight cores. Seed, lore, chime.

These syllables are atomic. We could build a periodic table of all the single-syllable words that constitute the irreducible building blocks of the world. This is the table that Gizzi draws upon.

The epigraph he chose for *The Outernationale*, Oppen’s

“I think there is no light in the world
but the world

And I think there is light”[11]

is an elegant demonstration of both this principle and its importance as a constructive foundation of Gizzi’s work — a statement of calm conviction anchored in eighteen single syllables. And most of them, among the most basic of the bases of the world: world, I, think, light. There.

And above all, *is*.

And above all, *and*.

To and. That it might among.

“world I think light there”— It hints at the first line of the Bible filtered through Descartes. And that’s Gizzi’s point of precarious balance, negotiating the dubious claims of reason against the equally dubious claims of faith. *But that they claim* — it’s the claim itself and the potential for that, or any, claim to constitute a *thing* that forms the basis of the metaphysical dimension of Gizzi’s work. It’s an important dimension in itself, but one of the most important and constructive things it does is to infuse the physical, creating a hybrid in which the *meta* gets grounded on and in and of the earth.

Earth. With. In.

NOTES

1. Peter Gizzi didn't really say it — I just imagined it — which goes for all other similar instances. The only quotations from P. Gizzi in this piece are from his poetry, and they are put in quotation marks and fully cited; all other allusions/illusions are strictly my imaginings. Other than that, the usual conventions apply: for example, poem titles appear in quotation marks, and book titles appear in italics.

2. "When Orbital Proximity Feels Creepy," *ARCH*, 26; quotation altered.

3. This he really said.

4. "Plain Song," *SVLW*, 89–90; quotation altered.

5. "A Panic That Can Still Come Upon Me," *OUT*, 1.

6. "Local Forecast," *SVLW*, 94.

7. "Field Recordings," *ARCH*, 6.

8. "Field Recordings," *ARCH*, 5, 7, 14, 15, 16, 18, 19, 21, 78.

9. "'the winter sun says fight,'" *ARCH*, 31.

10. "When Orbital Proximity Feels Creepy," *ARCH*, 27.

11. *OUT*, epigraph.

CONTRIBUTORS

CHARLES ALTIERI is Stageberg Professor of English at UC Berkeley. He teaches courses in aspects of twentieth-century poetry, modernism, history of ideas, and Shakespeare. His two most recent books are *Wallace Stevens and the Demands of Modernity* (Cornell, 2013) and *Reckoning with Imagination: Wittgenstein and the Aesthetics of Literary Experience* (Cornell, 2015). He is now writing a book on Hegel's concept of inner sensuousness in modernist writing as a critique of new and old materialism.

KACPER BARTCZAK is associate professor in the Department of American Literature, University of Lodz, Poland. His criticism includes *In Search of Communication and Community: The Poetry of John Ashbery* (Peter Lang, 2006) and *Swiat nie scalony* (Biuro Literackie, 2009), a collection of essays for which he received the award of the Polish literary journal "Literatura na Swiecie" in 2010. He has published five volumes of poetry, the latest of which, *Wiersze organiczne* (2015), has been nominated for two major Polish poetry prizes, the Silesius and Gdynia awards. His translations of American poets into Polish include John Ashbery, Rae Armantrout, John Yau, and Peter Gizzi, whose poems appeared under the title *Imitacja zycia i inne wiersze* (co-translated with Andrzej Sosnowski, Instytut Mikołowski, 2013).

DAN BEACHY-QUICK is a poet and essayist, author most recently of *gentlessness* (Tupelo, 2015) and *A Brighter Word Than Bright: Keats at Work* (Iowa University Press Muse Series, 2013). His work has been supported by the Lannan and Guggenheim Foundations, and he directs the MFA program at Colorado State University.

HANNAH BROOKS-MOTL is the author of the poetry collections *The New Years* (2014) and *M* (2015). Recent work has appeared or is forthcoming in the *Best American Experimental Writing*, the *Cambridge Literary Review*, and *Poetry Now*, among others. She earned her MFA at the University of Massachusetts, Amherst, and is currently a PhD candidate at the University of Chicago, where she is poetry editor of the *Chicago Review*.

OLIVIER BROSSARD is associate professor (American literature) at the University Paris Est (Marne-la-Vallée) where he has been running the Poets and Critics program with Vincent Broqua and Abigail Lang since 2011: www.poetscritics.org. A member of the

Institut Universitaire de France, he is currently at work on "A Collective History of American Poetry and Poetics." He has translated many US poets into French including: David Antin, Keith Waldrop, Frank O'Hara, Ron Padgett, Thalia Field, and John Ashbery, whose *The Tennis Court Oath* was recently published under the title *Le serment du Jeu de Paume* by éditions José Corti. An edited book of essays, *"Lovers of My Orchards": Writers and Artists on Frank O'Hara*, is forthcoming from the Presses Universitaires de la Méditerranée (2017).

ANTHONY CALESHU is the author of a study of the poetry of James Tate (Peter Lang, 2010), three books of poetry (most recently, *The Victor Poems*, Shearsman, 2015), coeditor of the essay collection *Poetry and Public Language* (Shearsman, 2009), and the founding series editor of Periplum, a small press publishing pamphlets, books, broadsides, and digital videos of poets in conversation. He is professor of poetry at Plymouth University (UK).

PHILIP COLEMAN is an associate professor in the School of English and a fellow of Trinity College Dublin, Ireland. His most recent books are *John Berryman: Centenary Essays* (coedited with Peter Campion, 2017) and *George Saunders: Critical Essays* (coedited with Steve Gronert Ellerhoff, 2017). Other recent publications include *Critical Insights: David Foster Wallace* (2015), *John Berryman's Public Vision* (2014), and *Berryman's Fate: A Centenary Celebration in Verse* (2014). With Calista McRae, he is editing a selection of John Berryman's literary correspondence for Harvard University Press.

SARA CRANGLE is a Reader in English at the University of Sussex, where she codirects the Centre for Modernist Studies. In addition to articles on James Joyce, Wyndham Lewis, Dada, and affective states such as sulking, she is the author of *Prosaic Desires: Modernist Knowledge, Boredom, Laughter, and Anticipation* (2010). She edited *Stories and Essays of Mina Loy* (2011) and coedited, with Peter Nicholls, *On Bathos: Literature, Art, Music* (2010; 2012). She is currently compiling a selected edition of the poems of Anna Mendelssohn (a.k.a. Grace Lake), and completing a book about Mina Loy and satire.

GRAHAM FOUST's most recent book of poems is *Time Down to Mind* (Flood Editions, 2015). With Samuel Frederick, he translated three volumes by the late German poet Ernst Meister, including *Wallless Space* (Wave Books, 2014), a finalist for the 2015 National Translation Award in poetry from the American Literary Translators Association. He works at the University of Denver, where he is director of undergraduate studies in English.

DAVID HERD's collections of poetry include *All Just* (Carcanet, 2012), *Outwith* (Bookthug, 2012) and *Through* (Carcanet, 2016). He is the author of *John Ashbery and American Poetry* and *Enthusiast! Essays on Modern American Literature*, and is the editor of *Contemporary Olson*. His recent writings on the politics of movement have appeared in *Almost Island*, *Los Angeles Review of Books*, *Parallax*, and the *Times Literary Supplement*.

He is professor of modern literature at the University of Kent and an organizer of the project *Refugee Tales.*

DANIEL KATZ is professor of English and comparative literary studies at the University of Warwick. He has published widely on modern and contemporary literature, including three books: *Saying I No More: Subjectivity and Consciousness in the Prose of Samuel Beckett* (Northwestern University Press, 1999), *American Modernism's Expatriate Scene: The Labour of Translation* (Edinburgh University Press, 2007), and *The Poetry of Jack Spicer* (Edinburgh University Press, 2013). He is also editor of the "Bloomsbury Studies in Critical Poetics" book series.

AARON KUNIN is the author of *Cold Genius* (Fence Books, 2014) and four other books of poetry and prose. He teaches at Pomona College in California.

RUTH JENNISON is associate professor of modern and contemporary American poetry in the English department at the University of Massachusetts-Amherst. She is the author of *The Zukofsky Era: Modernity, Margins, and the Avant-Garde* (Johns Hopkins, 2012) and articles and book chapters on twentieth- and twenty-first-century American poetics, Marxism, and the political economies of literary form. Her current book project, *Figurative Capital: American Poetry and the World System*, explores the relationship between poetry and uneven development.

BEN LERNER has received fellowships from the Fulbright, Guggenheim, and MacArthur Foundations, among other honors. He is the author of two novels, *Leaving the Atocha Station* and *10:04,* and three books of poetry: *The Lichtenberg Figures*, *Angle of Yaw*, and *Mean Free Path*. His most recent book is the *The Hatred of Poetry*. He is a distinguished professor of English at Brooklyn College.

PETER MIDDLETON is the author of several books, including *Distant Reading* (Alabama, 2005), and *Physics Envy: American Poetry and Science in the Cold War and Since* (Chicago, 2015), and many essays on modern and contemporary poetry and poetics. He is a professor of English at the University of Southampton, and was recently the Leon Edel Visiting Professor of English at New York University.

JEREMY NOEL-TOD is senior lecturer in the School of Literature, Drama and Creative Writing at the University of East Anglia. His poetry criticism has been widely published and he is the editor of *The Oxford Companion to Modern Poetry*, second edition (Oxford University Press, 2013) and the *Complete Poems* of R. F. Langley (Carcanet, 2015).

MARJORIE PERLOFF is Sadie D. Patek Professor Emerita of Humanities at Stanford University and Florence R. Scott Professor Emerita of English at the University of Southern California. She is the author of many books on modern and contemporary poetry, including *Radical Artifice: Writing Poetry in the Age of Media,* and *Unoriginal Genius: Poetry by Other Means in the New Century.* Her most recent book is *Edge of Irony: Modernism in the Shadow of the Habsburg Empire* (2016).

LYTTON SMITH is assistant professor of English at SUNY Geneseo and the author of the poetry collections *The All-Purpose Magical Tent* and *While You Were Approaching the Spectacle and Before You Were Transformed by It,* both from Nightboat Books. His coauthored essay, with Katherine Baxter, on translation and the poetry of Craig Santos Perez and Robert Sullivan recently appeared in *Literary Geographies*.

MICHAEL D. SNEDIKER is associate professor of English at University of Houston. He is the author of *Queer Optimism: Lyric Personhood and other Felicitous Persuasions* (University of Minnesota Press, 2009), which was nominated for the MLA First Book Prize, the Alan Bray Prize, and Phi Beta Kappa's Christian Gauss Prize. His second critical book, a reading of disability theory and aesthetics across the very long American nineteenth century, is titled *Contingent Figure: Aesthetic Duress from Ralph Waldo Emerson to Eve Kosofsky Sedgwick* (forthcoming, University of Minnesota Press). He is also the author of *The Apartment of Tragic Appliances* (Punctum Books, 2013), which was named a Lambda finalist for Best Gay Poetry and, most recently, *The New York Editions* (Fordham, 2017), winner of the Poets Out Loud prize.

COLE SWENSEN is the author of seventeen volumes of poetry and a collection of critical essays. A former Guggenheim fellow, she is also the coeditor of the Norton anthology *American Hybrid* and the founding editor of La Presse, a nano-press that specializes in contemporary experimental French letters. Her awards include the Iowa Poetry Prize, the S.F. State Poetry Center Book Award, and the PEN USA Award in Literary Translation. She divides her time between Paris and Providence, Rhode Island, where she teaches at Brown University.

LEE UPTON's most recent books are *Bottle the Bottles the Bottles the Bottles* from the Cleveland State University Poetry Center; *The Tao of Humiliation: Stories*, winner of the BOA Short Fiction Award, finalist for the Paterson Prize, and named one of the "best books of 2014" by *Kirkus Review;* and *Visitations: Stories* (2017, the Yellow Shoe Fiction Series, Louisiana State University Press). She is the Francis A. March Professor of English and writer-in-residence at Lafayette College.

NERYS WILLIAMS lectures in American literature at University College, Dublin. She is the author of *Contemporary Poetry* (Edinburgh University Press, 2011) and *Reading Error: The Lyric and Contemporary American Poetry* (Peter Lang, 2007). Her poetry volume *Sound Archive* (Seren, 2011) won the Irish Strong first volume prize in 2012. Recent articles and chapters examine how contemporary poetry represents the Iraq and Afghanistan Wars, the poetry of post-devolutionary Wales, and militarism and the dynamic between poetry and radio.

INDEX